Beyond Superpower Rivalry

Latin America and the Third World

Edited by John F. Weeks

NEW YORK UNIVERSITY PRESS
New York and London

© 1991 by Geonomics Institute for International Economic Advancement
All rights reserved
Manufactured in the United States of America

Library of Congress Cataloging-in-Publication Data

Beyond superpower rivalry : Latin America and the Third World
    / edited by John F. Weeks.
        p.   cm. — (Geonomics Institute for International Economic
    Advancement series)
    Proceedings of a conference held in Vienna in late spring of 1989.
    Includes index.
    ISBN 0-8147-9235-9 (cloth)
    1. Latin America—Foreign relations—Soviet Union—Congresses.
    2. Soviet Union—Foreign relations—Latin America—Congresses.
    3. Latin America—Foreign relations—United States—Congresses.
    4. United States—Foreign relations—Latin America—Congresses.
    5. Developing countries—Foreign relations—Congresses.   6. United States—
    Foreign relations—1989—Congresses.   7. Soviet Union—Foreign relations—
    1989—Congresses.   I. Weeks, John F.   II. Series.
    F1416.S65B49   1991
    327.8047—dc20
                                                                    91-13305
                                                                    CIP

New York University Press books are printed on acid-free paper,
and their binding materials are chosen for strength and durability.

Contents

CONTENTS

Acknowledgments

This book brings together the presentations of people from business, politics and academia, who met for several days in Vienna at the end of May 1989. The gathering was extraordinarily exciting, debating epoch-making events, events which some of the attendees were active participants in molding (particularly the Soviets at the conference). The gathering was also an organizational nightmare, involving two administering institutions, Instituto de Relaciones Europeo-Latinoamericanos (IRELA, in Madrid) and the Geonomics Institute (in Middlebury, Vermont), and a conference at a site common to neither organization. Participants came from four continents, and organizational details required multilingual exchanges.

The conference was a success in great part due to the extremely convivial working relationship established between Geonomics and IRELA. For that close and fruitful relationship we at Geonomics extend our thanks to Wolf Grabendorff, Director of IRELA, and Jorge Heine, Associate Director at the time of the conference. We also thank Gertrude Krause-Traudes of IRELA for her tireless efforts in organizing the conference from the Madrid end. We also are deeply indebted to the Central Bank of Austria for providing the facilities for the conference; their hospitality was beyond gracious. We also thank Leonard Santow, Geonomics board member, who in addition to his intellectual contributions arranged for the Central Bank to host the meeting. Two other Geonomics board members, Marcelino Garcia and Willard Jackson, contributed their precious time to the conference, bringing to it valuable insights. We also sincerely appreciate the cooperation that came from the Institute for the Study of the USA and Canada of the Soviet Academy of Sciences, with which the Geonomics Institute maintains long and cordial relations.

Finally, thanks go to Elizabeth Leeds of Geonomics for her administrative aid from the Middlebury end, and Nancy Ward and Colleen Duncan, also of Geonomics, who worked for months on the administrative details of the conference and arrived in Vienna a week in advance to ensure all went smoothly. Colleen Duncan ably oversaw production of this volume. These three should be given credit for overcoming my mistakes and bungling and ensuring the success of the meeting.

John F. Weeks

Foreword

Since its founding, the Geonomics Institute has dedicated itself to facilitating communication among scholars, policymakers, and business leaders. It does so with the hope that interaction among those who develop analysis, those who form the policies, and those who respond to such policies will contribute to solving the major economic problems of the late twentieth century. To this end, Geonomics organized in April 1988 a conference in Middlebury, Vermont, on external debt and economic policy in the Third World. The success of that conference prompted a second, more ambiguous conference, held in Vienna in May–June 1989, organized in partnership with the Latin American center of the Economic Community (Instituto de Relaciones Europeo-Latino-americanos, IRELA). The purpose of the conference was to provide an unusual encounter—to bring together Soviet and U.S. experts to listen to voices from the South.

This second Geonomics conference on North-South issues had a bold and what seemed in mid-1989 quixotic purpose: to explore practical steps required to end the Cold War in the Third World, with the focus on Latin America. With the new Soviet policy of "openness" and a new U.S. administration taking power in 1989, the moment seemed opportune to consider the concrete ways tensions could be reduced between the two superpowers in the Third World. As this conference was planned, there were clear signs of greater policy flexibility in Moscow with regard to conflicts and rivalries in the Third World, but little did we realize how rapidly events would unfold.

The basic hypothesis underlying the conference proposal was that the regional and national conflicts observed in the Third World essentially derived from the tensions and dynamics of Third World societies; and, further, that the intervention of the superpowers, in as far as it incorporated the East-West rivalry, rendered those regional and national conflicts more difficult to resolve. Conflicts would not end with the passing of Cold War rivalry; quite the contrary, regional conflicts have their own cause. But the end of U.S.–Soviet rivalry implied another issue, addressed by the conference keynoters: Would superpower disengagement or continued intervention through meaningful cooperation be the best course for the future?

To pursue the implications of this question we brought together an extraordinary group of experts. From Latin America came men who had served as president, vice president, and prime minister of their countries, in addition to several of the region's leading academicians. They were joined by representatives from the Soviet Institute for the Study of the USA and Canada, U.S. academicians and business representatives, and several leading West European experts. This prestigious group discussed and debated for four days, providing insight into a new world unfolding for Latin America and the rest of the Third World. Exploring the possibility of East-West cooperation rather than conflict in the Third World proved to be an idea whose time had come.

The Geonomics Institute is privately funded, nonpartisan, and not for profit. We welcome comments, reactions, and questions regarding the Institute and its programs.

Michael P. Claudon
President and Managing Director
Geonomics Institute

Introduction

The rivalry between the United States and the Soviet Union for influence in Latin America ended in the late 1970s. This extraordinary development did not result from any explicit or implicit agreement between the two great powers, nor did it involve a compromise in the usual sense. Rather, rivalry ended when the Soviet Union abandoned the field of conflict. Approximately thirty people, among them Latin Americans, North Americans, Europeans, and Soviets, met in Vienna in the late spring of 1989, when this epoch-making change was in the offing. For five days in formal conference sessions—and informally in restaurants, bars, and cafes—the participants discussed and debated the implications of a Latin America liberated from the shadow of the Cold War. This book, whose contributors include those who served as president, vice president, and prime minister of their countries, is the result of that discussion and debate. The consensus that emerges assesses the liberation as foretelling an uncertain future.

When the planning for the Vienna conference began in June 1988, the organizers cautioned themselves against undue optimism with regard to the changes in U.S.–Soviet relations and developments in the internal politics of what the Cold War generation called the "Eastern Bloc." Indeed, "Beyond Rivalry to Cooperation" was suggested as a title for the conference, then rejected on the grounds that to use the word "cooperation" would be wildly optimistic. Yet before this book would be published, the NATO heads of state meeting of July 1990 would proclaim the end of the Cold

1

War, announcing that the western powers and the Soviet Union were no longer "adversaries." And in late summer and autumn of 1990, the United States and the Soviet Union would act in concert in response to a crisis in Western Asia, an area whose oil resources made it for decades the focus of superpower rivalry. If the course of events over the two years from June 1988 to June 1990 suggest anything, it is that one's predictions should err on the side of the bold, even the outrageous, or they might fall behind the rush of history.

In those dim, distant days of mid-1988, the openness and self-criticism of our Soviet colleagues still struck one as extraordinary, and the revelations of policy changes seemed to come in waves. It is difficult now, with the phenomenal rendered commonplace by perestroika and glasnost, to appreciate the stunned reaction, particularly of the Latin American participants, as the Soviet speakers repeatedly stressed that class struggle no longer guided their country's foreign policy. The major theme that emerged during the conference was the dramatic change in Soviet policy toward Latin America and the Third World in general. Whatever term one cared to use—fraternal states, allies, clients, or puppets—the government of the Soviet Union had clearly abandoned the market. The military withdrawal from Afghanistan represented perhaps the most farsighted perception of self-interest by a great power in this century: abandoning a client-state on its own border with every anticipation that an anti-Soviet regime would follow in the short term (though such did not occur). Perhaps only Charles de Gaulle's decision to withdraw from Algeria would be comparable, and France was not then a great power.

In dramatic contrast, the policy of the government of the United States showed little sign of any "new thinking" in the 1980s. Thus, another theme of the conference was the enduring policy of the United States to maintain Latin America in its sphere of influence. And in 1989 and 1990, one saw a transition in justification for a U.S. military role in Latin America from the communist threat to the "drug war," in whose name the Bush administration invaded Panama shortly before Christmas 1989. One cannot help but be struck by the startling contrast in the relations between the superpowers and their neighbors. In 1989 and 1990, the Soviet Union was apparently prepared to accept a line of neutral, perhaps even hostile, border states in Central Europe and would presumably seek national security through some post–sphere-of-influence strategy. Simultaneously in the western hemisphere, the United States funded the Contras in their attempt to overthrow the Nicaraguan government, funded the Salvadoran military to prevent a government of the left, and invaded Panama.

The dramatic shift of Soviet policy and the tenacious constancy of the U.S. sphere-of-influence posture toward Latin America gave rise to a third theme, though it served more as a question to debate: With the Soviet Union withdrawn from the Latin American field, will the United States pursue its self-interest in the region with less restraint and concern for the sovereignty of its neighbors on the continent, or enter into a new tolerance for political diversity? The participants arrived at no consensus on this question, which itself suggests the anxiety with which the future should be viewed. In the papers by the three Latin American political leaders, one sensed this anxiety, derived in part from the tension between the constructive role that U.S. policy could play and the actual practice.

It fell to Frederick Heldring, banker and internationalist, to open the conference and this volume and articulate the optimistic theme upon which the gathering was based: a world undistorted by spheres of influence, with the extravagant waste in military expenditure redirected to raising living standards. But if events since the conference indicate anything, it is that reduction of superpower rivalry certainly has not represented the sufficient condition for a more rational allocation of the world's resources.

Chapters 2 through 6 are written by experts intimately involved in policymaking in their respective countries. Victor A. Kremenyuk, Deputy Director of the Soviet Institute for the Study of the USA and Canada (ISKAN), in Chapter 2 provides a clear and concise statement of the dramatic change in Soviet foreign policy toward the Third World. The keystone of this new thinking is the official rejection of class considerations as the basis of Soviet foreign policy. Of course, considerations of power politics and narrow national interest determined Soviet international relations to a great extent, notwithstanding ideology, a point made in several later chapters. However, ideology represents the justifying moral force behind the pursuit of national interest, so the shift described in this chapter is of major significance.

Osvaldo Hurtado, former president of Ecuador, addresses in Chapter 3 the epoch-making changes in international relations prompted by Soviet new thinking and considers their impact on Latin America. Here one finds a sentiment expressed by the other Latin American writers in this book: the profoundly distorting effect of U.S. Cold War obsession on the other countries of the western hemisphere. President Hurtado's essay provides both an analysis and a lament that this obsession resulted in the neglect of the major problems of Latin America, the debt crisis being the most obvious. Along with this neglect went a strong current of great-power arrogance, particularly during the Reagan administration, when U.S. policy focused on what President Hurtado calls the "Nicaraguan obsession." Almost without exception, the Reagan administration ignored the counsel of leaders such as President Hurtado in pursuing a unilateral policy of diplomatic and military confrontation with the Sandinista government.

A detailed analysis of the basis of U.S. foreign policy toward the Third World is offered in Chapter 4 by Tom J. Farer, expert in international law and former head of the Human Rights Commission of the Organization of American States. Few North Americans can treat this subject with the objectivity of Professor Farer, under whose leadership the OAS Human Rights Commission not only monitored abuses in right-wing dictatorships such as Guatemala and Chile, but also sent the first investigative mission to Cuba. Professor Farer's analysis suggests that one can hold out only limited hope for a more tolerant and enlightened shift in U.S. policy in the post–Cold War era. He contends that all U.S. governments since the end of World War II rejected the principle of reciprocal standards in superpower behavior, basing their actions on a putative and inherent virtue of U.S. motivations, such that U.S. national interests and the interests of the broader community of countries were treated as overlapping. Professor Farer's rather pessimistic judgment about the potential for flexibility in U.S. policy perhaps was verified by Secretary of State James Baker III in September 1990. In the context of the conflict with Iraq, Baker asserted the necessity of the United States to assume global leadership in the post–Cold War environment, reminiscent of the Pax

Britannica of a century before.[1]

In Chapter 5, General Edgardo Mercado Jarrin would appear to concur with Professor Farer's assessment of U.S. policymaking. The General, perhaps more than any other participant at the conference, could speak from experience of the difficulties a nationalist regime faced when dealing with the U.S. government, for he served as prime minister under President Juan Velasco during the Peruvian Revolution, and his government implemented a number of measures aimed at limiting the influence and power of U.S. financial and commercial interests in his country. As in the chapter by President Hurtado, General Mercado Jarrin stresses the distorting effect of superpower rivalry on Latin American politics. Especially important in his view was the tendency of groups on both ends of the Peruvian political spectrum to focus on the role of the United States and the Soviet Union in Peru's affairs rather than on national issues in their own right. General Mercado Jarrin is not optimistic that the end of the Cold War brings great benefits to Latin America. He expresses a sentiment that arose again and again in discussions during the conference: that in its economically weakened state Latin America would find itself marginalized from the centers of economic and political power; that, indeed, "the region is of little concern to the countries that have benefited from the Reagan-Gorbachev [and later, Bush-Gorbachev] accords." His solution to this possible marginalization would be regional cooperation, economic and political, but also military, to ensure regional security and autonomy in a rapidly changing international context.

Carlos M. Vilas, Argentinian social scientist, traces the long-term nature of the U.S. sphere-of-influence approach to the region in Chapter 6. He argues that U.S. hegemony in the region was only incidentally related to Cold War concerns, having a much longer history, reaching back to the Monroe Doctrine. In his view, U.S. governments maintained a constant policy of excluding other major powers from the region, beginning with the British

---

1. See the report of Baker's speech in the *Guardian* (London) and in the *International Herald Tribune*, September 7, 1990. At the subsequent "summit" between Bush and Gorbachev, apparently Gorbachev vigorously objected to being assigned the role of junior partner in the policing of the world, prompting Bush to retreat from Baker's ambitious assertion (reported in the *Guardian*, September 10, 1990, p. 5).

in the mid–nineteenth century. Central to this view is the argument that the Soviet Union never offered a serious threat to expand
its influence into Latin America, and the U.S. emphasis on the
Soviet Union as an adversary in the region provided a convenient
excuse for the continuation of a much older policy.

Chapters 7, 8, and 9 evaluate Soviet foreign policy in more detail. In Chapter 7, George Mirsky of ISKAN analyzes the course of
Soviet foreign policy after World War II, showing the pragmatic
resource to the development of the nonaligned movement, especially after the death of Stalin. The pragmatism of the Soviet
Union to nonalignment on one hand and the hostility of the
United States on the other reflected the diplomatic isolation and
relative weakness of the former. One of the most interesting
aspects of the chapter is the argument that "it would be wrong to
say . . . that the Soviet Union tried to use the Third World as an
instrument to undermine the West." Rather, the Soviets considered that capitalism would be undermined by its own internal
problems, and developments in the Third World might reinforce
that process but were secondary at best. Unlike several other au-
thors in this book, Dr. Mirsky arrives at the end of his chapter optimistic about the impact of the new détente on the Third World.

The focuses shifts to the Soviet role in Latin America and the
Third World in Chapter 8, written by the Mexican Sovietologist
Edme Dominguez Reyes. This analysis locates itself at a more concrete level than that of Dr. Vilas, considering the different interest
groups within the Soviet Union in the process of policymaking and
following the ascendancy of the Gorbachev faction within the
Communist Party. While Dr. Dominguez's discussion does not
challenge Vilas's conclusion that the Soviet Union played a largely
passive role in Latin America, it demonstrates the profound shift
that occurred in Soviet posture toward competition with the United
States in the Third World. The overwhelming trend in Soviet
policy under Gorbachev became disengagement, spectacularly man-
ifest in the withdrawal from Afghanistan, more subtle but still
fundamental in Latin America (for example, reducing assistance to
Cuba and Nicaragua). After explaining these changes, the author
ends with the warning that western politicians did not sufficiently
appreciate the profound nature of the Soviet policy shifts, nor did

they appreciate the risks, both domestic and international, involved for the Gorbachev government.

Nicely complementing the chapter by Dr. Dominguez is the focus of Boris Y. Yopo in Chapter 9 on Soviet "new thinking" initiatives toward Latin America. To an extent difficult to anticipate in the the early 1980s, the Soviet government under Gorbachev refocused its Latin American priorities from seeking short-run competitive advantage over the United States to the long-term normalization of state-to-state relations. The author explains the shift to be in part the result of Soviet perception that previous policy proved "insufficient to contain the 'neoglobalist' plans of the Reagan administration . . . while the costs of maintaining strategic parity with the United States in the existing climate of tensions and international polarization were rising." The overall effect of the new Soviet approach was the development of closer diplomatic and commercial ties between the Soviet Union and the major countries of Latin America, perhaps a foreign policy strategy more consistent with national self-interest in the long run.

Chapters 10 through 13 broaden the discussion to superpower relations with the rest of the Third World, offering an assessment of regional conflicts. Within Central America, the growing U.S. intervention in Nicaragua represented the greatest source of superpower tension (though the Salvadoran civil war ran a close second). The Soviet Union's leading Latin Americanist, Viktor Volsky, treats the Nicaraguan conflict in Chapter 10, emphasizing its terrible economic and social cost. While written before the electoral defeat of the Sandinistas in February 1990, the chapter's emphasis on national reconciliation between the protagonists in the conflict remains timely. Dr. Volsky contrasts the role of the United States, repeatedly working to undermine a regional accord, with the support that the Soviet Union gave to the Contadora Group and later the Esquipulas negotiations among the five Central American presidents. It could be argued that little virtue should be claimed for the Soviet position, for it could only gain from a regional accord. However, subsequent events suggest that self-interest was indeed laced with principle in this case, as Dr. Volsky suggests: Following the electoral defeat of the Sandinistas, the Soviet government announced that it would continue its economic aid, notwithstanding the change in government.

During the 1980s, Central America represented the most contentious region of the western hemisphere for the superpowers. The former Vice President of Guatemala and Rector of the national university, Francisco Villagran Kramer, in a quite complex and subtle argument, explores the degree of autonomy of the region's governments in determining their fates. Dr. Villagran demonstrates in Chapter 11 the overwhelming influence of the United States in the region—perhaps more overwhelming than in any other part of the world—and also shows that the ebb and flow of geopolitical tensions creates nooks and crannies in the international power game. Within these, under favorable circumstances, the governments of the small countries of the Central American region can act with some effect. The agreements among the five Central American presidents in 1988-1989 (the Arias Plan) represented successful exploitation of such a favorable moment.

The Soviet Union asserted itself in Africa in a much more aggressive manner than in Latin America, and the comparison between the two continents in the context of superpower rivalry is quite instructive. Colin Legum argues in Chapter 12 that after World War II, "Africa was seen by the Soviet Union and the United States as a key continent in determining the new balance of world power." While in Latin America the term "national liberal struggle" lacked precise meaning, in Africa its import was clear: anti-colonial struggles, which the Soviet Union supported (and the United States opposed) in Angola, Mozambique, and Zimbabwe, among others. When the Soviet Union's activities in Africa went beyond support for anti-colonial struggles to nurturing and maintaining particular regimes (for example, in Somalia and Ethiopia), the result varied from embarrassing to disastrous for both patron and client. The recounting of the unsavory regimes supported by Moscow in the name of anti-imperialism proves quite sobering; the U.S. role in South Africa and opposing independence struggles in Portuguese colonies, however, leaves little moral authority to be claimed by either superpower.

Also acute over the last three decades was the superpower contention in Asia, made more complicated than elsewhere by the national security interests of China. Sharam Chubin stresses in Chapter 13 that here, as elsewhere, the Soviet leadership demonstrated a new flexibility in the second half of the 1980s. Relations with Asian countries proved delicate because a number of these countries share borders with the Soviet Union, as well as ethnic groups also found within the Soviet republics. The chapter's emphasis on the revival of Islam in the Soviet periphery rings prophetic in light of the rise of ethnic group demands and unrest in the southern Soviet republics in 1990. Unlike most of the Latin Americans at the conference, Chubin sees cooperation between the superpowers as a source of stability and possible conflict resolution, at least in Asia.

V. B. Benevolensky of ISKAN also sounds an optimistic note in Chapter 14, an overview of the relationship between superpower competition and the growing international economic interdependence. His view is that "the importance of economic leverage [by the superpowers] as a foreign policy instrument increased" during the late 1970s and 1980s, "as the political potential of military force diminished." While this diminution certainly held true for the Soviet Union, it is unclear that the same applied to the United States in light of the invasion of Panama (December 1989) and the deployment of troops in Western Asia (the conflict with Iraq in 1990). Quite provocative is Dr. Benevolensky's hypothesis that the economy of the United States relied less than previously on imported raw materials, and this change would have a positive effect, favoring "more superpower tolerance to social and political developments in the Third World."

Chapter 15 addresses an issue of paramount importance to Latin America and the rest of Third World: development assistance from what in 1989 were called the "socialist countries." While Jozef M. van Brabant, Chief of Centrally Planned Economies at the United Nations (and one must wonder what his office will be called in the future), wisely avoids prophecies about such aid in years to come, he does provide a state-of-current-knowledge survey of the recent past. He demonstrates that trade and aid from the "socialist countries" were closely linked, though the former played a marginal role, concentrated with a few developing countries. While President Gorbachev has stated on a number of occasions his intent to multilateralize Soviet aid, Dr. van Brabant's contribution indicates the enormous practical obstacles to achieve this. Notwithstanding these obstacles, the Soviet Union has taken practical steps in this direction—through UNICEF, for example—and one can anticipate Soviet membership in the International Monetary Fund and the World Bank in the 1990s.

The Vienna conference sought to ride a rising wave of change in superpower relations. While events developed faster than perhaps any of the participants anticipated, the issues debated and themes developed stand out for their persistent timeliness. Rather than being overwhelmed and rendered moot by the race of events, rapidity of change has made these issues and themes all the more relevant. As further dramatic developments unfold in East Europe and the Soviet Union, the central question remains whether these imply for Latin America and the rest of the Third World a context more favorable for autonomous development or quite the contrary.

Part I

A New Beginning

1

Prospects for Cooperation
Over Competition

Frederick Heldring

It is a pleasure and honor for me to be invited to this conference, which brings together representatives from Latin America, West Europe, the Soviet Union, and the United States, to speak about ways we can bring about a better equation to manage the globe. I submit that the present generation is doing an extraordinarily poor job of managing, but there is nothing to be gained by pointing fingers. Whether one is from the Third World, the Soviet Union, or the United States, we can find ample cause to give ourselves poor marks. Of course, each of us must admit that it is difficult to manage anything, let alone the world, if there is no one in charge.

We are very far from a world government, but I think our international organizations—the United Nations, the International Monetary Fund, and the General Agreement on Tariffs and Trade—should be endowed with greater authority than they have presently. Apart from the matter of governance, a substantial stumbling block to effective management of the global community has been the Cold War, a situation that has caused and still causes an enormous dislocation of resources, specifically arms, which between the United States and the Soviet Union alone amount to US$600 billion per year, and in the world as a whole well over US$1 trillion.

This chapter is a lightly edited version of the keynote speech delivered at the Geonomics Conference in Vienna. No effort has been made to conceal the informality of the oral presentation.

The good news, however, is that we would not be here today if it had not dawned upon many of us throughout the world that it is time to build a new equation. While such an equation would of course be multifaceted, I would like to focus not on what separates the Soviet Union from the United States, but on what we have in common in general, and particularly what we have in common in relation to the Third World.

What do we have in common? The future leaders of the world will be those countries that manage their economies prudently, not those that have the greatest military capability. Both the Soviet Union and the United States possess the military might, but neither manages its economy particularly well. Both are debtor nations with rapidly increasing indebtedness, which will affect the ability to lead; and, generally, creditor rather than debtor nations are leaders. Both nations are faced with a very strong Europe that is in the process of future unification and strengthening. The United States counts on the European Community to assist in financing part of the current-account deposit on its balance of payments. Of a total deficit in 1988 of US$135 billion, which required financing by foreigners, the European Community provided US$32 billion. U.S. net indebtedness at present as we measure it is US$500 billion, and it is expected to reach US$1 trillion in the early 1990s if we stay on the course on which we have presently embarked. I do not know the statistics of the Soviet Union as thoroughly, but I believe it is a debtor nation and counts on foreigners to finance its current-account deficit.

Current-account deficits are a direct result of an insufficient savings rate, which in the case of the United States includes a budget deficit that in itself constitutes a negative saving. I believe the Soviet Union also suffers from a budget deficit. In this connection, let me cite a few revealing statistics concerning the percentage of GNP that different countries or areas of the world spend for military purposes: in the case of Japan, it is 1 percent; in Europe, 3 percent; in the United States, 6.5 percent; and in the Soviet Union, 18 percent. I suspect that there is some correlation between the degree of effectiveness with which an economy is run and the extent to which resources are diverted from productive investments to military purposes. I admit it is the banker in me asking these questions: Who are the debtors, and who are the creditors? Does the

extraordinary expenditure for nonproductive purposes have something to do with that?

While between the Soviet Union and the United States the problems and challenges are quite different, there are some very basic
factors both countries share. It is clear that the pressure on the
Soviet government to reduce the percentage of GNP allocated to
military purposes is great. I am pleased to note that those pressures
appear to begin to be felt as well by the Bush administration. I
note, incidentally, that the bond market did well when there
were rumors that President Bush would propose troop reductions in
Europe. The market interprets positively any situation that might
assist in reducing the U.S. budget deficit.

The second area on which we should concentrate is those factors
that unite us, rather than separate us, from the Third World. I
remember well in the 1960s reading and listening to the late
Barbara Ward, who so eloquently warned that the growing gap in
the standard of living between North and South would pose significant risk to the world. Matters have deteriorated since that time.
Excessive and injudicious lending on the part of the North—indeed, including the Soviet bloc, which has its own problems—has
led to austerity measures and an untenable reverse flow from South
to North in the form of export surpluses to pay interest on loans. I
am amazed that the situation has not caused more unrest than it
has, but I have no doubt that more of what we have witnessed in
Venezuela will occur if the debt crisis is not solved soon. Barbara
Ward would be shocked to observe how seriously the North allowed
conditions in the South to deteriorate. I am not, however, absolv-
ing the South; there was imprudent lending as well as borrowing.

Obviously, the Soviet Union and the United States have at least
in the long run an equal stake in an amelioration of the Third
World equation. In the long run, neither country benefits from a
continuation of the present condition. Thus, it seems that the
United States and the Soviet Union should deemphasize ideological
considerations in their economic development efforts. We should
focus together on what we can do to alleviate some of the problems,
working as partners in the Third World. Having made that determination, we should begin modestly but with concrete steps. I
suggest that we select initially two or three economic development
projects in which both the Soviet Union and the United States have

their unique expertise, and in which a joint project would produce a better result than a single effort. Ideally, the selection of the project would be made in consultation with an economic development organism capable of representing the Third World, perhaps the United Nations.

Governance of the whole concept is of paramount importance. Much in life fails on account of poorly conceived governance. The most effective instrument would be a small board to which both governments would appoint their representatives; the chairmanship of the board would rotate annually. Each project would also have its chairperson appointed by and reporting to the board.

As far as funding is concerned, I have above-average hopes for meaningful arms reduction agreements that will relieve our budget pressures in the next few years. One less bomber plane probably could go a long way to fund a project. In any event, both countries initially could divert funds to this effort from their ideologically motivated economic development projects.

Although I have spoken of economic development, I refer to it in the broadest definition of the term, one that includes the global environment. In this connection, I offer this quote from a report of the 76th American Assembly held in New York in April 1989:

> Sustaining the global environment provides a major new challenge in relations with developing countries. The apparent warming of the world climate is likely to widen the gap between the developed and developing world. Dealing with this issue will require urgent policy choices and new forms of cooperation by all nations. The implications of failing to act range from rising sea levels through the renewed threat of famine due to possible failures in agricultural production. Dealing with this issue will require urgent policy changes by all nations. Industrialized countries must reduce their use of energy; new energy strategies, based on highly efficient technologies, must be developed and transferred to the Third World; and developing countries must address the task of slowing and reversing deforestation.
>
> Great advances in improving well-being have been achieved in the past three decades, but much remains to be done to alleviate poverty in the foreseeable future. Sub-Saharan Africa, where explosive population growth is combined with severe environmental degradation, requires priority attention.

In an adequately managed world, it is very difficult to produce action in the absence of a crisis. A strong international institution is needed in the area of global warming, in which no one gains— not even Siberia. One of the initial projects might well be conducted in relation to such a challenge. The Sub-Sahara comes to mind, but the deforestation of the Amazon in Brazil is a candidate as well.

In conclusion, I again quote from the 76th American Assembly report. Its preamble states:

> Dramatic changes have taken place in the global economy—and the pace is likely to continue at a relentless rate. We see the next few years as a watershed—a significant turning point in post–World War II political, economic, and security relations. It is a uniquely promising moment in history.

> Yet, at a time that should be triumphant, the industrialized democracies have permitted dangerous trade and other economic imbalances to build up within the international system. Unless corrected soon, they could engulf the world in a new wave of protectionism and bring a financial crisis in the 1990s.

Indeed, a financial crisis is a distinct possibility. I do not know of a period in history in which so much excessive debt has accrued globally. It is not only the less developed countries' debt that presents a challenge—so too does the growing U.S. debt abroad, as well as internal U.S. debt, including debt owned by the savings and loan industry, debt created by leveraged buyouts of corporations, mortgage debt in general, and overall consumer debt. If such a financial crisis arrives, all creative effort will be required to deal with it, possibly at the expense of such a new initiative as I describe here, which leads me to suggest we should start soon.

At the same time, however, if we speak of crisis, we must think of the Chinese word for it, which combines the concepts of danger and opportunity. With the demise of the Cold War within our grasp, would it not be wonderful—indeed, full of wonder—if we could avail ourselves of the opportunity presenting itself in this new era by initiating some small joint projects such as I have suggested.

2

Soviet New Thinking on Superpower Rivalry

Victor A. Kremenyuk

New political thinking in the Soviet Union is closely connected to the domestic political and economic reform. This reform has been developing for more than three years through different stages and with unequal results. Its essence, however, is quite clear: democratization of both political and economic life; openness and encouragement of critical assessment of the Soviet past and present; growing respect for human rights; and growing concern over the consequences of the arms race and overindustrialization for both world peace and the domestic situation. The goal of the political reform is to create the rule of law, including democratic procedures at all levels of government, respect for human rights, and freedom of information and political expression, particularly free travel inside and outside the country. The direction of the economic reform is to restructure completely the system of political and economic management and to encourage peaceful and fruitful coexistence of state, cooperative, and individual property, which would lead to a significant increase in the standard of living of the population.

These are essentially revolutionary changes. The task is to make them as peaceful as possible without undue violence, which could only provide counterviolence and chaos. Support from a majority of the population should minimize disruption. The present Soviet leadership has pursued reform with remarkable skill, and it already has brought about significant changes. For example, the Congress of People's Deputies opened in Moscow on May 25, 1989. The new Soviet parliament will become the new power center in society, with all corresponding responsibility for the decisionmaking process for domestic and foreign policy. It is evident that the modus operandi of Soviet society will inevitably change if the current process of restructuring continues, and it will acquire new dimensions and unforeseeable forms in the coming years.

These changes in the Soviet Union will of course influence foreign policy decisionmaking, though significant changes have already taken place within the last several years, and they have contributed to the changing climate in international affairs generally and superpower relations in particular. If the internal reforms in the Soviet Union are sometimes regarded as inefficient and inadequate (as was publicly discussed at the Congress of People's Deputies in Moscow), foreign policy under Gorbachev has already registered remarkable achievements that have marked changing Soviet relationships with Europe, Japan, China, and the United States.

All these changes are connected with what has been called "the new political thinking."[1] The new approach has forcefully intervened in current world politics. It has become a major factor working for further accelerated changes in the global agenda and in the alignment of forces between those for change and those for maintaining the existing world political and economic order. The entire context of global politics was drastically changed with the advent of the new political thinking. It is too early to assess all possible consequences of its impact, for it will continue to evolve and produce new ideas that can change existing patterns of thinking.

The new political thinking was an audacious effort to practice the principles that long ago were formulated by different thinkers both in the East and West and in the North and South. These basic principles are: (1) the acceptance of integrity and interdependence of the world irrespective of divisions along ideological lines, levels of development, religious beliefs, and racial and ethnic conflict; (2) the recognition of the priority of human values, such as peace, prosperity, and freedom, over class values;[2] (3) disarmament, primarily

---

1. For a fuller treatment, see Gorbachev (1987).

2. For many years, the class values at the heart of Soviet foreign policy included world revolution, internationalist solidarity with revolutionary movements around the world, and purity of Marxism-Leninism, understood primarily as unchangeable dogma. For further discussion of the role of class struggle in Soviet new thinking, see Chapter 7 by George Mirsky in this volume.

in the area of strategic weapons, as the primary path toward world peace and security; (4) resolution of conflicts, with due respect to the interests of all parties; and (5) respect for human rights as a cornerstone of both national and international politics.

These were the major guidelines of the new political thinking in the Soviet Union, and they have formed the basis of Soviet foreign policy since 1985. In practice, they became the leading principles of the Soviet government in intermediate-range nuclear force (INF) talks, in settling the conflict in Afghanistan, in making unilateral decisions on reductions in nuclear and conventional forces, and in other areas. The new principles represent the reversal of rigid Soviet positions that were taken during Brezhnev's rule. The traditional Soviet "nyet" has become "da," which initially has puzzled other governments, for they were unprepared for the new dynamics of international affairs.

There are two ways to assess the importance of new political thinking in the Soviet Union. First, there is its foreign dimension, which created the possibility of breaking some of the major deadlocks in international relations. Second, there is its domestic role, for the new political thinking can be regarded as a function of the general change in the Soviet Union. It is in the latter context that its reversibility can be assessed. Quite understandably, one of the major concerns of western nations was and is the problem of stability and consistency of the current Soviet foreign policy. At issue is the possibility of the new policies being reversed should there occur changes in the Soviet leadership or should the present leadership change its foreign policy in response to unforeseen circumstances.

The problem for the West was epitomized by U.S.–Soviet Specialist G. Breslauer of the University of California at Berkeley, in the question: "Perestroika or 'Peredyshka'?" (Restructuring or a pause to catch one's breath?) The question holds vital importance for the West and also for the Soviets, who are concerned about the present and future of their country and have definitely declared themselves in favor of the complete restructuring of their nation, including its foreign policy. Thus, the domestic dimension of the new political thinking acquires crucial importance, for it is domestic Soviet politics that will guarantee that the new political thinking will not be simply a new propaganda campaign but will become a new strategy supported by the whole thrust of the Soviet state and of its allies. As a strategy, the new political thinking will continue to be one of the major factors of international development, which also include the problems of East-West security, North-South controversies, and regional conflicts as a part of contemporary international life.

The principles of the new political thinking have already been realized in many initiatives put forward by the Soviet government. Among these were the suggestions to discuss and negotiate a program of complete nuclear disarmament (Gorbachev's statement on January 15, 1986), followed by the acceptance of the "double-zero" option for the INF in Europe, with an agreement signed in Washington in December 1987. Initiatives also have dealt with cooperation on fostering development in the Third World,[3] strengthening the role of the United Nations in settling international problems,[4] and improving bilateral contacts with China, West Germany, Great Britain, and other countries.

Further, the new political thinking could not avoid addressing the problems of superpower competition in the Third World. For years, this competition has become one of the more urgent problems in international relations, contributing to the continuation of the arms race (both nuclear and conventional), mutual suspicions, mistrust, superpower rivalry, and alliance-building. It contributed to a significant extent to the aggravation of local tensions and regional conflicts throughout the world. Although both superpowers spent billions of dollars and rubles assisting the developing nations, this money largely went for arms purchases or for creation of local military establishments, contributing to economic stagnation, political repression, and local wars.

One of the main consequences of this rivalry in the Third World was its role in ending the Soviet-American rapprochement in the early 1970s. While at that time there was the possibility of starting an irreversible process of disarmament and cooperation, Soviet-American disputes and controversies over the Middle East, Angola, Ethiopia, Kampuchea, and, finally, the Soviet invasion of

3. See the statement by the Political Consultative Committee of the Warsaw Treaty, 1987.

4. Mikhail Gorbachev's speech at the United Nations in December 1988 was particularly important in this context.

Afghanistan, increased suspicions. As a result, the Cold War re-emerged in rhetoric and policies, leading to a new spiral in the arms race. The lesson from this experience has also been incorporated into the context of the new political thinking. Unilateral forays into the developing world do not pay; they always bring trouble to both the intervenors and the governments that are supported by the interventionist force.

Only a definite and successful development strategy can bring in the long run an end to wars and social conflicts in the Third World. That conclusion is basic to the new political thinking. Combatting hunger, poverty, disease, abuse of human rights, and homelessness can bring along political stability, economic prosperity, and social justice to the deprived people of the poor countries. Eliminating these will eliminate the potential for guerrilla wars, uprisings, revolutions, and coups. There is simply no other way to achieve peace and stability, and this is not only a sphere of responsibility of Third World nations, but it should be the goal of the entire global community. Once shared by developed and developing nations, it could form a consensus for the long-range goals of redressing superpower politics toward Third World issues.

To make this commitment to development, a common goal is not enough to discuss these issues at formal and informal unofficial levels. Such discussions give a positive stimulus to the search for common denominators in superpower relations. It is necessary to add to these discussions a set of specific actions that could increase confidence and mutual trust and subsequently bring a solution to the most heatedly disputed problems in the Third World. Such actions could be undertaken unilaterally as well as through constructive and well-organized negotiation.[5]

Four types of specific actions could be suggested as possible openings for the introduction of the new political thinking into the area of superpower relations with Third World nations. The first concerns the problems of superpower military presence and performance in the Third World. To date, both the United States and the Soviet Union have followed the practice of building alliances

5. As then Soviet Foreign Minister Eduard Shevardnadze put it in his United Nations speech in 1985, the mechanisms for such solutions could be devised through a mechanism of consultations both at the U.S.–Soviet level and within the structure of the United Nations.

and client relationships in the Third World. One of the main
purposes of this policy was to extend their military presence into
the areas that were considered strategically important. This expanded military presence was expected to provide base and logistical support for forces projected into those regions as a part of global
military rivalry. The pretext for these actions very often was support of the local governments, which were threatened either by
"communist" or "imperialist" subversion. As a result, there were
wide military networks created by both sides, including perma-
nently stationed troops (primarily on the U.S. side), vast amounts
of military advisers and other paramilitary personnel, base facilities, and local forces armed and trained by the respective superpower.

The results of this policy are well known. The United States en-
snared itself in Vietnam, where it lost almost 60,000 lives and
US$140 billion worth of material and suffered political and moral
consequences domestically and internationally. The Soviet Union
made the decision to invade Afghanistan, which cost almost nine
years of bloodshed, more than 13,000 lives, tens of thousands of
maimed and injured, an unknown but evidently significant
amount of money, and a loss of prestige and national consensus.
Both superpowers had to learn the lesson that military power in
today's world has its rather fixed limits and cannot, even when it
deals with a seemingly weak enemy, force a political solution. Not
surprisingly, both wars brought vast devastation and human suffering, without contributing adequately to the solution of domestic political and economic problems.

These events raise questions about the validity and relevance of
the direct use of force by the superpowers in the Third World.
Politically and militarily, direct use of force turns out to be counterproductive and inefficient, for it creates unnecessary crises, which
under certain circumstances can easily turn into broader crises affecting the whole international system. Direct intervention casts
doubt upon the effectiveness of international law and the ability of
the superpowers to follow its rules. It aggravates the rift between
the great powers and Third World countries because the direct use
of force undermines the sovereignty of the independent states.
Finally, it gives legitimate grounds to those in the world community who doubt the real intentions and interests of the superpowers

in their quest for power and influence.

All this taken into consideration, one concludes that there should be no direct use of military force by the superpowers in the Third World. This should be absolutely excluded as a viable contingency for the future, whether or not there exists legal justification for such actions. Of course, this is a step back from Franklin D. Roosevelt's idea of the great powers acting as "global policemen." There is simply not sufficient mutual trust for the superpowers to play such a role. Therefore, military interventions on the part of superpowers, and even of the secondary powers, including France, Great Britain, and China, should be reduced to nil. For the sake of keeping the global balance intact, they should, unilaterally or on the basis of multilateral agreement, cease their forays into affairs of Third World nations. This modus operandi should be maintained irrespective of political events in the Third World. Eliminating intervention would keep general issues of world security and strategic stability independent from the twists of local power struggles.

At the same time, there should be general agreement that the issues of the Third World cannot be settled through either foreign intervention or military force. There is sufficient evidence that the problems of Third World nations, being a part of their quest for a better standard of living, are not solved through military means but rather through a sustained international effort in food, health care, and development assistance. As a first step to achieve that goal, the abstention from using military force should be achieved as a part of a general understanding, including unilateral decisions of nonintervention and agreement achieved through intensive multilateral diplomacy.

The second set of actions concerns the general attitude on the part of the superpowers (as well as the secondary powers) toward the use of violence in settling Third World issues. The period of revolutionary romanticism has long ago ceded to the period of sober economic planning and calculation. There is also widespread and profound doubt that violent revolutionary changes can bring about the constructive solution of social problems. These doubts arise from the violence that brought Stalinism to the Soviet Union, the Cultural Revolution to China, the Pol Pot regime to the Khmer Rouge, and the Ayatollah Khomeini to Iran. At the same time, the consequences of supporting rightist regimes, such as Pinochet in Chile and Zia in Pakistan, also casts vast and legitimate doubt about whether this brings a solution to the peoples of the respective nations.

These considerations suggest that the superpowers should not foster violence as a substitute for direct intervention. This has undermined peace and security in these areas, very often provoking new wars and conflicts. Arms exports to the Third World have diverted large sums from civilian use, thus contributing to the aggravation of the social problems in developing countries. One of the latest examples of this policy, the Reagan Doctrine, proved by its failure that there can be no military solution to political problems, and any attempt to use force brings about new suffering. The superpowers should not only discuss these things between them, but also they should set an example for the other powers by promoting peaceful and democratic change in the Third World.

The third set of actions concerns the possible mechanisms that could effectively bring change into the superpower rivalry. There is already an established, though sometimes not very effective, pattern of U.S.–Soviet consultations, which made it possible to achieve an agreement on and withdraw Soviet troops from Afghanistan. Another success in negotiations has been the peaceful settlement in Southwestern Africa (Namibia). At the same time, all efforts to find a manner to negotiate a peaceful solution to the Arab-Israeli conflict or the conflict in Nicaragua have been unsuccessful. And, of course, there is no progress in putting an end to the forty-year-old Korean conflict.

A central problem retarding the solution to the regional conflicts and more general Third World issues is the lack of communication and understanding between the United States and the Soviet Union on how these conflicts should be solved. There are still strong remnants of rivalry and confrontation, suspicions, and "sphere of influence" thinking, even though it became clear long ago that these are counterproductive and self-damaging. The other major problem in this area is how to make compatible joint U.S.–Soviet approaches with the views and interests of other nations in Europe, Asia, Africa, and Latin America. Without giving a thought to this aspect of cooperation, it is easy to imagine a "superpowers' condominium," which would alienate other nations.

The fourth set of actions concerns our attitude toward the United Nations and its reemergence in the capacity of an effective world organization responsible for peace-keeping, maintenance of security, economic and social development, and respect for human rights. The essence of the new thinking, as stated by Gorbachev, is that the United Nations can become an extremely effective instrument for solutions of both regional and global issues concerning the Third World. For many years, the United Nations was largely paralyzed by the atmosphere of East-West and North-South confrontation. There was a real danger that the organization would turn into a podium of propagandistic campaigns and futile battles over resolutions that did not oblige anyone to do anything. It is absolutely urgent now to think profoundly about how this body can be used for joint problem-solving and imposition of international law regarding terrorism, drug trafficking, "good offices" in inter- and intra-state conflicts, peace-keeping operations, and verification of disarmament. These and many other functions would become necessary, provided that the new political thinking turns into a powerful vehicle of Soviet foreign policy. It must be recognized, of course, that changes are not easily achieved after years of a stifled approach and a closed decisionmaking process. But the new thinking gives hope that the existing world order will become more open, less violent, and more cooperative, even within the lifetime of the present generation. In conclusion, the new thinking is not just the product of one country, but it is in part the logical reaction to the dangers created by previous world tensions, and it should be shared by all those who are concerned about the life and destiny of future generations.

3

Latin America in the
New International Context

Osvaldo Hurtado

FROM PRESIDENTS REAGAN TO BUSH

At the end of the Reagan administration, several of his foreign policy objectives had not been achieved. Cuba not only preserved its independence and sovereignty, but it also broke out of the isolation imposed on it since the 1959 Revolution and succeeded in "legitimizing" itself vis-à-vis the new Latin American democracies, whose most important events—presidential inaugurations—were attended by Fidel Castro. Although Soviet presence has not increased in Latin America, neither has it been reduced. In El Salvador, despite substantial U.S. economic aid, the guerrilla forces reconstituted themselves, and to date it does not appear possible for the army to defeat them. Although the economy of Nicaragua was seriously eroded and declined substantially, the Sandinista government retained its power and political influence. It defeated the Contras, and it is unlikely that the Sandinistas can be overthrown by force, as the U.S. government attempted to do. However, if the objective of the Contras was not to overthrow the Sandinistas but to wear them down economically and socially to force them to negotiate, then their purpose was achieved.

"Reaganism" arrived in the White House beset by a "Nicaraguan obsession," which became a central and inseparable objective of U.S. foreign policy for eight years. This obsession led the U.S. government to neglect other parts of Latin America and the region's most serious problems, principally economic, which in the

long run imply greater risk for the hemispheric security that so
worries the United States.   For example, the Caribbean Basin
Initiative, conceived to provide greater access to the U.S. market for
the region's industrial and agricultural goods, never achieved its
purpose. Losses of the Caribbean countries due to restrictions on
their sugar exports, other cases of protectionism, and low prices
were greater than the gains from selling their new goods on the
U.S. market.[1]

The policy devised to deal with the Latin American economic
crisis was also a failure. After a moratorium on debt payments by
all the countries of the region, the U.S. departments of State and
Treasury maintained that this problem could be resolved through a
renegotiating process to postpone payments, austerity programs to
readjust the economies, and the renewed growth of the U.S. economy, which was then emerging from several years of stagnation.
According to President Reagan, stated during the visit I made to
the White House in 1982, the reactivation of the U.S. economy
would pull with it the Latin American countries, situating their
economic revival.

Since then, due to the shortcomings of the first debt renegotiating sessions, there has been no sign that a general Latin
American revival will last.   Despite the austerity programs that
have been implemented and sustained growth of the United States
and other industrialized countries for six consecutive years, the debt
problem remains, and the Latin American crisis is the same, if
not worse. Little has improved since world attention focused on
the Mexican announcement that it was unable to meet its debt payments.[2] In contrast, the creditor banks have significantly improved their position, accumulating reserves to protect against risk
of bankruptcy. At present, not even a moratorium by most of the
debtors would jeopardize private international banks.

This mistaken perspective on the debt problem and the preju-
dices of the Reagan administration vis-à-vis international organizations and multilateral agencies prevented it from accepting the
Latin American stance that the debt crisis needed a political response. Consequently, the administration systematically refused to

1. This is demonstrated statistically in Weeks (1989).
2. See United Nations (1989).

allow a dialogue with the debtor nations. Further, the Reagan administration did not appreciate the valuable role the development banks could have played in the search and execution of adequate and more efficient responses to the situation. The International Monetary Fund (IMF) and the World Bank imposed their free-market ideas indiscriminately on several Latin American countries through so-called conditionality. In addition, the Reagan administration deprived the Inter-American Development Bank (IDB) of resources by refusing to meet its financial commitments to increase the multilateral's capital. In reality, the great accomplishment of the Reagan administration was the culmination of the democratization process in Latin America that had been initiated by President Carter.

In contrast to events in previous historical periods, the U.S. government committed itself to the elimination of dictatorships and the establishment of constitutional governments. At the close of his term in office, President Reagan was able to display a map of an almost totally democratic Latin America, something that had not existed in the 170 years of the region's republican life. Only in Panama had there been a retreat from democracy.[3] In contrast, the last two dictatorships were defeated: in Chile, a plebiscite was won by the opposition, which prepared the way for the election of a new government at the end of 1989; and in Paraguay, the dictatorship of General Stroessner was overthrown, a successor elected, and at least a democratic transition government has been put in place. Not even the most optimistic Latin American would have imagined that all this would be possible so quickly.

The new international context and the problems of the U.S. economy are not entirely favorable for the economic reactivation of Latin America. Despite the economic growth attained during the 1980s, the United States was no longer the unequaled economic power of the 1960s. This was not only because Japan and a united Europe became major financial, economic, and technological powers, but also because the United States faced economic difficulties stemming from deficits in its budget and external account. In these conditions, it does not seem realistic to anticipate that the

---

3. In December 1989, U.S. troops invaded Panama, deposing the government of General Manuel Noriega and installing a new head of state.—(*Ed.*)

Bush administration will devise and execute an ambitious aid
program for Latin America. As much as it is needed, we cannot
expect an initiative like President John F. Kennedy's Alliance for
Progress, or a new Marshall Plan, which several Latin American
countries requested.

The tone of President Bush's electoral campaign and inaugural
speeches and his first official statements and acts show no signs
that Latin America is one of his priorities. Because the everyday
concern of the U.S. population for the region is slight, it is
understandable that its political leaders take little interest in the
region. No one wins an election in the United States with
speeches about Latin America. The U.S. government has historically been a sum of balances that have always impeded quick
changes in its political behavior. The force of this inertia and the
weight of the establishment perhaps have been what in the last instance defined U.S. foreign policy for Latin America. There is no
reason to expect President Bush to change a line of conduct that has
been maintained for the last decades with very few variations.
During these years, there has been a progressive loss of interest in
Latin America, in contrast to the greater preoccupation with
Europe, the Soviet Union, the People's Republic of China, and
Japan. The spectacular economic growth of Japan and Europe and
the U.S. rapprochement with China and the Soviet Union are
elements that substantiate these trends.

In regard to the so-called Third World, it is widely known that
the United States takes interest only when conflicts arise that could
alter the balance of the superpowers. If Soviet renunciation of its
former role in world revolution, which had been one of its principal dogmas, is really true, then the potential for confrontation in
the Third World will be reduced. With this reduction, U.S. interest in Third World countries, including those in Latin
America, could wane. But because in Central America the East-
West conflict still prevails, this area will be of particular interest
for President Bush, who, like his predecessor, probably believes
that Latin America's problems can be reduced to avoiding "communist penetration in El Salvador and Nicaragua."

Those who know President Bush describe him as being less
ideological than Reagan, more skilled in political terms, more
realistic, and vastly more experienced. All these characteristics

should enable him to better understand the complexity of Latin America and to value its strategic importance. However, for the reasons previously noted, it seems unlikely that there will be substantial changes in the White House and State Department perspectives on South and Central America. Further, the policy for the latter region has been clearly dominated by a military focus.

It could be said that the Brady Plan[4] demonstrates the contrary, and that it is a first sign that the Bush administration will revise President Reagan's low assessment of Latin America's economic problems. Indeed, this plan is the first acceptance on the part of the U.S. government that the debt problem should be treated politically, and that in some cases debts cannot be paid. Secretary Brady acknowledged this by admitting the possibility of what until recently was systematically denied: the reduction of the amount of the Latin American debt.

The proposal at best contains general guidelines for action and entails the participation of various actors in a manner not concretely specified. One hopes that such an important initiative will not meet the same fate as the so-called Baker Plan, which, as everyone now knows, was an improvisation of the then Treasury Secretary at the IMF Conference in Seoul in 1985. It is often said that in Latin America words are not always accompanied by deeds. Unfortunately, what Latin Americans have so often been criticized for is precisely what has happened in the United States, with both the Caribbean Basin Initiative and the Baker Plan.

EUROPE AND JAPAN IN LATIN AMERICA

If the United States does not wish to play, or cannot play, an important future role in Latin American development, and if Japan and a united Europe emerge as new economic powers, one should ask if they would be willing to commit themselves to the region's development. The present situation in Europe does not appear favorable for Latin America. Perestroika has fundamentally altered relations among European countries. There is nothing of greater im-

---

4. U.S. Secretary of the Treasury Nicholas Brady announced in early 1989 a new initiative to deal with the debt of the most heavily indebted countries. Over a year later, the plan had been applied only to Mexico, with uncertain results.—(*Ed.*)

portance than banishing the spectre of World War II, a fear under which the old continent has lived for almost half a century. For the united Europe that will be born in 1992, the need to take advantage of the economic opportunities opening up in the Soviet Union and East Europe will be a priority, along with maintaining growth. These concerns will lead European leaders to make relations with the other two world economic giants—the United States and Japan—the first point on their work agenda. Finally, Europe's traditional and favored treatment of its former colonies in Asia, Africa, and the Caribbean obviously will be strengthened. In these conditions, I believe that there will be little possibility that Europe will place great importance on its relations with Latin America, except, perhaps, and in a limited way, for Germany, Italy, and Spain.

Moreover, there is the risk that the constitution of the so-called European Fortress in 1992 will turn the continent into a bastion of protectionism. Although the trade balance continues to be favorable for Latin America, in recent years there has been a tendency toward a reduction of exports to Europe. If it is not reversed, protectionism could become more pronounced with the birth of the united Europe, bringing restrictions on Latin American exports and a worsening of the region's crisis.

By the end of the century, only the U.S. economy will exceed that of Japan. As a financial power, Japan will be second to none. This immense economic power will internationalize Japan, whose commitments with the world are increasing. There are already signs that Japan is willing to assume the leadership role that its privileged economic position gives it, via greater participation in the decisions that shape international trade and finance. Japanese interest in Third World matters is shown by the increase of its quota in the IMF. Further, the Brady Plan was derivative of the innovative initiative devised by Japanese Prime Minister Takeshita on the debt problem. With these antecedents, Latin America should pay greater attention to its economic relations with Japan and also to the "four Asian Tigers": South Korea, Singapore, Taiwan, and Hong Kong.

Europe and Japan could make an important contribution to Latin America's development if they decided to contribute to increasing the capital of the World Bank, the IMF, and the IDB.

For its part, the United States should finally honor its commitment to make a US$25 billion contribution to the reposition fund, which would permit the IDB to almost double its loans.

SOVIET RESTRUCTURING

The political and economic phenomena touched off by perestroika surely constitute the most significant developments in international postwar politics. The conflicts between the United States and the Soviet Union, grounded in the debate over "totalitarianism-democracy" and "capitalism-collectivism" and by the "East-West" confrontation, whose most extreme manifestation was the Cold War, soon may be coming to an end. With the advent of perestroika, those realities are changing at a dizzying speed. International relations based on fear, suspicion, and the desire to exterminate the adversary are giving way to relations based on trust, dialogue, tolerance, and cooperation. As such, it is not an exaggeration to say that since World War II, and perhaps in the modern history of humanity, we have never been closer to peace than now.

The agreements between the United States and the Soviet Union for the reduction of arms open the way for eventual nuclear disarmament and the elimination of the threat of world war, with unimagined positive economic, political, and social consequences for the future of humanity. Only a few years ago, few would have thought that the Soviet Union would unilaterally withdraw important military contingents from Europe and Asia and abandon its occupation of Afghanistan, and that its leader, Mikhail Gorbachev, would visit China, against whom the Soviets had waged so many ideological and political battles for thirty years. This Sino-Soviet rapprochement opened the door to an end to Vietnam's intervention in Cambodia and peace in Southeast Asia. The bloody war between Iran and Iraq has ended, the Palestine Liberation Organization has renounced violence, Cuban troops have begun their withdrawal from Angola, and agreements have been signed for the pacification of Southern Africa. If these trends continue, the vestige of war will remain only in Lebanon and the tormented Central American region.

If the processes of political democratization and economic liberalization in the Soviet Union continue for several more years, they will surely unleash forces in favor of extending freedoms and establishing real political pluralism and new economic reforms. These processes, once in motion, are difficult to stop. Restricted democracies cannot remain static indefinitely, without pressure for innovation and change.

For the Soviet Union, the Third World continues to be of concern because of strategic interest. In the specific case of Africa, important relations exist with several governments or political parties of that region. One objective of perestroika is the modernization of the Soviet economy, and it is obvious that the Soviet Union is interested in increasing economic relations with Japan, the United States, and Europe, an indispensable step for obtaining financial resources and technology, without which the progress of the Euro-Asian giant would not be possible in the terms set forth by its new leaders. These regions and countries, not Latin America, would seem the priority of the Soviet government.

LATIN AMERICA AT THE CROSSROADS

Latin America has been economically stagnant for the last ten years. If there is an area of the world where the concept of a "lost decade" is relevant, it is Latin America. The standard of living at the end of the 1980s was no higher than what it was ten years before.[5] An analysis of the situation reveals that there is no possibility for these downward trends to undergo any changes in the 1990s. Therefore, it is not pessimistic to warn that Latin America will discover in the year 2000 that the final decades of the twentieth century were lost in terms of progress and development. In contrast, South Korea is now the tenth largest exporter in the world, but it lagged far behind Argentina, Brazil, and other Latin America countries barely twenty years ago.

Latin America's economic stagnation is compounded by its loss of influence in the international world. The decolonization of Asia, Africa, and the Caribbean multiplied the representation of

5. See the table in IDB (1989).

countries in the United Nations, its agencies, and in the Organization of American States (OAS). Latin American political and economic leadership has also declined. In light of the economic emergence of other regions of the world, it is unlikely that it will regain its former influence.

The crisis, in addition to the negative economic and social effects, gave rise to structurally worse effects in the political realm. There has been a decomposition of public institutions and loss of the state's capacity to fulfill its most basic functions, such as the preservation of civil order, the exercise of justice, the administration of essential public services, and the important economic activities that Latin American governments traditionally have provided. The underground economy and black markets are substituting for the legitimate economy, and cities are turning into immense markets of street vendors. In these economic activities, laws and government authority hold little meaning. If this process of state decomposition, of which there are signs in Peru and Argentina, is not curtailed in time, the possibility of anarchy is real.

If the Latin American state is incapable of fulfilling its elemental functions, it is even less able to execute more complicated functions, such as the formulation and execution of economic policies to overcome economic and social crises. Among the many lessons that the debt crisis has taught the region is that an abundance of financial resources does little good if there are no political institutions and public organizations to take full advantage of them.

Despite the spread of democracy, Latin America is still unstable. The changes of governments and ministers mean significant modifications in the principal public policies and in the high levels of the techno-bureaucracy. Under these conditions, it is difficult to implement the long-term programs that historically have been necessary for initiating true development. The stability and continuity of economic policies were essential to the development of the United States, Japan, Europe, and most recently the Asian economies. Even in the case of Brazil, a country that has a modern state structure, the weakness of its political party system has prevented the adequate functioning of its state agencies, thus limiting the full realization of an immense economic potential. This instability is the region's biggest obstacle to attracting foreign investment. Despite the region's efforts, foreign investment slowly declined, while capital flight increased, representing losses amounting to more than half of the Latin American debt.[6]

To emerge from the crisis, Latin America must seek a consensus among political parties and social groups to define fundamental economic policies and obtain a commitment to their long-term implementation. An agreement of this nature cannot be reached at present in a majority of the countries because there are no credible representatives. Therefore, it is imperative to modify the situation of political parties in Latin America, in the sense of promoting a system of majority parties, which would uphold democracy and give real sense to the opposition.

A further prerequisite for renewed economic growth in Latin America is the resolution of problems related to the debt and international trade. The main responsibility for this falls on Europe, the United States, and Japan. Thanks to new less ideological and more realistic leadership, virtually all Latin American countries have implemented austerity programs and evolved toward policies that are less interventionist and more open to the world economy. Acting with great responsibility and varying degrees of success, they have done everything possible to put their houses in order. Nevertheless, the crisis has not been resolved, nor will it be resolved solely by the actions of Latin America. The developed world must find a solution to the debt problem, which requires its reduction. Further, the restrictions to trade practiced by Europe, Japan, and the United States must be eliminated and financial inflows reestablished so that Latin America can cease being a net exporter of capital. Unless these steps are taken, the problems will continue and worsen.

Trends, however, are negative. For example, the most recent U.S. trade law indicates an increase in obstacles for Latin American exports. According to Barber Conable, president of the World Bank, the trade restrictions in the industrialized countries have cost the developing world twice what they receive in aid. And that aid falls far short of Latin America's payments to foreign banks, US$170 billion over the seven years of the debt crisis.

Latin American democratic institutions have demonstrated surprising vitality at a time when constitutional governments can of-

---

6. "The Net Transfer of Resources Abroad," *CEPAL News* X, 1:1, January 1990.

fer only austerity, administrating scarcity and not the abundance enjoyed by the earlier dictatorships. During the troubled 1980s, Latin American democracy was besieged by extremely grave problems, mostly the consequence of the economic crisis and extremist violence. These problems would have caused the fall of constitutional governments a few years ago, but now their effect has been to weaken the governments by diminishing their credibility and reestablishing military tutelage. The case of Argentina shows the danger: The government of President Alfonsín began with a total subordination of the armed forces to civil authority but ended with a renewed military presence in the political life of that nation.

Notwithstanding these difficulties, Bolivia and Argentina, for the first time in many decades, changed governments in a constitutional and orderly manner. Despite devastating guerrilla actions in El Salvador, free elections were held, and power was peacefully transferred from one party to another in 1989, an unprecedented event in this century. The same was true of Guatemala, Peru, and especially Colombia, which faced an extremely severe economic crisis exacerbated by the violence provoked by guerrillas and drug traffickers. In the past, governments were invariably overthrown for less serious reasons.

At the same time, the changes occurring in the socialist world were felt in Latin America. The Soviet Union has always been regarded by the majority of Latin American socialists and communists as an example, an ideal to be emulated. Since the October Revolution, ideas formulated in Moscow became a catechism for Latin American revolutionaries. For some Marxists, perestroika has meant the crumbling of a large part of the ideological structure that sustained their thinking and actions.

Endogenous factors have also brought about this ideological redefinition among some Latin American Marxists. The dictatorships, particularly those in the southern cone, and the bloody consequences modified the visions of these groups of what they pejoratively called "bourgeois democracy," leading them to moderate their criticisms. They have changed their views now because they realize that without it there can be no guarantee of human rights or political freedom.

These political changes are also the result of certain attitudes of moderation, such as those now present in Cuban foreign policy.

Fascination for the Cuban model is a thing of the past. To this must be added the negative economic results of the Nicaraguan Revolution. Although attributable to the U.S. boycott and the Contra war, economic problems are leading Latin American revolutionaries to reflect on the possibility that similar situations might occur if they succeed in winning power in another country. This is particularly the case because of clear indications of Soviet and Cuban withdrawal from Latin American commitments. Under these circumstances, it is possible that the Latin American Marxist parties will evolve in the same direction as their West European comrades, who adopted parliamentary democracy as their sphere of political action.

But social tensions have increased in the region. The popular outburst in Caracas in reaction to the austerity program implemented by the president of Venezuela has been the most dramatic demonstration of the profound social malaise suffered by those living in extreme poverty. They and the middle classes know that the impoverishment they have been suffering for the last eight years may well continue until the end of the century. These spontaneous manifestations of discontent will seek some form of political expression. For now in Latin America populism is again the expression of the frustrations and anguish of the pauperized populations. It is widely known that these political movements leave behind worse problems at the end of their mandate than those they inherited.

Despite the responsibilities that Europe and Japan could assume in the development of Latin America, the role of the United States will continue to be preeminent, albeit within the framework of the changing new world conditions. Latin America and the United States have historically oscillated between two extreme positions: confrontation or subordination. Any country adopting an international policy independent of the United States necessarily became its denigrator; countries following a policy that coincided with that of the United States were subordinated to its orders. These old realities are changing. Latin America is evolving toward positions that are less polemical and more constructive in its relations with the United States. This favorable mood should be used to lay the foundations of a fruitful program of cooperation between North America and South America, two close but distant regions.

On our part, we Latin Americans must convince ourselves that only by our own efforts will we succeed in emerging from this stagnation, and only if we persevere for many years. At the same time, if the risk of nuclear war is finally eliminated, why not devote at least part of the enormous resources once reserved for preparing a nuclear holocaust to the development of the Third World?

REFERENCES

IDB. 1989. *Economic and Social Progress in Latin America, 1989 Report.* Washington: IDB, 463.

United Nations. 1989. *Preliminary Overview of Latin America and the Caribbean, 1989.* Santiago: ECLAC, December 29.

Weeks, John F. 1989. "Central America towards 2000: Crisis sin Salida." In Michael Conroy, ed. *The Future of the Central American Economies.* Austin: University of Texas Press. Published in Spanish in Mats Lundahl and Wim Pelupessy, eds. *Crisis Economica en Centroamerica y el Caribe.* San José, Costa Rica: Editorial DEI.

Part II

Evaluating U.S. Foreign Policy

4

Continuity or Change
in U.S. Perspectives on
Superpower Competition?

Tom J. Farer

Particularly in the case of powerful states enjoying, by virtue of their power, a theoretically wide range of choice, foreign policy may often look like the mere aggregate of largely extemporized responses to particular cases. And those responses are, no doubt, influenced by the need to improvise settlements among parochial bureaucratic and other constituencies intent on institutional or domestic political objectives. But anyone who has closely observed the foreign policy decisionmaking process is struck by the extent to which a normally unexamined world view (which for purposes of easy reference I will call an ideology) shapes the agenda of policy options in any given instance.

The source of any national elite's ideology was nowhere better summarized than in British historian L. B. Namier's observation:

> To treat them [political ideas] as the offspring of pure reason
> would be to assign to them a parentage about as mythological as
> that of Pallas Athene. What matters most is the underlying
> emotions, the music, to which ideas are a mere libretto. (1955)

I will at a later point suggest the character and origins of the regnant ideas about America's relationship to the world. I now simply underscore the proposition that the wide-ranging influence of any governing elite's world view hinders if it does not utterly preclude important changes in policy without some concomitant change in the silent melodies to which our leaders dance.

DÉTENTE I

One way to end superpower competition[1] is for either the Soviet Union or the United States to alter its behavior to satisfy the other's perceptions of propriety. Alternatively, either by agreement or reciprocated unilateral acts and omissions they might grope their way to a single new standard of propriety. Following the second course probably requires revision of long-settled ideas about the world. It will be easier to anticipate the conditions for "new thinking" by U.S. foreign policy elites if we have a firm purchase on the nature and sources of "old thinking."

Through their complaints about the behavior of other states, governing elites reveal the operational substance of their ideology. Over the past four decades, official Washington has condemned as "provocative," "destabilizing," and evidence of "aggressive" or "hos-

---

1. This paper was written in 1988, when it was not yet possible to envision the extraordinary rate at which Soviet power would erode and the corresponding introversion of state policy. At the close of 1990, in the middle of the Persian Gulf crisis, cooperation is more evident than competition and, to the extent that it endures, competition is conducted largely through diplomatic rather than military and economic instruments.

Only a fool will confidently predict either how long semi-anarchy will prevail within the Soviet Union or what sort of political arrangements will finally crystallize. What does seem likely, however, is that at some point a powerful state will reemerge in the territory constituting the Soviet Union. Although shorn of traditional Marxist ideology, it will retain the interests and aspirations induced by history and geography. Like any great power, this new state will attempt to shape a congenial global political environment, and it will demand insignia of respect and a prominent place in the management of world politics.

The United States, for its part, will remain at the center of the international management structure because its interests are global and it is still the only state with the resources, reputation, and will to organize consequential multilateral initiatives. Meanwhile, Germany and Japan at the global level and a number of regional powers are in a position to demand equal protection of the law, to demand, in other words, that they be able to enjoy all the latitude the United States may seek for itself in world affairs. Hence, my effort in this essay to identify rules of the game for the United States and the Soviet Union after the Cold War retains, I believe, its original relevance.

tile" intent the following Soviet initiatives, which I have selected for illustrative purposes from a vast cluster of prospects:

1. military assistance to the widely recognized (albeit brutal and loathsome) government of Ethiopia in repelling a Somali invasion designed to sever a substantial slice of Ethiopian territory;

2. military assistance to that same government for purposes of suppressing a separatist rebellion in Ethiopia;

3. following Portugal's withdrawal, military assistance to one Angolan faction engaged in a struggle for control with factions aided by the United States and its proxies;

4. various forms of assistance to the African National Congress and the Southwest African Peoples' Organization, political-military organizations recognized by the United Nations as legitimate national liberation movements;[2]

5. military assistance to the universally recognized government of Nicaragua in defending against an insurgent movement based outside the country and trained, armed, and funded by the United States;

6. military assistance to Arab countries opposing settlement of the Arab-Israeli conflict in terms satisfactory to the United States, said assistance tending to reduce the power asymmetry between said states and Israel;

7. deployment of naval forces beyond the sea approaches to the Soviet Union, particularly Indian Ocean deployment; and

8. arms sales to the nonaligned government of Peru.

I have selected these particular cases for two reasons: first, because most of them involve behavior that is indisputably allowed by that broad consensus among states we call "international law"; and second, because multiple instances of all the indicted actions, other

---

2. "National liberation movements" are recognized in various U.N. General Assembly resolutions as enjoying the status of belligerents with all attendant legal rights. U.N. recognition has been extended only to those insurgent political/military organizations struggling against "alien" (racial or ethno-religious) domination in territories occupied by European colonial powers before 1945 and in which the indigenous population, presumably (or should I say presumptively) represented by the insurgent movement, has never exercised its right to self-determination.

than aid to national liberation movements, can be found in the record of postwar U.S. policy.

Assistance to Ethiopia in its war with Somalia would seem no less a paradigm of collective self-defense than U.S. aid to South Korea in 1949. The direct antecedent of Soviet-Cuban support for Ethiopia's war against the Eritrean national liberation movement[3] is U.S. support for the Ethiopian armed forces throughout the 1960s and early 1970s, when the secessionist effort flowered. Another precedent is western-bloc assistance to the federal government of Nigeria in its successful struggle with secessionist forces in the area known briefly as Biafra.

Assistance to the government of Nicaragua in its conflict with the Contras has among its many antecedents U.S. assistance to the government of South Vietnam prior to 1964, when North Vietnamese troops entered the war. And, of course, there are innumerable examples of U.S. global deployment of naval forces and arms sales to Third World countries, including those such as Indonesia, with dubious records of compliance with international human rights norms.

Considered in isolation from their historical context, these illustrative complaints imply that, at least prior to the Gorbachev era, the Soviet Union could not satisfy Washington's ideas of responsible behavior merely by using international legal standards and U.S. precedents as its guides. And Washington still seems to reject those guidelines as a sufficient basis for accommodation. In April 1989, Secretary of State James Baker III declared with apparent anger that "our hemisphere is not a dumping ground for Soviet arms or a failed Soviet ideology" and added, apropos Moscow's arms shipments to Nicaragua, that Soviet "responsiveness" to U.S. concerns in resolving regional conflicts, particularly in Central America, "may be one of the best indications of real change in Soviet behavior" (Ottaway 1989).[4]

---

3. This immensely effective organization is not recognized by the United Nations as a "national liberation movement." At least until recently, most governments have chosen to perceive the Eritrean struggle as separatist rather than anticolonial in character. The grounds for rejecting the conventional view are elaborated in Farer (1979).

4. Iraq's invasion of Kuwait has, of course, shifted the locus of the "test" Secretary Baker announced. It appears that, in Baker's judgment, Moscow has passed.

Failure of the 1972 Moscow Principles

Does such rejection imply a hierarchical conception of the international system, that is, a conception allowing some states to enjoy rights and opportunities denied to others? The conventional view among Americans relatively attentive to international relations is that détente involved a U.S. concession of coequal superpower status to the Soviet Union and a concomitant agreement to play the game of nations by a common set of norms. As expressed formally in the Moscow Declarations concluding the Nixon-Brezhnev summit of 1972, each side committed itself not to seek unilateral advantage in areas outside their respective spheres of influence.

In the very face of this principle of peaceful coexistence, again according to the conventional view, the Soviet Union exploited domestic conflict and war weariness in the United States by intensifying its campaign to alter the global balance of power. Over the next seven years, the Soviet Union underwrote North Vietnam's conquest of the South, deployed Cuban proxy forces in East and West Africa, supported North Vietnam's occupation of Cambodia, gave Nicaragua the means requisite for an aggressive regional policy, and invaded Afghanistan. The nub of the matter, then, is that having purported to accept symmetrically applicable standards of proper conduct, Moscow proceeded with its unrelenting effort to effect a change in the international balance of power by fomenting or aggravating regional conflict in the Third World. According to this view, the issue is not whether superpower behavior should be judged by a common standard, but whether the Soviet Union is prepared to abide by the standard agreed on seventeen years ago.

An advocate for the Soviet Union would, no doubt, offer a very different view of the rise and fall of détente. Drawing on, among other sources, Henry Kissinger's memoirs, one would contend that at the very moment it signed the Moscow Declaration, the U.S. government remained fixed in its determination to reduce Soviet influence. Early in his first volume, Dr. Kissinger criticizes the State Department for "injecting us into the Middle East conflict in a way that magnified rather than reduced Soviet influence" (1979, 136). A few pages later, recalling his response to Ambassador Dobrynin's question—"Supposing the [Vietnam] War was settled, how would you go about improving relations?"—he writes:

The best answer I could come up with was a summit and an unspecified promise to improve trade. In the Middle East our interest ran counter to Moscow's; it was the goal of our strategy,
after all, to reduce Soviet influence in the Middle East, that of
the Soviets to enhance or at least preserve it. (1979, 161)

This attitude, Moscow could argue, was incompatible with a pledge
not to seek unilateral advantage. Paradoxically, Moscow might cite
the U.S. response to the disorder in Angola incident to Portuguese
withdrawal as further evidence of Washington's refusal, despite
the Moscow Declaration, to treat the Soviet Union as an equal.
According to ex-CIA officer John Stockwell (1978), from the
moment it was clear that Portugal intended to withdraw,
Washington, acting in concert with its Zairian client, sought victory for its preferred faction. From the Soviet point of view, then,
the worst that can be said of its behavior is that both superpowers
leaped at a perceived opportunity to implant an ideologically congenial client. Their common reluctance to seek a joint approach
implies common belief either that the other party would not comply with the Moscow principles or that the principles did not cover
this case.

Once the competition was joined, each sought victory through
the introduction of powerful proxies, South Africa and Cuba, respectively. By virtue of the former's proximity to Angola, the United
States could maintain a low profile. Perhaps no more than a wink
was necessary. Cuba's distance from the scene entailed large-scale,
high-profile logistical support from the Soviet Union. The superpowers differed not with respect to any matter of principle, but
rather in their assessment of costs and benefits from enhanced investment in the conflict. Moscow, in my view having done its
sums badly, imputed more value to an MPLA (in English, the
Popular Movement for the Liberation of Angola) victory than the
U.S. Congress could envision from orchestrating its defeat.

As for Afghanistan, Soviet counsel might argue that while the
invasion was inexpedient and undoubtedly a violation of the
United Nations Charter, it was essentially indistinguishable from
U.S. intervention in Vietnam, an intervention that American public opinion condemns retrospectively more on grounds of prudence
than principle. In both cases, insurgent forces enjoying outside
support were about to sweep away a superpower's client regime. In

both cases, the regime's leader resisted his patron's advice and came to be an obstacle to victory over the insurgents. Also in both cases, the superpower took those measures necessary to secure a more tractable associate and thereafter took over the main burden of the war. The U.S. occupation of the Dominican Republic in 1965 and of Grenada in 1983 are two additional American-created precedents for direct military intervention to establish or preserve ideologically congenial governments in Third World states. Claims to have acted in those cases basically to protect U.S. citizens are frivolous. Any effort to distinguish them on the grounds of invitation or authorization from regional or sub-regional organizations is equally frivolous.

How might counsel in the service of Washington rebut the charge of a double standard of propriety? Perhaps a threshold question is whether U.S. leaders do or should see any need for a rebuttal. A double standard is morally condemnable when applied to persons, because under now-dominant religious and philosophic conventions, individuals are morally equal. Whether seen as abstractions or huge collectives, states are very problematical subjects of moral rights and obligations. Their formal equality, that is, their right to equal application of the "law,"[5] is a legal convention, albeit one justified by moral ends, including the maintenance of peace and the enhancement of human rights. The formal equality of states is, in other words, instrumental in character and thus susceptible to modification without moral objection if such modification is better calculated to achieve the same ends.

If there is no moral objection to a double standard, there is, I think, a prudential one that has profound moral implications. It is, in brief, that the United States, whether acting alone or in conjunction with other states, lacks the means to compel or induce Soviet acquiescence. Refusal of the United States to accept reciprocally applicable standards of propriety would guarantee repeated superpower collision, spreading disorder in the Third World.

---

5. Here I use the term "law" to cover both formally recognized norms such as those embodied in the United Nations Charter and informal understandings such as those incorporated into the Moscow Declaration.

WORLD VIEW I: DEFENSE OF NATIONAL INDEPENDENCE

But can such a refusal really be induced from U.S. behavior? Certainly nothing in Kissinger's memoirs or the reminiscences of other members of the U.S. foreign policy community evidences an intention so to order the world. What both official and private writings do exhibit is a conviction that controversial actions undertaken by the superpowers are in fact distinguishable under a common standard of propriety, and that appearances to the contrary fade when these cases are placed in historical context. Once placed there, the argument goes, they expose Soviet behavior as a pattern of aggressive assaults on the postwar normative system embodied in the United Nations Charter, while revealing American behavior as fundamentally defensive in character. While it may be appropriate in a legal case to deny the jury knowledge of past behavior, the requirements of order in the politically decentralized international system make it essential to assess each occurrence as one instance of a larger pattern either of compliance or resistance to previously agreed standards that continue to enjoy broader support.

The principal jurisprudential expression of this view can be found in the writing of Myres McDougal and his colleagues, sometimes referred to as the "Yale School" of international law (1960). There are, McDougal announced at the height of the Cold War, two distinct systems of public order in the world. One, championed by the United States, is the public order of freedom marked by respect for individual and national autonomy. The other, dominated by the Soviet Union, is the totalitarian order committed to centralization of life-shaping choices. In identifying and applying international legal norms, the scholar should choose to advance the cause of freedom, he argued. Thus, in the Cuban missile crisis the appropriateness of a forceful response could not be judged solely in terms of expectations about whether use of the missiles was imminent. What made a partial blockade appropriate was the whole postwar record of Soviet efforts to overthrow or subvert undeferential regimes, thereby altering the international balance of power to endow Moscow with global political hegemony.

McDougal's view of the Soviet Union as a relentlessly expanding, aggressive state, augured by George Kennan's immediate postwar call for "containment," remained an essential element of the American foreign policy catechism at least through the first half of the Reagan presidency. Kennan wrote:

> [One of the Kremlin's guiding concepts] is that of the innate antagonism between capitalism and socialism. . . . It has profound implications for Russia's conduct as a member of the international society. It means that there can never be on Moscow's side any sincere assumption of a community of aims between the Soviet Union and powers that are regarded as capitalist. . . . [The Kremlin's leaders have endeavored] to secure and make absolute the power which they seized in 1917. They have endeavored to secure it primarily against forces at home. . . . But they have also endeavored to secure it against the outside world. For ideology . . . taught them that it was their duty eventually to overthrow the political forces beyond their borders. (1947)

Soviet behavior abroad, Kennan concluded, must therefore be seen as "a fluid stream which moves constantly, wherever it is permitted to move, toward a given goal. Its main concern is to make sure that it has filled every nook and cranny available to it in the basin of world power" (1947).

Kennan's article appeared in 1947. That same year, President Harry Truman, declaring himself "fully aware of the broad implications involved," called on Congress to appropriate US$750 million in aid to Greece and Turkey and to authorize the detail of American civilian and military personnel to those countries for, among other purposes, "the instruction and training of selected Greek and Turkish personnel." The aid was required, he said, to help them preserve their free institutions and their national integrity. And it would constitute, he added, "a frank recognition that totalitarian regimes imposed on free peoples, by direct or indirect aggression, undermine the foundations of international peace and hence the security of the United States. . . . [W]e cannot allow changes in the status quo in violation of the Charter of the United Nations by such methods as coercion, or by such subterfuges as political infiltration" (Truman 1947). Thus, the war for influence in countries deemed natural dependencies of the western alliance was joined.

This view of the Soviet Union as inherently committed to assault on the postwar normative system remained official wisdom from 1947 at least until the middle of Ronald Reagan's second term. A

1981 speech by Alexander Haig, then Secretary of State, evidenced
the continuity of Washington's world view:

> As the Soviet arsenal grew and the West failed to keep pace,
> Moscow's interventionism increased. . . . Today's Soviet military
> machine far exceeds the requirements of defense; it under-
> mines the balance of power on which we and our allies depend,
> and it threatens the peace of the world. . . . The most persistent
> troubles in U.S.–Soviet relations arise from Soviet intervention
> in regional conflicts, aggravating tensions and hampering the
> search for peaceful solutions. . . . The Soviet Union must under-
> stand that it cannot succeed in dominating the world through
> aggression.

The Beginning of Doubt

Until the war in Vietnam, this view of the United States as de-
fender of the postwar normative system (characterized by respect for
national independence and the prohibition of force as an instrument of change) against relentless Soviet challenge encountered
virtually no effective domestic opposition. But as the Indo-Chinese
conflict escalated, a fraction of the American elite, based primarily
in the universities, began sketching an alternative interpretation
of U.S.–Soviet conflict. The new dissenters did not launch a single
integrated assault on the fortress of opinion. For a while united in
opposition to the war and to what they all perceived as reflexive
American hostility to left-wing movements and regimes in the
Third World, they divided on questions both of diagnosis and prescription.

To oversimplify for the benefit of brevity, one group—which
came to be seen as well as openly to define itself as the new
American Left—was characterized by a gloomy view of American
history and society, capitalist modes of development in the Third
World, and by a correspondingly sunny one of Third World revolutionaries (though not of the Soviet Union). Strongly influenced
by Marxist thought (particularly by its explanation of imperialism),
this fraction of dissenters saw in the whole of American history an
imperial policy, first to occupy the continent, then to subordinate its
Latin neighbors, and finally to dominate the world to make it safe

for American trade and investment.

Left-wing dissenters from established thought tended to see the Soviet Union as a problem for Washington mainly because its very existence as an ambitious superpower enhanced the freedom of choice and thus the autonomy of Third World elites. If Soviet power was neutralized, the U.S. and its allies would have the field free to maintain an economic order beneficial primarily to the capitalist core of the world economy. Rather than fostering economic development, it was argued, the liberal trading system (the "Empire of Free Trade") inhibited the kind of growth that would ameliorate mass poverty and make Third World states more independent of resource-allocating decisions made in the foreign ministries and board rooms of the First World. Barnett and Mueller's (1974) book on the multinational corporation, *Global Reach,* typified the New Left's perspective. The policy prescription issuing from this type of analysis was a generalized opposition to U.S. activism in the Third World. New Leftists assumed that activism of any form would inevitably be on behalf of regimes and social classes hostile to domestic equality and therefore willing to subordinate the interests of their states to those of the capitalist democracies.

The second fraction of dissenters differed sufficiently among themselves so that they formed less a group than an agglomeration. Nevertheless, they tended to share certain themes. Unlike the New Left, they did not attribute U.S.–Soviet conflict in the Third World exclusively to a conscious effort by the United States to sustain a global empire of free trade. Rather, they tended to interpret the conflict in part as induced by the structural fact of a world with two dominant states, structural tendencies toward competition and paranoia being enhanced in this case by radically different historical experiences, ideologies, and geographic positions.

As a group, these centrist dissenters tended to devalue political change in Third World states. Most governments, they argued, are driven by nationalist ambitions and voracious domestic constituencies to sell their resources to the highest bidder. Markets rather than ideology channel the Third World's natural resources. Ideology might marginally influence decisions on matters such as military bases. But changes in technology have radically reduced the value of such bases. And where they are still valuable, the West in general could bid higher than the Soviet bloc for their acquisition.

Change from a conservative to a leftist regime may tend for a time to discourage foreign investment and to place existing investment at risk. But with the exception of a few oil-exporting states, U.S. direct investment in Third World countries is modest compared to investment in the First World. And the economic furies unleashed by countries that expropriated without compensation is an inhibiting lesson to the next generation of leftist leaders.

On the other side, it is not clear that the Soviet Union should expend wealth, prestige, and internal unity to preserve a regime previously aligned with the West, when regimes of all ideological stripes regularly display ingratitude toward their superpower patron whenever a better deal can be struck. Somalia is a case in point. For all its declared commitment to "scientific socialism," despite all the students trained in Soviet universities, despite the half-billion dollars in modern weapons bestowed on its armed forces, the government of Somalia showed itself immune to Soviet advice and interests by attacking Ethiopia when it was a latent addition to the Soviet client stable, and then in extremis transferring its affections to the West.

The Soviet Union's acquisition of additional clients in the Third World and the corresponding loss of some by the West does not appear to have had any effect on the overall balance of power between the two great inheritors who emerged forty-four years ago from the abattoir of World War II. All that seems to have been achieved by their respective efforts to affect the political evolution and alignment of Third World regimes is the sapping of their own economic strength. The dubious reward has been to reduce the influence of both in a world where medium powers are beginning to grasp for regional hegemony and where, in any event, military power does not consistently translate into usable influence, much less tangible accretions to national welfare.

This centrist view also disputed the Cold War wisdom that located the Third World in the western camp. Perhaps one can find the origin of this western possessiveness in the fact that the older Third World states had long danced to tunes played in one or another western capital. And, of course, the new ones frequently filled spaces previously occupied and to a great extent defined by western colonial administration. The departing European masters often influenced the selection of the first generation of post-colonial leaders and shaped the institutional structures they occupied. Being seen from Washington (and other western capitals) as members of the "Free World Camp" confronting a monolithic Marxist opponent, their prospective displacement by Marxist-sounding counter-elites was naturally experienced in western capitals as a threat, even a challenge, to the resolve of the West to maintain an inherited, natural, and indefinitely sustainable status quo (in the absence of Marxist subversion). Hence, a threatened change in the ideological character of a Third World regime was deemed significant regardless of its immediate material consequences.

Implicit in the writings both of centrist and leftist dissenters was a very different view of the Third World. Rather than occupying a fixed place within the perimeter of the western camp, it was huge, sprawling, and wildly diverse terrain located outside both camps. Despite their efforts to build stable alliances, the superpowers found their influence ebbing and flowing. This results in part because conflict and competition within and among Third World states inevitably led to a superpower currying favor with one group or government, which provoked the opposing side to look to the other superpower for compensating support.

Seen from this perspective, Soviet efforts to displace or reorient Third World associates of the West should not in most instances be characterized as threatening. They are neither probes of western resolve to defend vital ground nor dangerous destabilizing assaults on the normative status quo. Rather, they are moves in an endless and indeterminate game of influence projection that powerful states have always played in the no-man's land between them. What matters is that the game be played according to rules that prevent a general breakdown of international order.

As noted, the Soviet Union's Third World interventions in the wake of the Moscow Declaration are susceptible to several interpretations. One is that they indicate an insistence by the Soviet Union on an equal right to compete for influence and participate in collective efforts to manage regional conflict. Another more ominous interpretation is that Moscow saw an opportunity to alter the global balance of power in the Vietnam-induced breakup of the Cold War political consensus in America and the consequent constraints on the exercise of American influence. According to this second interpretation, Moscow began acting according to permissive rules of intervention largely in response to its perception that President Jimmy Carter was the herald of American self-constraint.

Even under the former, more benign interpretation, the United States could not have achieved in the 1970s a lasting understanding with the Soviet Union about the terms of their competition, not one that left the United States with greater latitude for intervention in the affairs of Third World states. I presume the Soviet Union remains reluctant to make that concession, notwithstanding President Gorbachev's reorientation of Soviet priorities, a reorientation based on a recalculation of the costs and benefits from adventures among the developing countries.

WORLD VIEW II: DEFENSE OF HUMAN RIGHTS

One obstacle to a U.S.–Soviet accord on guidelines for superpower activities in the Third World has been the U.S. conviction that its behavior is essentially defensive,[6] while Soviet behavior is designed to undermine American security and overthrow the postwar order. Occupants of the right wing of American politics will surrender that conviction gradually and grudgingly, if at all. But it seems to have lost its grip on a majority of the electorate and the foreign policy elite, so it is no longer an insuperable obstacle.

A second obstacle has been the perception, rarely challenged in American discourse before Vietnam, that governments (or movements) in the Third World professing pro-western sentiments, purporting to favor market economies and elections, or simply declaring themselves hostile to Marxism, are moral siblings of the United States. Close scrutiny of the shifting guard the United States sought to defend in Saigon dealt rather a sharp blow to the naive notion that all governments making friendly noises belonged literally in the "Free World Camp." Yet the notion might have survived Vietnam had it not been compounded by well-reported orgies of misanthropy organized by ferociously anti-communist governments in Washington's own hemisphere. The murderous order imposed by Pinochet in Chile and his counter-

---

6. Defensive viewed in terms of both superpower security interests and the norms embodied in the United Nations Charter, above all that of national independence.

parts in Argentina and Uruguay, imposed by armies on which the U.S. had lavished training and advice about the virtues of democracy, narrowed to a group of true believers the conviction that our thugs were necessarily better than theirs. And if they were not, then did it follow that the extension of American power and the corresponding contraction of Soviet power necessarily promoted human rights?

To the end of stilling doubts aroused by the pathologies of certain anti-communist regimes, conservative publicists like Jeane Kirkpatrick, Reagan's first Ambassador to the United Nations, reaffirmed and elaborated the distinction between merely authoritarian and totalitarian governments. Kirkpatrick and other conservative writers drew some dissenters back to the traditional faith. Their arguments were facilitated by widespread concern over continued growth in Soviet arms, the brutal war in Afghanistan, and disgust and disillusionment with postwar developments in Vietnam, as well as a general call for a restoration of national pride. At the same time, optimism was prompted by the restoration of civilian governments in much of Latin America and the evident consolidation of democratic regimes in Spain, Greece, and Portugal. While the number of agnostics remains substantial, press and congressional reaction to developments in Nicaragua indicates a strong residual inclination both among political elites and the general public to judge leftist authoritarian regimes by harsher standards than rightist ones.

Reagan and his coterie were hardly the first Americans to conflate the enhancement of national power and human rights. It is a very old tradition, extending back beyond even the man who lent his name to moralism in foreign policy, Woodrow Wilson. Historian Michael Hunt traces it back virtually to the founding of the Republic:

> By the early twentieth century, three core ideas relevant of foreign affairs had emerged, and they collectively began to yield a strong influence over policy. *The capstone idea defined the American future in terms of an active quest for national greatness closely coupled to the promotion of liberty.* It was firmly in place by the turn of the century, after having met and mastered a determined opposition on three separate occasions—in the 1790s, the 1840s and the 1930s. [Emphasis added.] (1987)

Cuba has been a repeated target of our moral fervor. In the mid-1890s, when Cubans renewed their revolt against Spanish rule, "free Cuba" rallies occurred throughout the United States.[7] If the United States failed to act on behalf of Cuba, one senator warned, "the time will come when there will be retribution upon us as a people, because we have not been true to the task assigned us by Providence" (Dallek 1983, 26). Speaking eight decades later, President Jimmy Carter seemed to echo the senator's sentiments when he concluded his address with the statement:

> Our policy is based on an historical vision of America's role. . . .
> Our policy is rooted in our moral values, which never change.
> Our policy is reinforced by our material wealth and by our military power. Our policy is designed to serve mankind.

Not surprisingly in light of their experience, the seminal human right for most Americans has been democratic government. Generally, U.S. policymakers have been willing to find it wherever multiparty elections are conducted by regimes that extol the virtues of private enterprise. It was holy writ for the Reagan administration that democracy, however imperfect, reigns in El Salvador and Guatemala. As a practical matter, neither satisfies Joseph Schumpeter's now-standard definition (1947), because in neither case did elections determine who would have the power to decide the central issues of national power; nor could elections compensate for the absence of an effective system of justice, that drive-shaft of real democracies. As one Central American educator put it not long ago, North Americans think they are hearing an entire democratic symphony when all that is being played is the single note of elections.

TOWARD NEW PRINCIPLES AND PROCEDURES: DÉTENTE PLUS

In designing guidelines for moderating U.S.–Soviet competition in the Third World and promoting cooperation in the restraint of

---

7. According to Robert Dallek (1983), "The issue let loose cascades of imperialistic and moralistic oratory."

regional conflicts, account must be taken of the long tradition of moralism. Woven as it is into the warp and woof of our political culture, it cannot be altogether abandoned. Nor does it seem likely that the Soviet Union could eschew its declared value preferences summarized in its praise for "wars of national liberation." Mere national interest is a dubious basis for the policy of a multinational state such as the Soviet Union. To find legitimacy, the governors of such a state in this age of rabid nationalism must offer themselves as the champions of a universally relevant ideal. Classical Marxism-Leninism once provided it. As changes within the Soviet Union and certain of its close allies so vividly illustrate, the old model has lost its glamour. The old model corresponds neither to what is (except in a few stagnant political ponds that will soon be absorbed into powerful fresh streams) nor to what most people hope will be.

Apparently, Gorbachev and his colleagues had not at the end of the 1980s found a concise, normative statement that described, justified, and comprehensively explained the rapidly changing reality over which they preside. Probably that was because they were in mid-course on a journey whose end could be but dimly seen. Their predecessors, who paid a high price for prematurity, often spoke of "socialism with a human face." Optimistic observers could point to three elements of the emerging changes: (1) a market-driven economy tempered by strenuous efforts to equalize opportunity and safeguard the interests of those unable to compete effectively; (2) a political order that institutionalized a relationship between political power and popular preference; and (3) a respect for autonomous social institutions such as the church, trade unions, and professional societies.

Socialism with a human face could serve as a distinct ideal. It would be distinguishable in more than name from the forms of capitalism found in most Third World countries. Certainly it would contrast with the harsh ideals espoused by western conservatives and to some degree practiced in the United Kingdom in the 1980s, if not the United States itself. As an alternative model to that articulated by the Reagan and Thatcher administrations, it could claim distinction in terms of the following roles for the state: (1) as the guarantor of a level economic playing field for all sectors of the population;[8] (2) as the guarantor of a level political field, for example by assuring relatively equal access to the media of communications;[9] and (3) as the guarantor of a dignified existence for all those citizens who, for one reason or another, have no market value.

So defined, socialism with a human face would place a balanced emphasis on economic and social rights no less than political and civil rights. To the extent it addressed the demands of its own national minorities, ceding them a substantial measure of local autonomy, it could claim for itself leadership in the field of cultural rights. The idiom of human rights offers a bridge between a post–Marxist-Leninist socialism and free-enterprise capitalism.[10] A common idiom, if it corresponds reasonably with superpower behavior at home and with the behavior urged upon clients, would draw some of the virulence from superpower conflicts in the Third World.

A common idiom would create a more benign environment. It would not dissolve inherited conflicts of interest and sentiment that attach themselves to great powers as mollusks adhere to rocks. Beyond atmospherics, there must be substantive and procedural rules of the road.

A detailed proposal for such rules would require another paper. As a point of departure, however, I would suggest that the United Nations Charter offers a satisfactory constitutional framework for governing the behavior of the great and regional powers. Above all, it has stood for the proposition that no state may employ force for any purpose other than self-defense against an actual or imminent armed attack upon its territory, its officials, or its citizens, and the defensive force employed must be proportional to the threat. It also prohibits attempts by whatever means to effect the overthrow of a recognized government unless authorized by the Security Council or a regional organization acting within the terms of its constitution. For better or worse (often for worse), it has been widely con-

8. This would be in contrast, for example, to the state in a country such as Guatemala, which guarantees, when it does not enhance, the concentration of capital and wealth in a very few hands.

9. The western conservative approach mechanically assumes that if the media are in private hands, they will for market reasons reflect all sectors of opinion.

10. See Chapter 2 by Victor A. Kremenyuk in this volume, where such is suggested.

strued to tolerate foreign military assistance to recognized governments attempting to suppress rebellions. Unfortunately, such assistance has often been extended without reference to the beleaguered government's compliance with human rights norms.

United Nations Charter restraints on unilateral coercion are bound to evoke frustration in an ever more tightly connected world. Rogue regimes that mutilate their populations, assault their neighbors, or tread on the rights of other states by exporting pollutants or terrorists must be disciplined. But the medicine of unilateral action may be more dangerous than the disease. As the world's two most powerful states, enjoying vast natural resources and possessing large parts of the earth's surface and the adjacent atmosphere, the United States and the Soviet Union have an enormous common interest in making the United Nations work to deal with these delinquents, which is why Détente II must be only a station on the line to entente.

REFERENCES

Barnett, Richard, and Ronald Mueller. 1974. *Global Reach: The Power of Multinational Corporations.* New York: Simon & Schuster.

Dallek, Robert. 1983. *The American Style of Foreign Policy.* New York: New American Library.

Farer, Tom J. 1979. *Warclouds on the Horn of Africa.* 2d rev. ed. Washington: Carnegie Endowment.

Haig, Alexander. 1981. Address to the American Bar Association, Department of State Bulletin, 10-12.

Hunt, Michael. 1987. *Ideology and Foreign Policy.* New Haven: Yale Press.

Kennan, George. 1947. "The Sources of Soviet Conduct." *Foreign Affairs,* July.

Kissinger, Henry. 1979. *White House Years.* Boston: Little, Brown & Co.

McDougal, Myres. Among the principal works applying and elaborating the jurisprudential view of the Yale School are the following: Myres McDougal and Associates, *Studies in World Public Order* (1960); McDougal and Florentino Feliciano, *Law and*

Minimum World Order (1961); McDougal and William Burke, *The Public Order of the Oceans* (1962); McDougal and Harold Lasswell, *The Interpretation of Agreements and World Public Order* (1967); McDougal and William Reisman, *International Law in Contemporary Perspective: The Order of the World Community* (1981).

Namier, Sir Lewis Bernstien. 1955. *Personalities and Powers.* London: Hamish Hamilton, 4.

Ottaway, David. 1989. *Washington Post,* April 16, A35.

Stockwell, John. 1978. In Search of Enemies: A CIA Story. New York: Norton.

Truman, Harry S. 1947. *Congressional Record* 93, part 2, March 12.

5

The Rivalry Between
the Superpowers:
A Latin American Perspective

General Edgardo Mercado Jarrin

This chapter treats the rivalry between the two superpowers in Latin America from a Latin American perspective. The discussion is divided into three parts: the first analyzes the new phase in the global situation; the second examines the Latin America scenario in which the rivalry between the superpowers takes place, with extrapolation of trends for the future; and the third reviews the effects of this rivalry in the spheres of ideology, the economy, and military security.

A NEW PHASE IN THE WORLD SITUATION

World War II divided the world geopolitically into spheres of influence. What happened in Poland was the preserve of Moscow, and what occurred in Latin America was the concern of Washington. Each superpower expected its control over its area of influence to be respected. Exceptions such as South Korea and Cuba have been acknowledged by both sides, but when spheres of influence began to be encroached upon, as in the case of Nicaragua, the risk of confrontation was inevitable. This was corroborated in the Kissinger Commission Report on Central America, which asserted that "the United States cannot accept any Soviet military

participation in Central America nor in the Caribbean, beyond
what is already tolerated in Cuba."

The Soviet Union accepted the role of Latin America as the
strategic rearguard of the United States. Its approach was prudent
and cautious, and it was designed to avoid political risks.
Moreover, Soviet might has not been capable of interfering with
the South American maritime lines of communication, despite an
increased naval presence in the South Atlantic. Former President
Ronald Reagan disclosed that Soviet President Mikhail Gorbachev
had expressed to him his desire that the Central American Peace
Plan succeed and had promised to halt aid to the Nicaraguan government. This statement was consistent with the Soviet policy of
not selling offensive arms to Nicaragua; those sent were aimed at
improving the combat efficiency of the Sandinista army against the
Contras. In sum, the Soviet Union kept a "low-profile" policy for
South America, avoiding risks. It appears that this role was recognized by U.S. strategic planners.

Of course, the United States has understandable security interests
in the hemisphere. Latin America is important to Washington as
a resource supplier, which does not require extensive lines of communication, and because it is a region flanked by strategic maritime routes in the Caribbean Basin, the South Atlantic, the
Southern Straits, and the South Pacific. The political stability of its
strategic rearguard, the absence of any real Soviet threat to this
area, and the lack of economic and military risks to U.S. security
originating from Latin America free U.S. strategy from the need
to deploy significant forces to this region, allowing their utilization in the central theater of operations. Nevertheless, the emergence of new threats in the 1990s—subversion and drug trafficking—could force the United States to divert its defense resources to
South America.

International relations remain characterized by the dominant
position of the two superpowers, which continue to set the tone for
world events. The current existence of mutual interests bolsters the
belief that the world has entered a long period of détente and is
not merely going through one of the brief cycles of successive periods of tension and rapprochement that have marked relations between the two superpowers. The two biggest sources of tension between the two countries—the arms race and regional conflicts—

have begun to be addressed: a disarmament treaty has been reached for the first time, and numerous conflicts have been resolved.

A long period of détente between the United States and the Soviet Union will make it possible to attenuate the distortions that the rivalry inflicted on the political and economic development of Latin America. Although the world has entered a period of détente different from the high tension between the superpowers that prevailed after World War II, the changes that are occurring do not modify U.S. strategic interests in Latin America. Soviet naval power has increased notably in the last few decades, and its presence has been growing in the South Atlantic and the South Pacific. North American naval superiority is indisputable, but as a priority Washington must maintain its maritime lines of communication. Therefore, North American strategic interests in Latin America—predominantly maritime—involving access to markets and primary materials remain unchanged. Nor have its other security interests in the region altered, such as maintaining political stability in the area compatible with these interests and preventing the presence of hostile extra-hemispheric powers in the zone. Consequently, the strategic importance of military bases in the region, such as in Panama[1] and other areas of the Third World (for example, the Philippines), must be reevaluated, with as yet unclear implications for Latin American interests.

The major dangers of superpower rivalry are behind us, but Latin America finds itself weakened and marginalized vis-à-vis the new situation resulting from détente. In a certain sense, the lengthy and generalized economic crisis in which it has been immersed, including the lack of a solution to the debt problem, shows that what occurs or will occur in the region is of little concern to the countries that benefited from the Reagan-Gorbachev accords. Therefore, regional integration and the deepening of political consensus among the governments of Latin America are all the more imperative.

---

1. Some have argued that U.S. Panama policy, including invasion, was prompted by a desire to maintain bases in that country beyond the year 2000, when the Torrijos-Carter treaties require their removal.—*(Ed.)*

THE SOUTH AMERICAN SCENARIO

In Latin America, the trends indicate an increasingly stronger regional identity, a better articulation of interests, and the growing conviction that only in this way will the region minimize its vulnerability to external factors. In the global confrontation between the superpowers, Latin America has been characterized by its relative strategic and geopolitical marginality, which has tended to become more accentuated. It is not considered to be a possible major theater of operations by either superpower, which is manifested in a certain degree of calm. The region has passed through an unfavorable decade with loss of status due to new factors, among which are the declining capacity of energy suppliers, notably OPEC, to regulate prices; decreasing prices for primary materials; the lack of a unified response to the external debt problem; obsolescence of traditional development models; and the general deterioration of the standard of living. The last applied to most of the countries of the region and affected the poorest groups most, which has debilitated Latin America, reducing its margin for power and negotiations in the international context.

The political-strategic tensions among the Latin American countries originating from present and potential interstate conflicts are losing vigor. Many of the old border tensions—for example, the cases of Brazil-Argentina, Argentina-Chile, and Peru-Chile—appreciably decreased in the 1980s and will probably continue to do so. In addition, the tensions between Colombia and Venezuela could enter a new period of calm.

The new Latin American democracies are being affected by the weakness of their institutions, a phenomenon that frequently deepens divisions instead of moderating and resolving conflicts. Nonetheless, the 1980s was a period of democratic consolidation in which harmony and coexistence were sought. There are no foreseeable armed conflicts, except for the subversive movements affecting Colombia and Peru. In the economic sphere, there is a growing awareness that the Asian development model is not viable for Latin America under the present conditions. This perception will lead the new generation to critically review the traditional antagonisms among our countries, and then to initiate formation of a Latin American Common Market. In the meantime, Argentine-

Brazilian cooperation is clearing the way for the emergence of a power center capable of making a South American defense alternative viable. There has been progress toward making the South Atlantic into a Peace Zone, and attempts are being made to do the same in the South Pacific. The Andean Pact, the Amazon Pact, the River Plate Treaty, the maintenance of the Treaty of Tlatelolco,[2] and the recent proposal by the Group of Eight for a dialogue with the United States are creating a new culture of cooperation and peace in Latin America. All these factors are shaping the new Latin American framework, one in which the rivalry between the superpowers will continue to take place.

The Latin American countries are seeking a greater degree of political independence from the United States. Many of them are determined to act with autonomy in the international arena. In these relations, the Latin American countries are demanding recognition of their national interests, fundamentally linked with aspirations for economic and social development that they themselves must define in a sovereign manner, without pressures of any sort. Defending their national interests has made them more conscious of their relations with other groups of countries, especially with the European Economic Community, Japan, the Soviet Union, the countries of Central Europe, and the People's Republic of China.

One of the most pressing tasks before Latin American governments at present is the formulation of a long-term development policy. This task is extremely complex, owing to the region's internal diversity and unequal social development. The groundwork was laid by the Group of Eight's efforts to coordinate regional cooperation and integration policies and to address the region's external vulnerability. These efforts will generate greater capacity for negotiation and responsibility in cooperative efforts in the coming decade to help maintain world peace and security as well as to shape a just international order of hope and progress.

Latin America and the United States perceive their interests in the region very differently. As a world power, the U.S. perception of its security role in Latin America is heavily influenced by how

2. The Treaty of Tlatelolco (named for the part of Mexico City where the meeting was held) prohibits the stationing of nuclear weapons in Latin America. All Latin American countries signed, except Argentina and Brazil.

these interests fare globally. The United States is particularly sensitive to the possibility of the expansion of Soviet power in the
Caribbean Basin and the South Atlantic. The nations of Latin
America view their interests in a different context. For many
countries, sustained economic growth and social transformation
are decisive in promoting domestic stability. Due to these differences in perspectives, the internal changes in the region, especially revolutionary changes, are perceived differently by Latin
American countries and the United States. The United States often
views these changes as a threat to its national security. In contrast,
the Latin American countries do not consider them dangerous to
the United States, and as such they reject U.S. intervention as a
proper response.[3] These differences could be reconciled by a reappraisal of the problem on each side. If not, the specific problem of
Panama, which intermingles U.S. strategic interests, nationalist
aspirations for social change, and aspects of international ethics,
could escalate tensions in the region.

RIVALRY BETWEEN THE SUPERPOWERS
IN LATIN AMERICA

In this period of superpower détente and cooperation, relations between the United States and Latin America are going through
their most critical period since the end of World War II. Beyond
questions of ideology and politics, there is a generalized malaise
in the region over the present state of these relations. At least two
concerns gave rise to this situation: that the United States showed
decreasing interest in resolving Latin American problems, and
that it seeks the same degree of support as it did forty years ago, despite its actions with regard to the Malvinas, Grenada, the Central
American crisis, and Panama.

Of those problems affecting relations between the United States
and Latin America, the debt is a central issue. The Brady Plan[4]

3. This was shown by the virtually unanimous opposition to the U.S. invasion of
Panama in the Organization of American States.—(Ed.)

4. U.S. Secretary of the Treasury Nicholas Brady announced in early 1989 a new
initiative to deal with the debt of the most heavily indebted countries. Over a year
later, the plan had been applied only to Mexico, with uncertain results.—(Ed.)

represents a slight change in U.S. policy toward the debt because previous policy consisted of little more than attempting to create conditions for the total payment of the debt. The real issue— shared responsibility implying partial payment—was never recognized by the Reagan administration.

The notion of reducing the debt represents a change of criteria and timid recognition that the problem should be dealt with politically. Nevertheless, the Brady Plan places too much emphasis on the conditionality of the International Monetary Fund and the World Bank. Further, the plan favors Mexico and Venezuela, both of which are in a better position to begin negotiations with the U.S. government and the multilaterals. Moreover, these two countries are located in the Caribbean Basin, the area of greatest security interest for the United States. The impression is that the Brady Plan is motivated more by security reasons than by a desire to resolve the socioeconomic problems of Latin America as a whole. The vulnerability of international banks vis-à-vis the biggest debtors in the region is part of the security concern, and the medium-sized debtors may be excluded.

On the other hand, the Brady Plan is also indicative of the new role the United States could assume in Latin America given current relations with the Soviet Union. The United States may decide to cooperate selectively with the countries in the region most compatible with its economic and security interests. Taking competition from Japan and West Europe into account, U.S. policy in the future could seek a preferential rapprochement with Mexico, designating the greatest amount of aid to this country and disassociating itself from those that do not bring it greater benefits. One cannot rule out the possibility that the United States would extend to Mexico an accord similar in scope to that signed with Canada to create a new opportunity for integration.

The problem of the debt is connected to the processes of democratic consolidation, a link that to date the United States has refused to accept. The stability of Latin American democratic governments is jeopardized by the serious economic problems they are confronting. The application of adjustment policies, a prerequisite to negotiations and obtaining credits, has eroded the social base and stability of governments seeking to consolidate democracy. Thus, there is a contradiction in U.S. foreign policy between what is considered the "Reagan legacy"—active support of democracy—and the failure to accept that democratic consolidation requires economic stability and social support.

It is true that the political map of Latin America and the Caribbean has been transformed. Today more than 90 percent of the population of the region lives in democratic societies. But it would be an exaggeration to conclude that this is due to the policies of the Reagan administration, in particular to cite El Salvador and Chile as cases of active support to democracy. It cannot be ignored that there exists the danger of a return to authoritarianism in several countries (Argentina and Peru, for instance).

The issue of drug trafficking was highlighted in the 1988 electoral campaign and promises to be an obligatory theme from a U.S. standpoint in hemispheric relations. The new drug agency head was instructed by President Bush to present a new global antidrug policy by September 1989. A problem that should have been a motive for cooperation has ended up becoming a source of friction because of the unilateral posture adopted by the United States.[5] Washington's focus on combatting the drug problem at its source has shifted the burden of responsibility and placed the brunt of the pressure on the Latin American countries, without making any significant progress in reducing demand or attacking the U.S. drug trafficking network.

In the case of Peru, the U.S. government has provided some US$70 million in the last ten years for the eradication of cocaine and the curtailment of drug trafficking. This aid, however, which amounts to less than US$10 million per year, is insignificant in proportion to the magnitude of the problem. Not only is the amount meager, but the programs are inadequate. As a consequence, while in 1970 only 15,000 hectares were estimated to be used for cocaine production, the estimate was 150,000 in 1990. The Peruvian economy has become "narcodollarized," with cocaine generating some US$1.2 billion annually. Drug trafficking and terrorism have colluded in the valley of Huallaga. With the 10 percent share they get from the drug traffickers, the guerrillas

5. This was indicated by the reaction of the Colombian government to the unilateral attempt of the Bush administration in January 1990 to patrol Colombian waters, and the rather amorphous outcome of the "Drug Summit" in February 1990.—(Ed.)

could acquire sophisticated arms to become a formidable fighting force. If there is no significant change in the U.S. approach to drug trafficking, the issue will become a major point of conflict in hemispheric relations.

Of all of Latin America's problems, the one that has received the most attention and interest in recent years has been the Central American crisis. President Bush is facing a major challenge in this area, primarily because of the failure of Reagan's policy. All the countries in the area are experiencing serious political and economic problems. The electoral victory of an extreme right-wing regime in El Salvador did not pave the way for peace. Further, the guerrillas endured perhaps stronger than ever. In Guatemala, the Cerezo government became increasingly weak relative to the military. And in Nicaragua, elections brought conflict as well as democratization as the economic crisis deepened. On the other hand, the Contras, previously the key to U.S. policy, deteriorated as a military force. Revising U.S. policy would mean emphasizing dialogue and negotiation instead of a military solution, but President Bush said he would continue Reagan's policy. The Bush administration did not take substantial initiatives in this area, did not modify strategy, and did not abandon the Contras. It would seem that President Bush's policy for Central America sought to maintain a military threat alongside the new front—the domestic civilian opposition—in the fight against the Sandinistas.

Given the low point of U.S.–Latin American relations, it is not surprising that the presidents of the Group of Eight, at their meeting in Punta del Este in mid-1989, decided to redefine these relations as a priority of the first order. The new phase in the world situation, the emergence of new economic blocs, and a new U.S. president seemed to provide an opportunity for resuming a dialogue that would recognize the problems and mistakes that cooled relations in the hemisphere. The realization of such a dialogue would imply U.S. acceptance of a new mechanism for Latin American integration, more representative than those of the present inter-American system. However, the initiative presented by the Group of Eight received no response.

At points during 1989, both Secretary of State James Baker III and President Bush alluded to the need for increased dialogue and cooperation. However, the continuity demonstrated by the Bush

administration in its treatment of various hemispheric matters—
Central America, drug trafficking, the debt, Panama, bilateralism
versus multilateralism—impeded the implementation of a different policy for the region.

Superpower Rivalry and Ideology

The United States, Japan, and countries of the European
Community exert strong ideological pressure on concepts of the
economy and society, which serves to promote their own economic
and social philosophies. This ideological pressure, with or without
the direct participation of the superpowers, is echoed in the multilateral organizations, which have become in their own right a
source of pressure for the application of economic policies based on a
rigid, doctrinaire framework. This approach neither respects the
structural heterogeneity of developing economies nor applies its
prescription of painful recessive adjustment processes to developed
countries that show the same symptoms.

As a consequence of ideological pressures, there have emerged
in Latin America market-oriented approaches that conspire
against the very definitions of development. The reduction of the
state demanded by in-vogue neoliberal concepts could in the long
run compromise the institutions and skilled people that ensure the
continuity of economic and social development processes. Latin
America has been the target of an ideological counteroffensive by
the industrialized countries, led by the Reagan administration in
the 1980s, aimed at having a single development model prevail.
This model does not allow state intervention in the economy and
rejects all multilateral negotiations for development cooperation.
Multilateral negotiations would be permitted only for new issues
in which the industrialized countries have comparative advantages,
such as services, investments, and copyright protection.

The question is whether this stage of détente between the superpowers will eliminate or at least mitigate the influence of ideologies in the national decisions of the countries of the region. The
answer is negative: Latin American leaders are too influenced by
ideology and not sufficiently pragmatic.

A pathetic example of how decisions are influenced by opposing ideological positions and the projection of the East-West confrontation could be observed in Peru in two cases. The first involved the exploitation of natural gas in Camisea, and the second involved fishing accords with Cuba and the Soviet Union. Successive proposals by Shell (an Anglo-Dutch enterprise) to exploit Camisea were rejected by leftist parties. While they raised some reasonable objections, ideological positions prevailed in their arguments. On the other hand, Peru had signed several important fishing agreements with Cuba and the Soviet Union. Undoubtedly, there are questionable aspects of the accord signed with the Soviet Union, but it is evident that the ongoing attempts by political leaders to annul these accords were influenced by ideological positions, this time from the right.

These examples indicate a more general point: The rivalry between the superpowers exacerbates the ideological differences in Latin America, polarizes positions, and results in domestic confrontations on major issues. With regard to the role of the state, there are two ideological opinions in the region. One argues that the state should assume productive functions, while the other maintains the state's role should be supplementary to the efforts of the private sector, that its mission should be the provision of social services and the construction of infrastructure. To what extent do the superpowers influence these opinions? To answer this, one need only recall a speech by President Bush on May 2, 1989, in which he praised the historic turn in political and economic thinking that Latin America is undergoing, evidenced by democratic elections and steps taken toward a market economy. This view of President Bush's involves a narrow concept of democracy. The South American definition of democracy is based on the western model, but it is becoming increasingly open to a more integral notion of a political system in which the concept of democracy cannot be divorced from the issue of social justice.

For the reasons mentioned above, it is increasingly necessary to enter a stage of reducing the role of ideology. To this end, the superpowers should put their ideological rivalries behind them and accept the following criteria in relation to the developing countries:

1. The economic and political development of Latin America has its own peculiarities and is autonomous from the competition and rivalry between the two socioeconomic systems, capitalism and socialism. All that occurs in the international arena should not be attributed to the East-West confrontation.
2. Latin America's external relations are based on the principles of nonintervention and self-determination. The region's freedom to choose its own options must be zealously respected.
3. The disjunctive proposition that argues "either Latin America is with capitalism or it is with communism" is false and dangerous.

The Latin American stance is that the rivalry between the two superpowers should not turn the region into an arena for their disputes. Latin American governments should be treated as actors with equal rights. For this to happen, it will be necessary for both Washington and Moscow to collaborate to end regional conflicts and refrain from considering the area a propitious place for extending their spheres of interest.

Superpower Rivalry and Latin America's Trade and Industry

Latin American exports are confronting unusually low prices, world markets for agricultural products distorted by subsidies, trade restrictions, and a growing resistance by producers in the developed countries. Moreover, the external adjustment of the region makes it necessary to maintain a positive balance of trade to service external debts. The effects of this process were manifested in the severe economic crisis in Latin America. In the face of this situation, there is a growing current of opinion in favor of increasing trade with the Soviet Union and seeking markets in the Pacific Basin, particularly in Japan and the newly industrialized countries. Indeed, the Soviet Union sought to expand trade with Latin America at the end of the 1980s. It signed commercial accords establishing favored-nation clauses and the use of convertible currency with several Latin American countries.[6]

6. This point is discussed in Chapter 8 of this volume by Edme Dominguez Reyes.

At this stage of world détente and the severe crisis in Latin America, it is very unlikely that even extremist conservative groups would propose cutting off such trade relations. For the future, a relative intensification of commercial relations of the region with the Soviet Union would seem likely. These relations will be influenced by various factors, such as the priorities of Soviet domestic development, the success of the economic reforms of perestroika, and the extent to which western capital appears to serve Latin American interests.

Latin American industry developed based on western technology, which was much more advanced than Soviet technology, making close competition unlikely. The U.S. and European industrial pattern, models, and technology will continue to prevail in Latin America for the future. Nevertheless, the need for diversification of markets and a new industrialization-oriented strategy would give rise to the Soviet Union's increasing participation in the region's industrialization. Although the field of action of the Soviet Union remained small in the 1980s, it expanded its activities in a few fields, notably hydroenergy. Cases in point were the construction of the Salto Grande Hydroelectric Plant in Argentina and the studies undertaken in Peru for the irrigation of Olmos.

The experience of many years revealed certain advantages to economic relations between Latin American countries and the Soviet Union. First, the Soviet Union provided completed industrial plants, directly transferred to recipient governments, financed by low-interest credits and grace periods. Payment could be made with goods produced by the plant in question. Second, the Soviet Union was an important supplier of capital goods, with excellent technology in some activities, particularly for the development of basic industries and infrastructure.

Rivalry, Arms, and Security

Arms purchases in Latin America have not been influenced greatly by the rivalry between the superpowers. Further, due to the new phase in the world situation and perestroika, the Soviet Union in the future will be much more cautious in its arms sales to the region. On the other hand, it can be said that many of the arms

purchases made by Latin American countries in markets other
than the United States, including the Soviet Union, have been a
consequence of the restrictions or sanctions imposed by the United
States on arms flows to the region.

According to figures provided by the U.S. Agency for Arms
Control and Disarmament, the Soviet Union, France, the Federal
Republic of Germany, Italy, and the United States, in that order,
are the principal arms suppliers to Latin America. During 1979-
1983, the Soviet Union was the leading supplier of arms to Latin
America, receiving US$3.6 billion of the US$11.8 billion spent by
the region on weapons.

There were significant changes in the 1980s in Latin America's
acquisitions of military equipment and material. More sophisticated conventional arms were acquired, and governments bought
appreciably less second-hand and surplus equipment (because of
their relatively quick obsolescence). The traditional suppliers, the
United States and England, lost their places as preferred sources for
modern weapons. By the 1980s, governments no longer based
arms purchases on blocs, alignments, or zones of influence. This
evolution marked Latin America's greater military and political
autonomy with regard to suppliers and ended a cycle in which the
United States sought the standardization of arms and equipment in
its traditional zone of influence. Parallel to this situation, South
America became an exporter and efficient competitor on an international level of the manufacture and commerce of arms, including sophisticated models.

Arms purchases by several Latin American countries indicate
the nonideological shift described above. Nicaragua was the exception, though the Soviet Union refrained from selling offensive
arms, restricting itself to defensive weapons. The MIG 19 helicopters from the Soviet Union are for short-radius use and were
sold after the signing of the friendship accord between the Soviet
Communist Party Chief and the Secretary General of the FSLN.
Ideological reasons and the East-West confrontation obviously influenced the decision reached by the two countries. However, it is
likely that arms shipments to Nicaragua will be halted under the
new Gorbachev foreign policy.

In the case of Peru, the decision to purchase Soviet arms in the
early 1970s was the result of two factors: the need to replace obsolete

equipment, and Peru's exclusion from the U.S. and western arms markets. It is possible that if the United States had maintained arms sales to Peru, they would not have been acquired from the Soviet Union. Peru's decision was not the consequence of the rivalry between the superpowers, rather it was prompted by coercive measures on the part of the United States in response to the nationalization processes in Peru. As for the Soviet decision, it might have been influenced by the escalation of the Cold War during that period. Peru is currently going through a severe economic crisis, and its scant resources are being directed to alleviate it. A hypothetical question that comes to mind is, if the country tried once again to acquire a similar quantity of arms as that purchased in 1974, would the Soviet Union demonstrate the same willingness to make the sale? In light of the Soviet Union's new foreign policy, such a sale would be unlikely.

The military industrialization of Chile was not the consequence of the rivalry between the superpowers but the result of a misguided U.S. policy. After the U.S. Congress approved Senator Edward Kennedy's proposal to close the arms market to Chile, that country launched the development of a military industry to meet its arms supplies needs.

At present, the United States is attempting to restore bilateral relations in the region by reopening the sophisticated arms market as an expedient tactic to win the support of military elites by satisfying their aspirations to modernize their equipment. Examples of these attempts can be observed in the offers made to the Brazilian, Argentine, and Chilean militaries. In the 1990s, therefore, the United States might well try to snatch the lead in arms sales that the Soviet Union currently enjoys in Latin America.

Related to weapons sales was the issue of the effect on Latin America of the superpower negotiations over arms reductions. Governments in the region considered that these efforts were undertaken outside of the multilateral system, especially the Geneva disarmament conference. As such, they needed to be complemented with the actions of the mechanisms provided by the United Nations Charter (the Declaration of Acapulco). Latin American governments strongly believed that the entire world community should participate in the objectives of guaranteeing security and maintaining peace and collaboration. Nuclear disarmament should not be the concern solely of the superpowers.

A consequence of bilateral agreements between the superpowers could be the growth of a Latin American security and defense system of its own. The traditional concept of collective security had lost relevance in the new world situation. The need to formulate a new concept of the region's collective security is one of the challenges confronting Latin American democracies. This was explicitly acknowledged in the Declaration of Acapulco. Another effect of détente and nuclear disarmament could be the greater participation of the region in positions similar to those of the Group of Six[7] to contribute to collective declarations in favor of peace and nuclear disarmament and to cooperate in this realm with the countries of West Europe, Asia, and Africa.

Another consequence would undoubtedly be the need to reaffirm the Treaty of Tlatelolco. Twenty years after it was signed, there remained well-founded skepticism with respect to the Treaty's validity. Success depends on a demonstration of political will by Argentina, Brazil, Chile, and Cuba, which had yet to take the necessary steps to demonstrate a true commitment to Latin American denuclearization.

The heralded imminence of international disarmament that will free enormous resources would create possibilities for alleviating world poverty. Pressure from the Third World to channel freed resources to a development fund emerged immediately, and the aid could be used to facilitate recovery from the crisis in which poor countries find themselves.

CONCLUSION

During the period of East-West confrontation, the Latin American links generated within the system of international relations were based on the strategic importance of its minerals, petroleum, and maritime lines of communication, particularly for the United States. With détente, vis-à-vis the new framework of world dé-

---

7. The Group of Six was an ad hoc group of Latin American governments that sought in the 1980s to mediate the Central American conflict.

tente, Latin America is left weakened, isolated, and unprotected. The attenuation of the rivalry between the superpowers during the 1990s will not become the means to extract the region out of the neglect in which it finds itself.

Everything seemed to indicate that world détente was not accompanied by a corresponding political-economic change to redress the deficiencies of the postwar institutional framework created at Bretton Woods (the IMF, the World Bank, and the General Agreement on Tariffs and Trade). Without such a change, Latin America will continue to be excluded from the benefits of a new structure of economic power and international technology.

6

Imperfect Competition:
The Superpowers in Latin America

Carlos M. Vilas

Latin America is the area of the Third World where the hegemony of the United States has been maintained most openly and
unyieldingly throughout this century.[1] This hegemony was related to several factors: changes in the configuration of domestic
economy and policy of the United States; the internal dynamics of
Latin American and Caribbean societies; the global dynamics of
the international system; and the manner in which the United
States as well as the Latin American countries are articulated into
that system. But beyond all the changes brought by different periods and alternating political parties in office, the most salient
aspect was the permanence of this unequal relationship. The manner in which the United States has viewed its relations with the
region also remained relatively unchanged. Without dismissing
the explicit importance assigned to these relations, they have been
perceived by successive U.S. administrations as a dimension or
aspect of relations with third, extraregional powers.

This approach has been the case since U.S. policy for Latin
America was first formulated. The first explicit manifestation, the
so-called Monroe Doctrine, had as its objective to foil European intentions to reverse the new political situation unfolding in the
western hemisphere as the result of the independence of the
former Spanish colonies, and particularly to block British designs

1. For the sake of brevity, this paper includes the Caribbean under the
denomination of Latin America, despite historical, ecological, and cultural
differences.

on the Mosquitia Coast of Central America. Subsequently, the Caribbean became center stage for U.S. confrontations with Spain, and at the turn of the century confrontations with Germany were the backdrop of U.S. military operations against Nicaragua, Haiti, and the Dominican Republic. Beginning in the 1950s, the region became a chapter in U.S. relations with the Soviet Union.

This way of perceiving Latin America, subordinated to relations with extraregional powers, was based on the assumption that there in fact existed a competition between the United States and these powers for the region or, at the least, in the region. At the same time, it assigned Latin America an eminently geopolitical value, beyond its economic or commercial importance. Especially in Central America and the Caribbean, the most significant economic and commercial investments generally came after Washington's political and military expansion. Military interventions preceded the arrival of investors and created the conditions for the economic integration of both areas to the dynamics of the U.S. economy (Vilas 1974, 117-77). In the more developed countries of South America, the political interest in maintaining existing international alignments was soon coupled with the greater magnitude of economic interests. For its part, dominant domestic groups in these countries limited the opportunity for direct, gunboat-diplomacy-style actions and forced Washington to devise more sophisticated policies to keep these countries away from influences from outside the continent.

This primacy of strictly geopolitical factors became more evident after World War II. The majority of U.S. foreign investments and trade has never been in Latin America,[2] it has been in the developed world. At the same time, however, Latin America is the Third World region of greatest direct economic importance for the United States, excluding the Persian Gulf. Moreover, it is a region of great interest to various U.S.-based transnational corporations.

Economic links had great bearing on U.S. relations with the region. The importance of certain countries and areas for particular corporations, together with their low priority from the standpoint of the U.S. government, has permitted these companies to de-

2. This is documented in Weeks (1985, chap. 2). The Latin American share of U.S. direct investment declined continuously after 1960.

cisively influence U.S. policy toward countries in which their investments are located. The preponderant role of the United Fruit Company (UFC) in Central America is the clearest example of this situation. The company's opinions and objectives were able to define U.S. government policy toward certain countries out of proportion to UFC's weight in the U.S. economy. This power was a consequence of the economic importance of the Central American countries for the company. Similar recent cases were the Grace Company in Peru and ITT in Chile, countries considerably more developed in economic and political terms than the Central American region.

It is possible to state, therefore, that the central interest of the United States in the region was of a geopolitical nature and consisted of maintaining the international alignment of the area within the matrix of U.S. relations with the Soviet Union and the socialist countries.

The perception that U.S. administrations have had of relations with Latin America, and the policies based on these perceptions, had basically an anachronistic nature. The policies reflected a view that evolved during the first half of the nineteenth century in a world vastly different from the one about to enter the twenty-first century. Also, it was a profoundly reactionary stance, opposed to any substantial political and socioeconomic change in the countries of the region. Change, and particularly revolutionary change, would be seen as a path that will lead to the loosening of a given country's subordination to the United States. This, in turn, would be defined as shifting a country toward the sphere of influence of powers from outside the hemisphere. This approach led U.S. governments to feel more comfortable with those Caribbean and Latin American governments with which the peoples of the countries were the most uncomfortable. Programmatically, U.S. policy implied pressure against the political movements that championed demands for sovereignty and national self-determination.

Latin America is the Third World region farthest from the Soviet Union. This distance is as much historical and political as it is geographical. The political distance was the result of Latin America's traditional place in the U.S. sphere of influence (and prior to that, Spain's and Britain's). Further, the Soviet Union entered late into the international system, the basic characteristics of which already had been shaped by the leading capitalist powers. During the 1920s and 1930s, the Soviet Union made several failed attempts to establish trade relations with South American countries. It was not until the 1940s that the situation began to change. Only after the triumph of the Cuban Revolution in 1959 did the Soviet Union and the other socialist countries assume a major presence in the region.

It is important to be particularly careful to distinguish facts from words. In its international political rhetoric, the U.S. government and its leading intellectual exponents have portrayed the Soviet presence as the result of growing expansionism in the western hemisphere. The facts were very different. At the end of the 1980s, Soviet participation in Latin America's commerce, and vice versa, was of limited scope except in Cuba. Changes in Nicaragua's foreign policy since the triumph of the Sandinista Revolution in 1979 did not substantially alter the Soviet role. Soviet trade, economic assistance, and military aid were especially important for Nicaragua and Cuba, but they represent a very small proportion of Latin America's external economic and political relations.

There are various reasons for the small Soviet role. First, there was little complementarity between the Soviet and Latin American economies. Since the 1920s, the Soviet Union and Latin America's most developed countries underwent processes of industrialization and import substitution, but in different manners and with different stress. The Soviet Union initially placed great emphasis on heavy and medium industry, that is, on the means of production and development of infrastructure. Production of consumer and final-use goods was postponed or received less attention. Even in the 1980s, there was still a very evident contrast between the high quality and performance of heavy industrial machinery and the unsatisfactory quality of everyday consumer goods. In Latin America, more effort went to the production of medium industry and products for final use rather than to the development of infrastructure and the means of production. This pattern was not unrelated to the role of foreign corporations in the region's industrialization. Different styles of development and sociopolitical and institutional frameworks gave rise to different patterns of supply and demand of industrial goods, technological options, and distribution of earnings. During the 1970s and 1980s, the increased economic attention given to the demand for consumer goods in certain East European countries opened the doors to merchandise from a few more developed Latin American countries, though in relatively small quantities from the standpoint of the total volume of imports.

Second, the enormous geographic distances would make transportation and operating costs very expensive. Shipping goods and machinery from the Soviet Union's main ports to any Latin American port, and vice versa, involves much more time than shipments between Latin American and West European, Japanese, or U.S. ports. These disadvantages were compounded by the low productivity levels in Soviet industry in comparison to capitalist countries. In some cases, production cost differences could be balanced by more favorable conditions for financing from the Soviet Union.

Third, the mechanisms for marketing and distribution of machinery and spare parts in the East European countries suffer from rigidities that rendered them incapable of responding to urgent demands or filling orders promptly. The Soviet economy, like that of its neighbors and allies, operated with mechanisms for medium- and long-term centralized planning. This contrasted with what many Soviet officials viewed as the improvisation and lack of foresight in the Latin American economies. It must be added that until very recently, Soviet enterprises lacked, and will continue to lack for years to come, the autonomy to facilitate trade. Enterprise officials did not have the authority to adopt decisions without prior consultation with their respective central administrations. In the eyes of Latin American officials, Soviet commercial and economic missions tended to be slow and powerless to make decisions.

Fourth, there was the factor of inertia. Latin American enterprises—state, cooperative, private, and mixed—and bureaucracies were more familiar with western markets than with those of the Soviet Union, East Europe, and China. Technology and consumer tastes in Latin America were derived from western influence. For example, in Nicaragua, as a result of a U.S.–imposed trade embargo, a proportion of mass basic consumption and of the needed parts and spares could be provided only by very inexpensive imports or donations from the socialist countries. It was evident, however, that the people and even many officials preferred U.S. brands and products that had disappeared from the marketplace. That this was clearly a manifestation of cultural and ideological dependency did not mean that it was not a real problem with real repercussions.

Soviet commerce and economic assistance certainly offered advantages, among them softer financing terms, lack of corruption, and stability of agreements. To the considerations mentioned above, however, must be added political pressures exerted on the Latin American governments not to expand trade and economic relations with the Soviet Union. Thus, it was not difficult to understand why in the late twentieth century Soviet participation in the region's affairs was so limited. An increase in trade and cooperation with the Soviet Union would involve for the Latin American countries modifying their production apparatus and technological and planning systems and strengthening their capacity to resist external pressure.

For these reasons, the Cuban experience could not be generalized to the rest of the region. A great number of specific factors particular to both countries led to the development of close relations between the Soviet Union and Cuba. The rapid unfolding of the Cuban Revolution, the early confrontation with the United States, and the Revolution's capacity to resist this confrontation by its own means at the outset were all important factors. Also relevant, however, was the political climate in the Soviet Union stemming from the 20th Congress of the Communist Party of the Soviet Union, as well as the Soviet Union's ability to supply Cuba with oil quickly, massively, and cheaply after the United States unilaterally halted its supplies and the refineries were nationalized. Also facilitating assistance was the suspension of Soviet aid to China in 1961, which left the idle capacity of which Cuba was able to take advantage. In light of these factors, the Soviet Union quickly became Cuba's primary commercial and economic partner, with a presence quickly felt in virtually all spheres of society. The breadth and depth of these relations contrasts notably with Cuba's growing isolation from the rest of Latin America as a result of Washington's policies.

Nicaragua's experience was different from Cuba's, as Grenada's was from both. It is evident that neither the present Soviet leadership, its predecessors, nor the Sandinista leadership were interested in having the Soviet Union assume the role it played in the Cuban Revolution; certainly, the conditions were not favorable for this to happen. As for Grenada, Soviet response to requests for cooperation and assistance from the government of Maurice Bishop was generally low profile.[3] Notable in both cases was the importance of Cuban economic and military aid. Cuba is Cuba, however, and not the Soviet Union. The hypothesis that the Cuban revolutionary regime acted as a Soviet agent or beachhead fails to account for Cuba's autonomy in conducting its international relations in the Third World, especially in Latin America and the Caribbean. At the outset of the 1990s, one could not still argue that domestic or foreign policy in Cuba was derivative of Moscow.

The particularities of each of these three situations stem from the very different experiences of each country in terms of the respective revolutionary process and the link to the international system. Also important in explaining diversity were the different dimensions of the respective societies, the disparate endowments of resources and levels of development, and the possibilities for economic complementarity with the Soviet Union.

Finally, Cuba's experience could not be likened to that of the Popular Unity government in Chile. Chilean trade with the Soviet Union under Allende never exceeded 10 percent of foreign commerce, and Soviet credits granted Chile totaled approximately US$350 million. There was no large-scale Soviet investment in development projects, and Soviet provision of military equipment and training was inconsequential. In fact, the low profile of Soviet cooperation in economic policy and other spheres of the Popular Unity government stands in strong contrast to the subsequent role that the Soviet Union assumed in the international solidarity campaigns in condemning human-rights violations by the regime of General Pinochet.

It seems clear that the establishment of revolutionary or leftist regimes would not suffice to bring a significant increase in the Soviet economic, commercial, or, to a lesser extent, political presence in the region. On the contrary, a careful analysis of the experiences of Chile, Grenada, and Cuba reveals the low proclivity of the Soviet Union to increase its involvement in areas of potential conflict with the United States. Soviet foreign policy was not and in the future is unlikely to be characterized by the radical dogmatism that marked Ronald Reagan's approach to the region.

3. See, for example, Pryor (1986, 43).

The Soviet approach appeared to consist of seeking opportunities for establishing specific economic relations, including military equipment sales, and expanding its cultural, political, and diplomatic presence. At the same time, the strategy avoided provocations that could lead to direct confrontation with the United States. In each case, Soviet leaders adapted their approach to the specific circumstances of the Latin American counterpart, taking advantage of conflicts or tensions between the country in question and the United States. An excellent example of this flexibility was the relations established in 1980-1982 between the Soviet Union and Argentina's military government. These relations arose as a result of the January 1980 embargo on wheat sales declared by President Carter in reaction to flagrant human-rights violations. The approach of the Soviets to Argentina showed the preeminence of specific factors of realpolitik over abstract ideological criteria in the formulation of foreign policy for the countries of the region.

In 1974, the Soviet Union and its allies signed commercial and economic cooperation agreements with the Peronist government of Argentina totaling US$950 million (US$500 million of which was directly from the Soviet Union). These pacts were part of a policy of greater openness launched by presidents Campora and Perón, which began with the normalization of relations with Cuba in 1973 that led to trade and economic assistance agreements. The military coup of March 1976 did not invalidate these accords. By 1978, Argentina had become the Soviet Union's leading economic partner in Latin America, excluding Cuba.

When President Carter announced the embargo on the sale of U.S. grain, beef, and dairy products to the Soviet Union as sanctions against the military intervention in Afghanistan, Argentina rushed to fill the gap. The decision of the Argentine military was undoubtedly due to the need to expand exports to new markets and use the hard-currency earnings from Soviet trade to reduce the deficit in its balance of payments. But it was also a way of indirectly confronting the Carter administration, which had been particularly active in denouncing the massive human-rights violations in Argentina. For its part, the Soviet Union had the opportunity to meet its demand for basic staples. In addition, the Soviets could consolidate their political position with a regime that was being sought by the United States to create a South Atlantic military organization, in which South Africa was the other potential member. This was a period during which indirect confrontations with China on the other side of the world were still intense. Thus, good relations with the Argentine military dictatorship permitted the Soviet Union to counterbalance in Latin America's southern cone China's excellent relations with Pinochet's military regime in Chile. In the diplomatic sphere, Moscow did not condemn the overthrow of the constitutional government in Argentina. On the contrary, it attempted to block or discourage motions in the United Nations to condemn the military regime for its human-rights violations and even decorated several Argentine military chiefs. After the constitutional regimen was reestablished, these same officers were brought to trial for their implication in those human-rights violations.

In 1980, approximately 80 percent of Argentine grain exports went to the Soviet Union. Trade between the two countries tripled, with the absolute balance massively in Argentina's favor.[4] The situation was maintained through 1981-1982, but the United States in 1983 again became the leading grain supplier to the Soviet Union when President Reagan suspended the embargo.

The important point that emerges from the comments above is the caution with which the Soviet Union traditionally managed its relations with Latin America. In virtually all cases it avoided involvement that could significantly escalate the potential for conflict with the United States or in political situations with uncertain prospects. There were certain general principles in Soviet foreign policy for Latin America that were part of its general approach to the Third World as a whole: self-determination and nonalignment; development of commercial and economic relations with no political preconditions; and adherence to the principles of the United Nations Charter. The application of these general guidelines, however, is subordinated to a host of factors and conditions related to each specific situation. The principles were integration with the needs and objectives of the Soviet Union at each specific moment in time, within the framework of the central goal of avoiding direct confrontation with the United States on Latin

---

4. See, for example, López (1983) and Sizonenko (1981).

American territory. The October 1962 Cuban missile crisis was not and would not be repeated.

Does this mean that deep down the Soviet Union's approach to Latin America was similar to that of the United States, that is, purely a dimension of the relations between the superpowers? An unqualified affirmative would be excessive. Soviet relations with the western world were obviously determined by its relations with the United States, and by its various aspects, whether military—encompassing such issues as arms limitation and control and deployment of NATO troops—or economic. Latin America did not directly constitute a dimension of this relationship, except in the sense that the development of economic, commercial, and other relations with the Soviet Union could appear potentially more beneficial than the type of unequal relations that existed with the United States, thus reducing relatively the traditional influence of Washington. In this, Cuba's case was not an exception. Relations between the Soviet Union and Cuba are not an aspect of Soviet–U.S. relations; rather, they are the result of a broad set of particular factors, among which U.S. relations with Cuba evidently played a decisive role.

It would be wrong to deny the existence of Soviet interest in expanding and deepening relations with Latin America, but this interest did not seem to be high on the list of priorities. In any case, it was not pursued to the point of jeopardizing gains achieved in disarmament, coexistence, and other main issues in relations with the United States. At the same time, there existed in Soviet policy an appeal—symbolic in some cases, real in others—to certain principles of international relations important to the Third World, including the principle of nonintervention. The Soviet Union, however, maintained a low profile in important matters for Latin America, including the foreign debt, the Central American crisis, and international trade in primary products. Even this low profile acted indirectly to counter the aggressiveness that characterized White House policy toward the region during the 1980s, and it helped to advance regional approaches for the management of these issues.

The Soviet Union appears fundamentally interested in consolidating and expanding its relations with the more developed countries of the region. It would be with these countries that prospects for economic and commercial agreements appear more feasible and promising. One would expect such agreements to be applied according to the principle of nonintervention; the character of the respective governments would not be a consideration. The image of the Soviet Union fomenting subversion of the established order in Latin America was always questionable and is increasingly ridiculous at the outset of the 1990s. At the same time, no change would seem likely in the Soviet position in two cases at opposite poles of the political spectrum: support for Cuba and the condemnation of the Pinochet regime.

Between the two poles, many things would be possible, and the experience of the 1970s and 1980s attested to the versatility of the Soviet Union and its capacity to adapt itself to changing situations in a region, which in any case lay too close to Washington and too far from Moscow.

REFERENCES

López, J. A.   1983.   "Relaciónes Comerciales Argentina-USSR: Balance y Perspectivas." *América Latina* 8: 55-64, August.

Pryor, Frederick L.   1986.   *Revolutionary Grenada: A Study in Political Economy.*   New York: Praeger.

Sizonenko, A.   1981.   "URSS-Países Latinoamericanos: Resultados y Perspectivas de las Relaciones Interstatales." *América Latina* 1-2: 5-20.

Vilas, Carlos M.   1974.   "Notas sobre la formación del estado en el Caribe: La República Dominicana."   Estudios Sociales Centro-americanos 24, October–December.

Weeks, John F.   1985.   *The Limits to Capitalist Development: The Industrialization of Peru, 1950–1980.*   Boulder, Colo.: Westview Press.

Part III

Evaluating Soviet Foreign Policy

7

New Principles and Old in Soviet Policy

George Mirsky

PSYCHOLOGICAL ORIGINS OF MISTRUST FOR NEUTRALS

In the years immediately following World War II, there was no nonalignment because there was no Third World in the present sense of the term. The emancipation of colonies gained momentum with every year, but the newly independent countries were too preoccupied with internal and regional issues to coordinate a common foreign policy. Because the Cold War was already in full swing and competition between the superpowers was steadily increasing, a visible trend for neutrality in global affairs began to develop among the Third World states. Political leaders started to emphasize that their priorities would be national interests, economic development, and, in many cases, irredentist claims and networks of regional relationships. Many leaders made it clear that they would prefer to avoid involvement in the superpowers' struggle.

This thinking met with the distinct disapproval of the United States, especially when the conduct of American diplomacy was in the hands of John Foster Dulles. It was he, of course, who said that neutralism was immoral. His black and white world did not allow shades of intermediate positions. The essential task was to prevent the free world from falling into the hands of a totally evil force, namely, the godless communism. There could be no justification for refusing to stand up and be counted on the part of countries devoted to western values. And there was no doubt on the part of Dulles and like-minded people that only western values should inspire the Third World nations. It is unlikely that the genuine feelings of the population of those countries, their mentality, and their spiritual values concerned American policymakers. The spirit of the anti-communist crusade made it both impossible and irrelevant to try to understand real needs and interests of Third World governments, which were feeling their way in the terribly complicated and bitterly divided world.

Thus, it was inevitable that the first steps of the emerging non-aligned movement provoked hostile American reaction. Let us not forget that those first steps, eventually leading to the creation of the movement in its present form, were taken by such Third World leaders as Nehru, Nasser, and Sukarno, who were at that time worried that their countries might be drawn into military alliances organized and presided over by the United States and Great Britain. The Baghdad Pact (later known as SENTO) and SEATO (Southeast Asia Treaty Organization) presented in the eyes of most leaders precisely the danger they dreaded most: the subordination of their national interests and independent policies to a grand western scheme designed to combat communism and Soviet influence, which particularly Asian and African countries categorically refused to consider a real threat. Moreover, those pacts and alliances tended to jeopardize the very independence of nations. Being transformed into junior partners of imperialist states, they were virtually doomed to lose freedom of maneuver in the field of foreign policy. Also implied was more and more reliance on economic, political, and military cooperation with the West. Further, the sincerity of the West in dealing with the Third World was open to doubt. Third World leaders could not but suspect that under the guise of the anti-communist crusade the western powers really sought to restore some form of semicolonial domination in Latin America, Asia, and Africa.

The combination of the above-mentioned reasons made the Asian and African leaders reluctant to join western-sponsored alliances. Their common political interest gradually took shape as organized movement, basically directed against what they regarded as western encroachments on their sovereignty. The nonaligned movement, while loudly proclaiming its refusal to join either of the two great power blocs, in reality was a resolute opposition to just one of these blocs, namely the western one. This focus resulted because the so-called Soviet bloc expressed no intention of establishing military-political organizations similar to the Baghdad Pact, the Rio Pact, or SEATO. This asymmetrical approach to the nascent Third World on the part of the superpowers naturally brought about asymmetrical, differentiated responses from the new states, basically anti-western, though formally it looked even-handed and quite balanced. In fact, this anti-imperialist bias of the emerging movement was immediately noticed in the West and, due to the prevalent black-and-white world view, was dubbed as essentially pro-Soviet.

It was the basically anti-imperialist content of the ideology of the new movement that was at once noticed and duly appreciated in the Soviet Union. The implicit anti-western content tipped the scale in favor of the movement, overcoming the natural ideological distrust of anything neutral. The traditional ideological view in the Soviet Union, though motivated by a diametrically opposite outlook, almost exactly mirrored the American attitude vis-à-vis neutrals and those nonengaged. This predilection against neutralism can be explained both by a certain interpretation of the Marxist doctrine and by the influence of that unique pattern of development that was characteristic of Soviet Russia. Soon after the 1917 triumph, the dominant theme in Soviet ideology was world revolution. Although the prospect for such a revolution receded as years passed, there remained the view that capitalism was unstable and transitory, as well as the conviction that the imperialist rulers would wipe the first socialist country off the face of the Earth at the first opportunity. These views were not only expressed by the leadership, they were also widely believed among Soviet citizens.

"Capitalist encirclement" was an undeniable and all-important fact of life deeply rooted in the minds of the Soviet people. It was not a fantasy but reality; up until World War II, the Soviet Union *was* encircled by enemies of communist ideology. Of course, this did not mean that those neighboring states were actually preparing to attack the Soviet Union, but the fear of such an attack was precisely what the Stalinist propaganda wanted people to believe. The legitimate concern for security of the country was reinforced by artificially generated war hysteria, designed to justify enormous sacrifices demanded of the people. Victory in World War II effectively ended the traditional notion of "hostile encirclement." Now it was argued that a new anti-communist alliance led by the United States awaited an opportunity to destroy the Soviet Union.

Soviet citizens were brought up with an unshakable conviction that capitalism was not only a thoroughly vicious system, but one that was unquestionably doomed. Further, the more it approached its inevitable end, the fiercer and more dangerous it became. The threat of a new world war, according to prevailing opinion, was not receding but actually growing as the nuclear arms race began in the late 1940s. In this eventual life-death struggle, there was no room for taking a middle course. "Who is not with us, is against us" was the motto. Newly independent countries were regarded as the "reserve" of world socialism. Later, after Stalin's death, when emphasis slowly but definitely began to change, the term "reserve" was quietly dropped. National liberation movements became one of several currents of global anti-imperialist revolutionary process instead of an ally of world socialism.

It was not easy at first to reconcile this notion of brotherly alliance with oppressed peoples with the concept of neutrality, of a "middle ground" between the two blocs. Natural aversion to neutralism and nonengagement had to be overcome. It might have been impossible but for the fact that the anti-western aspects of nonalignment became apparent to Soviet policymakers and scholars alike. The "anti-both-camps" rhetoric of the nonaligned leaders could be disregarded, while taking advantage of their anti-imperialist stand in practical politics. The concept of an alliance with nations struggling against colonial and neocolonial domination proved after all to be compatible with the idea of nonalignment once it was demonstrated that the latter was inspired essentially by desire to avoid involvement in western-dominated blocs. Enough common ground was found for mutual goals to be proclaimed, namely liberation of peoples from imperialist domination, aggression, and exploitation.

LEARNING TO LIVE WITH THE NONALIGNED

The Berlin blockade and the Cuban missile crisis proved quite convincingly that any attempt to forcibly change the status quo "on the frontline" would be so risky and fraught with danger to mankind as to be beyond the limit of sane politics. Precisely because of this, secondary, or peripheral, frontlines grew in significance. The Third World was being transformed into a major battlefield. Once it became clear that significant changes in the zones controlled directly by NATO and the Warsaw Pact were out of the question, temptation emerged to gain ground in the "gray zone" of the Third World. Only there a war of maneuver seemed possible, for in Europe both sides were firmly dug into their trenches.

Motives of the two sides were different. The Americans were preoccupied with the necessity—as they saw it—to counterbalance growing Soviet military might and political influence in the Third World. However, this proved impossible to achieve by means of building political-military blocs and alliances reminiscent of colonial domination in the eyes of Asian and African leaders. Consequently, another approach was chosen: to come to terms with the Third World nationalism that to a growing degree was expressing itself in terms of nonalignment. A common ground seemed to be found, namely the fear of communism felt by many of the Third World regimes committed to a capitalist pattern of development. Playing upon this understandable fear of the privileged classes, the West tried to prevent the spread of leftist trends in the developing countries. Simultaneously, U.S. policy sought to promote capitalist patterns of development and to perpetuate dependence of the world periphery on the powerful centers. Within the framework of the new approach, it was inevitable for such blocs as SENTO and SEATO to fade away. The West abandoned attempts to draw the Third World into formalized alliances, and it recognized the legitimacy of its desire to steer clear of both powerful camps. Neutralism was no longer immoral; John Foster Dulles was forgotten.

Along with fear of communism, economic considerations—dire need of foreign assistance, credit, and technology—were powerful motivations for the dominant classes in the Third World for compromise and accommodation with the West. Moreover, as political conflicts with the West became less acute and the center of gravity in the nonaligned movement steadily shifted to economic matters, attention turned to grandiose schemes of creating a new world economic order. The Group of 77 was created mainly for this purpose, and it was closely linked to the nonalignment movement. Hopes for a rapid transformation of the world economy on a just and equitable basis were soon shattered, however. Deep contradictions between the Third World and the main capitalist centers continue to exist, and the gap between backward nations and developed nations is widening. But it is not automatically reflected in the political relations between the West and the Third World. Few western politicians would now openly attack the nonaligned.

Attitudes in the Soviet Union vis-à-vis the Third World also have undergone significant change. The potential political importance of the Third World was fully appreciated, as was the strength of nationalism. It was accepted that not all developing countries would immediately follow the socialist path, but this was not considered a barrier on the road to cooperation. Capitalist development in some cases possessed a considerable anti-imperialist potential in view of inherent contradictions with capitalist monopolies of the West and, accordingly, the countries in question might be regarded as objective allies of world socialism (such as India).

It would be wrong to say—as many western observers did—that the Soviet Union tried to use the Third World as an instrument to undermine the West. That idea was alien to Soviet political thinking and much more consistent with the Maoist view of a "world countryside encircling the world city and driving the latter to surrender." The main battlefront in Soviet eyes remained in the sphere of confrontation (albeit peaceful) between world capitalism and world socialism, movement of liberation being a natural and potent ally of the latter. In the Soviet analysis, the combined pressure of the socialist community, the workers' movement in the capitalist world, and the national liberation movement was capable of effectively curtailing aggressive imperialist designs and weakening in a decisive way the entire capitalist structure. It was believed that ultimate collapse of capitalism would come about as the result of its own internal contradictions, with external factors being of secondary importance.

In the 1960s and 1970s, Soviet policy did not treat the world as black and white. Nevertheless, the main problem of world development continued to be "who will beat whom." With world war out of the question, this bitter struggle between capitalism and socialism was analyzed as taking diverse forms, such as peaceful coex-

istence. The exact duration of this period of struggle was never determined, but it was felt that sooner or later inevitable sharpening
of contradictions inherent in capitalism would accelerate its down-
fall. Until that capitalist collapse, competition between the two systems would go on, mainly in the economic sphere. More countries, especially in the Third World, would gather under the ban-
ner of socialism as a result of the failure of capitalism in backward
areas. The fiasco of capitalism in the developing countries was
taken for granted, its rare cases of success considered temporary
and uncharacteristic. Eventual transition to socialism in the Third
World countries was never in doubt. Those countries would turn
socialist earlier than the developed capitalist states, doomed to be
the last bulwarks of the bourgeois society.

Nonalignment fitted perfectly in this scheme, as it was a shield
protecting the developing countries from imperialism and guaranteeing their independence. Independence and autonomy would
allow those countries to choose freely their own path of development. The freedom of choice in its turn was considered to be basically favorable to the socialist pattern of development because there
was no doubt that, left to themselves without imperialist pressure,
the developing countries would choose socialism. From the point
of view of realpolitik, nonalignment was quite useful because it
blocked the West from establishing military bases in the Third
World. As for the Soviet Union, there was no need for it to seek
military facilities in Asia, Africa, and Latin America. And so, for
different reasons, both superpowers came to tolerate the nonalignment movement, learning to live with it.

DEIDEOLOGIZATION OF INTERSTATE RELATIONS
AND NONALIGNMENT

Change of leadership in the Soviet Union in the 1980s brought
about emergence of new political thinking, the cornerstone of
which is the concept of freedom of choice. It is a principle long
recognized by the Soviet Union, so what is new in this respect?
The difference is that in earlier periods implicit in this idea was
its relevance to one group of countries only, namely those of progressive social orientation. While never clearly expressed, it was

understood that free choice, made by the people, would naturally be for a noncapitalist pattern of development. There was no similar recognition of the other possibility, that the people could favor a nonsocialist road. What we have now is a just, equitable, and even-handed approach: any choice made by any given nation is to be respected.

A new look at capitalism has been in evidence in the Soviet Union in the last year or two. It has been recognized that the capitalist system is much more viable and resilient than previously supposed. The end of capitalism is not in sight. Official opinion now holds that the change of social formations will occur within a wider historical space than was previously believed. The prospect of socialism definitely replacing capitalism on a world scale is beyond the foreseeable future. Thus, the socialist countries will have to live side by side with capitalist states for an indefinite period. There is no possibility—other than a suicidal attempt to use force—for either side to change this situation. Accordingly, peaceful coexistence is not a form of class struggle. The significance of this change of theory may elude a westerner not very well versed in Marxist ideology, but it is enormous. Class struggle means just that—struggle—and its goal is victory. So the world—prior to introduction of our new political thinking—remained in our eyes more or less rigidly divided; it was always "we" and "they." And although assuring victory of socialism by force of arms had been discarded at least three decades ago due to the realities of the nuclear age, the goal of defeating the capitalist enemy remained. Peaceful coexistence represented a strategy to create favorable conditions for the success of socialism in this great struggle.

Now the position is different. We accept the diversity of the present-day world, the plurality of its development forms, and the legitimacy of these forms (even ones we do not like). The concept of class struggle—a cornerstone of Marxist thinking—has not been discarded, but it no longer applies to peaceful coexistence between states with diverse social systems. Moreover, peaceful coexistence is regarded now as active in nature, permitting cooperation in global problems. Many of these cannot be resolved without mutual effort, without participation of states regardless of their ideology. Take, for instance, the problem of the environment; air and water know no frontiers, and it would be foolish to refuse aid to an ideological adversary in trouble in the ecological sphere. Paramount, of course, is the nuclear danger, which cannot be put aside by "passive" coexistence, without dialogue with the opposing side, without permanent negotiations on disarmament. To achieve meaningful results in this field, one must treat the other side not as an enemy, but as an opponent. It is impossible to cooperate on global problems or to solve regional conflicts while retaining the traditional spirit of ideological intransigence. A line must be drawn between the two spheres: class struggle, including ideological struggle, is one thing, and relations between states is another.

In his speech to the United Nations on December 8, 1988, Mikhail Gorbachev said: "We do not renounce our conviction, our philosophy, our traditions, and we do not demand of others to renounce theirs." Pleading for "honest struggle of ideologies," the leader of the Communist Party of the Soviet Union stressed that this struggle "should not apply to relations between states." The spiritual values of the competing world systems have to be put to the test in different fields, including the international one, but not in the sphere of interstate relations. The two terms "international" and "interstate" are not identical. International relations cover a much wider field, including the whole network of relationships between parties and movements that cannot be deprived of ideological content. One cannot refuse people, parties, classes, and states the right to feel sympathy for groups or movements ideologically and spiritually close to them. Relations between states are quite another matter; these relations should be free from ideological debate because our world in the nuclear age is too fragile for ideological differences to be settled by states in the way reminiscent of religious wars.[1] The problem is the confrontational approach to peaceful coexistence, and the goal is to get rid of it.

The nonaligned movement represented perhaps the first example of the practical realization of taking ideology out of interstate relations. Inside this movement, diverse and often contradictory forms of social and ideological organization managed to establish a working model of cooperation for decades. India and Cuba, Yugoslavia and Iran, Vietnam and Morocco—just to mention these

1. This point was made officially by Vadim Medvedev, then Secretary of the Central Committee of the Communist Party of the Soviet Union.

states is to realize the enormous heterogeneity of nonalignment. Incompatible and even diametrically opposed ideologies have not prevented the member states from fruitfully cooperating in dealing with problems facing Asia, Africa, and Latin America. The non-aligned movement proves the possibility of deideologization of interstate relations.

What about the attitude toward the movement on the part of the superpowers? Some say that both powers are trying hard to woo the nonaligned. No one can afford at present to belittle or downplay the influence of this movement, its vitality, its staying power, and its importance in the life of the international community. The movement has become a permanent, stable, and powerful factor in world affairs. But is its role diminishing in the field of international relations?

Some arguments could be advanced in favor of a weakening role for the Third World. If the superpowers reject the goal of defeating each other and subsequently move on to nonconfrontational foreign policies, the importance of the Third World as a prize in the game of world politics will decline. Gone would be the treatment of the developing countries as the soft underbelly of the opponent (to use Churchill's description of Southern Europe during World War II), where small investments can reap great dividends in enlarging spheres of influence. Further, the new Soviet emphasis on dealing directly with the West (especially the United States) and on establishing a cooperative relationship means that the bargaining power of Third World countries will weaken.

I believe both arguments are correct only to a certain point. It is undoubtedly true that the capacity of the Third World to play on contradictions between the superpowers diminishes as new détente sets in, especially if the division of the world into spheres of influence becomes obsolete. However, Soviet–U.S. competition is not likely to disappear altogether. Nonconfrontation is not synonymous with noncompetition. Neither side will presumably try to gain more military facilities in the Third World nor create bases or bridgeheads with the aim of encircling the other. At the same time, however, neither is likely to abandon attempts to strengthen its political influence, to encourage friendly regimes, nor to prove its superiority in dealing with problems of backward countries. It would be premature to assert that the days of Soviet–U.S. rivalry in the Third World are gone. It would also be rash to assume that with the advent of the new détente the Third World has altogether ceased to be a prize. It is only the meaning of the prize and its ultimate use that have changed.

Generally speaking, the network of international relationships in the present day is bound to become richer and more complex. Having rejected the primitive black-and-white, friend-and-foe vision of the world, the United States and the Soviet Union are likely to find it necessary to conduct more flexible and subtle foreign policy, to play on more instruments than before, to seek new alliances, and to look for compromise solutions. The world picture has become multicolored; instead of two hostile monoliths facing each other across the globe, many independent actors have entered the arena. Seen in this light, the importance of the Third World is certain to increase rather than to diminish.

On the level of practical politics, the Soviet Union recognized the legitimacy of nonalignment long ago, but only now has it been theoretically confirmed through the official adoption of a concept of ideological pluralism. Once nonalignment was tolerated as a phenomenon not exactly welcome but to be reckoned with; now it is recognized as a powerful and organic force of our time.

8

The New Soviet Foreign Policy: An Evaluation

Edme Dominguez Reyes

BACKGROUND

Accustomed as we are to analyzing Soviet foreign policy in Manichean terms, with an ideological focus such as that used by the Soviets to study the western world, the revolutionary restructuring undertaken by President Mikhail Gorbachev has left us virtually without a framework for analysis. The objective of this paper is to provide a broad outline of the main points of the new policy, its roots and evolution, and to explore the significance for Latin America and other parts of the Third World. Given the breadth of the subject matter, an exhaustive analysis is not possible. I will focus instead on the more important aspects from a Latin American viewpoint.

From a historical point of view, Soviet foreign policy has been shaped by two interrelated factors: ideology and state interests. The ideological factor sometimes produced a deformed vision of the outside world; at the same time, it justified certain actions that largely responded to the survival needs of a socialist society in a hostile world. Early on, the policy of world socialist revolution had to be modified to that of socialism in one country (and later, socialism in one region). Relations with the West, always contentious, have gone through periods of tactical alliance (World War II), then latent conflict (the Cold War), briefly interrupted by periods of eased tensions (Khrushchev's peaceful coexistence, Brezhnev's détente). Soviet diplomacy, particularly between the two world wars, frequently adapted a realpolitik style, exemplified by Brest-Litovsk in 1918, Rapallo in 1922, and the Ribbentrop-Molotov pact in 1939. However, the inevitable putative nature of the confrontation with capitalism (and therefore the West), culminating with the ultimate triumph of socialism, has always been the basic ideological principles of Soviet foreign policy. This ideological background, along with the closed nature of Soviet society to the western world, distinguished the Soviet Union's foreign policy from that of other countries. Ideology and limited contact gave rise to speculation about the defensive character and/or expansionism underlying Soviet policy. In practice, the pragmatism of most of its actions made its foreign policy comparable to that of any of the western powers.

The history of the Soviet Union's relations with other countries, as well as the relationship of its Communist Party with the international communist movement, has been dominated by the struggle against underdevelopment and the effort to occupy a place among the industrialized nations, with the purpose of becoming a world power. A rivalry with the West emerged with a basically military facade. The importance of achieving nuclear parity was an example of this. At the heart of this conflict was economic competition, as Soviet economic potential grew by leaps and bounds at the cost of countless sacrifices in an attempt to become a model for the Third World and a challenge to the advanced capitalist countries.

During the 1970s, after a long period of growth that brought severe hardships for most of the population, economic prosperity was achieved, allowing a distribution of material benefits to society. The rise in the standard of living and the growth of the armed forces occurred simultaneously. Strategic military parity with the United States was attained along with international prestige and influence within the Third World. A climate of international détente favorable to economic relations with the West was achieved during this decade. This prosperity was based on an economic strategy of massive investments, however, with little emphasis on efficiency. Consequently, the economy began to "overheat" as more was undertaken than could be achieved. Signs of crisis—scarcity of consumer goods, corruption, squandered investments—began to appear. Growth of GNP fell from 41 percent in the period from 1966-

1970 to 28 percent in 1971-1975, then to 21 percent in 1976-1980, and 16.5 percent in 1981-1985 (Karlitsky 1988, 89; Aganbegyan 1988, 64-65). For a time, all these problems could be compensated for by the increasing links with the West. Détente became a vital necessity for the Soviet leadership, a way of avoiding reform (even considera-tion of reform) of the overall economic strategy. As long as raw materials such as oil and gas could be exported and western equip-ment and technology imported, reform was not imperative.

Despite certain corrective measures (decline of imports and prompt debt payments) after the Polish problems in the early 1980s, the Soviet position in the world market became increasingly precarious. Détente entered a crisis during this period. Angola and Ethiopia, Carter's human-rights offensive, and the invasion of Afghanistan were antecedents of a new cold war, and they were seized upon by western neoconservatives.

The arms race regained its former pace, but in contrast with the preceding decade the Soviet Union found itself economically weak-ened, and the new U.S. challenge confronted the Soviet leadership with its technological backwardness and the inefficiency of its eco-nomic system. ("Star Wars" technology epitomized this chal-lenge). Together with the expectations that had been raised in the population by the prosperity of the early 1970s, this U.S. challenge made a change inevitable. By the early 1980s, four groups emerged within the Soviet political elite, each with a differing opinion on what the strategy of Soviet foreign policy should be.

First, there was an anti-détente group that saw the West as a united front against the Soviet Union. According to this group, the Soviet military budget required strengthening in order to face the North American nuclear threat. This group, however, faced the fact that increasing the military budget would not solve the prob-lem of Soviet technological backwardness. This faction was associ-ated with the newspaper *Red Star* and the journal *International Life*. It is unlikely at present that this current has many followers, though some do remain, especially in the army.

Second, a pro-détente group favored a cooperation between the blocs with U.S.–Soviet relations as the central axis. For this group, spheres of influence were acceptable and desirable, as were mili-tary alliances. For example, NATO was seen as playing an impor-tant role in restraining the power ambitions of Germany and

Japan. Those holding this position feared profound economic re-organization and preferred the easing of external tensions to min-imize domestic deficiencies by importing technology. This group was made up of the old guard, which disappeared by the end of the 1980s: Chernenko, Brezhnev, Gromyko, and Ustinov.

Third, an activist, outward-oriented position viewed the U.S.–Soviet relationship as central but, in contrast with the previously described group, favored greater Soviet integration in the world. The proponents of this position felt it necessary to break the im-passe in the arms control negotiations with more flexible Soviet proposals. Also central to this approach was the desire to reach agreements that would reduce tensions in the Third World. The members of this group included many Soviet specialists in U.S. af-fairs.[1]

Finally, there was the anti-American, pro-European, and pro-Japanese position, which emphasized the division of the western world. According to this position, it was necessary to formulate a more nuanced policy toward Europe and Japan, and even to seek rapprochement with China. Implied was the accelerated integra-tion of the Soviet Union with these countries, which would require concrete concessions.[2]

The influence exerted by these factions could be traced through the promotions or demotions of their adherents after the death of Brezhnev. During the brief period of Yuri Andropov's leadership, A. Yakovlev and A. Tolkunov were promoted, and official policy seemed to lean toward the pro-Europe/Japan position.[3] Under Chernenko, it seemed that this position continued to gain until the summer of 1984. Events consistent with the rise of this position

1. Including Georgi Arbatov, Director of the Institute for the Study of the USA and Canada of the Soviet Academy of Sciences; F. Bourlatski, former foreign policy adviser to Yuri Andropov; and Anatoly Dobrynin, former Soviet Ambassador to Washington, later appointed by Gorbachev to head the international department of the Central Committee, and currently his adviser for international affairs.

2. Proponents of this position were academicians such as A. Tolkunov and A. Yakovlev, a close ally of Gorbachev, who as director of the Institute of International Relations and World Economy went on to join the Secretariat of the Central Committee as head of propaganda for overseas. He was recently appointed to the Central Committee Politburo, the highest Soviet leadership body, as a full member, and he is currently Gorbachev's chief adviser for foreign affairs. For a detailed account of these positions, see Hough (1985).

3. See Andropov's declarations in *Pravda*, September 23, 1983.

were the boycott of the Los Angeles Olympics, the promotion of relations between the two Germanys, and an interview with General
Ogarkov (then Chief of Staff) in *Red Star* in May 1984.[4] By
September 1984, however, Chernenko had recuperated from an
illness, and the Soviet Union returned to a policy of more traditional détente: the speeches of a reinvigorated Gromyko recalled
the war alliance; contacts between the two Germanys were limited;
internal reform came to a halt; and Ogarkov was relieved of his
post in September (Hough 1985). However, the seed of change had
taken root in Soviet society and awaited a more propitious time to
make its appearance.

GORBACHEV AND THE REASSESSMENT
OF THE OUTSIDE WORLD

The challenge that Gorbachev inherited appeared even more
formidable because his strategy to deal with it could not help but
question a decades-old ideological legacy. Soon after his accession
to power, Gorbachev seemed to follow the line of confrontation
without concessions toward the United States. However, several developments seemed to indicate that a change of tactics, if not strategy, was underway: changes in personnel (Shevardnadze in place
of Gromyko), a summit with the United States, and the unilateral
declaration of a moratorium on nuclear arms. During the Geneva
summit meeting in late 1985, Gorbachev first suggested that it was
possible to reach an accord on intercontinental missiles independent of the talks on the Strategic Defense Initiative (SDI). For the
changes proposed by the new leader to crystallize, however, his
domestic political position had to be consolidated.

The first dismissals of high Soviet leaders occurred almost immediately after Gorbachev's accession.[5] The persistence of both
hard-line and centrist factions that supported a continuation of the
status quo in Soviet foreign policy blocked the change in strategy

---

4. He stated in this interview that the Soviet economy was not prepared to keep up
with the U.S. military challenge.
5. These included Romanov, Tikhonov, and Grichin.

Gorbachev had in mind.[6] Nonetheless, in January 1986, Gorbachev announced a new initiative for phased arms reduction and the elimination of all nuclear arms by the year 2000. During the 27th Congress of the Soviet Communist Party, he declared that growing world interdependence required a radical improvement in East-West relations through political understanding.[7] In this new approach, security became a political rather than a military problem, and the expansion of military strength was seen not only as useless, but counterproductive. This approach implied a criticism of diplomacy under Brezhnev, which was judged to be inflexible and dependent on excessive use of military force (Parrot 1988, 8).

Between February and March of 1986, new Soviet foreign policy changes occurred. Ponomarev was replaced as head of the international department of the Central Committee of the Communist Party of the Soviet Union by Anatoly Dobrynin. This official, the former ambassador to the United States, was a firm supporter of a more flexible diplomacy, "reasonable compromises" with the United States, and linking arms control and human rights. To promote these ideas and break the monopoly on defense policy by the military, Dobrynin created new teams of civilian experts on military matters. In the diplomatic corps, by August 1986 only one of eight deputy ministers of the Foreign Affairs Ministry remained from the Brezhnev period (Hough 1987, 34). Among the new policies developed by the Gorbachev team was the concept of "reasonable sufficiency" of the Soviet defense apparatus.

For the resolution of these and many other issues, unprecedented importance was placed on international organizations, particularly the United Nations. In addition to paying its contributions in arrears to the United Nations, the Soviet Union expressed its desire to participate in various international activities, which it had previously criticized, including peace-keeping forces. It acknowledged that the jurisdiction of the International Court of Justice was binding on all nations and conceded a key role to the United Nations in the settlement of regional conflicts (Bertrand 1988). Simultaneously, the Soviet government sought membership in international organizations such as the General Agreement on

6. These included Scherbytsky, CPSU First Secretary in the Ukraine; Chebrikov, of the KGB; and Head of Cadre and Ideology Yegor Ligachev.
7. *Izvestiya*, February 26, 1986.

Tariffs and Trade, the World Bank, and even the International Monetary Fund, though this would require internal reforms to make convertibility of the ruble possible. Further, by 1986 a new Soviet policy of maintaining a low profile in regional conflicts and Third World revolutions was evident. At the 27th Congress, solidarity with the liberation movements was discussed, but the emphasis was placed on the need for collective and negotiated solutions to regional conflicts (Gorbachev 1986, 87).

The external policy changes were only a reflection of the struggles for perestroika within the country. The Chernobyl tragedy played an important role in this struggle, for it demonstrated the need for administrative, technological, and, by extension, economic reforms. Apart from the errors that produced it, the accident brought to light the lack of competent emergency crews, the information gaps, and other inefficiencies. The first real manifestations of glasnost occurred during this tragedy, which opened the way for a more public examination of other problems affecting Soviet society. The flow of information to the outside also increased, and the West received detailed reports on the accident, along with the promise of greater cooperation with international agencies to prevent future accidents. This would be a precedent for future applications of glasnost and the democratization of the Foreign Affairs Ministry and other government agencies.

Little was achieved by Gorbachev at the Reykjavik summit, despite major Soviet concessions. Not to be deterred, Gorbachev took another dramatic step in October 1986, asserting the priority of social development and "universal human values" over the interests of any one class.[8] That is, he asserted that the Soviet Union renounced an international policy based on class conflict in favor of the "interests of humanity," in the face of global threats such as nuclear and ecological destruction. After 1987, Gorbachev succeeded in his new policy of concessions and more flexible diplomacy through the signing of a treaty on intermediate-range nuclear-force (INF) missiles, which eliminated an agreement on SDI as a precondition to other agreements. At the same time, he consolidated his control by continuing to replace officials in the Foreign Affairs Ministry and the KGB.

---

8. *Kommunist,* no. 16, November 1986, p. 12.

Under the new Soviet policies, the political strategy of negotiation prevailed over military power. Steps were taken to break with the traditional secrecy surrounding Soviet institutions, partly to comply with the verification requirements in the new treaties. A reappraisal of the outside world that no longer portrayed it as a threat facilitated greater influence of the public on security policy. This new "openness" required a renovation of the link between domestic and foreign policy. Traditionally, the quest for national security had been coupled with control of the population at home. In contrast, for Gorbachev a policy of negotiation and cooperation with the West was indispensable for domestic economic restructuring. The principal elements of this restructuring began to be revealed during the January 1987 meeting of the Central Committee of the Communist Party.

After the INF treaty was signed in Washington in December 1987, Gorbachev pressed his initiatives for disarmament, which included his announcement at the United Nations in December 1988 of a unilateral 10 percent reduction in Soviet army troops, in accordance with the "sufficient defense" doctrine.[9] Moreover, in early 1989 Shevardnadze announced the unilateral destruction of the Soviet Union's complete arsenal of chemical weapons. Soon after, a decision was announced to halt production of enriched uranium for the manufacture of nuclear arms. As another aspect of nuclear reduction, Gorbachev committed the Soviet Union to a unilateral reduction of 500 nuclear missile heads in East Europe and a detailed plan for the withdrawal of troops and conventional arms.[10]

9. This reduction applied to the 500,000 men and more than 5,000 tanks in the contingents stationed in the German Democratic Republic, Czechoslovakia, and Hungary. Also proposed were reductions of Soviet contingents stationed on the European and Asian parts of Soviet territory during the next two years. The majority of the troops stationed in Mongolia would return to the Soviet Union. In East Europe and Soviet European territory, there would be total reductions of 10,000 tanks, 8,500 artillery systems, and 800 combat aircraft (*El País*, December 8, 1988).

10. See *El País*, January 9, April 8, and May 10 and 13, 1988. They would consist of 500 nuclear warheads (284 missiles, 166 airborne projectiles, and 50 nuclear capacity cannons), in addition to all nuclear arms (from now until 1991), depending on U.S. plans for arms reductions. Moreover, Gorbachev proposed that by 1997 there be parity between both alliances, each having 1.35 million soldiers, 1,500 combat aircraft, and 20,000 combat vehicles. Each alliance would have a maximum of 1,700 helicopters, 24,000 artillery pieces, and 28,000 armored transport vehicles. (The Warsaw Pact would make the greatest reductions.)

The professed goal of these initiatives was to create a favorable climate for the creation of a global international security system based on a low-level military balance and humanitarian, ecological, economic, and political cooperation (Dobrynin 1988, 9-15). Without consolidation of the new leadership's power and political and economic reforms, a new foreign policy would not have been possible. Soviet new thinking toward the other countries of the world developed against a backdrop of a struggle among reforming, conservative, and centrist tendencies that led to a painful reevaluation of policies, practices, and concepts established over many decades.[11]

A NEW REGIONAL STRATEGY

In addition to the disarmament initiatives, the Gorbachev team undertook a reevaluation of Soviet strategy for different regions of the world. Priority was placed on finding a common language with the United States in terms of negotiation and cooperation. The search for this language extended to the rest of the industrial world as well, especially Europe and Japan.

The notion of a "common European home" synthesized the Soviet Union's aspiration to regain its place on the continent on which half of its territory lies. This notion also includes stressing the community of interests between East and West Europe and possibly the differences separating Europe from other external actors, for example, the United States (see Bertram 1988). The bulk of the disarmament initiatives dealt with Europe, and they were aimed at substituting the image of the Soviet Union as a military threat with a search for coexistence and cooperation at all levels.

On an economic level, Gorbachev was interested in West Europe as a potential source of technology that the United States refused to provide. Further, the Soviet market seems attracted to the Europeans, though they remained divided in their expectations of the changes occurring in the Soviet Union. In 1989, these divisions deepened, especially between the Federal Republic of Germany and Great Britain, on the issue of modernization of short-range

---

11. For a detailed account of this faction fight, see Parrot (1988).

missiles on German territory.   With the revolutions in East
Europe, however, this issue became an anachronism.

Rapprochement with West Europe began relatively soon.
Gorbachev's first visit to Paris in October 1985 was followed by subsequent visits to other European capitals and reciprocal trips by
European leaders to Moscow.   Relations with France improved
quickly, especially in the economic domain.   When Francois Mit-
terrand made his third trip to the Kremlin at the end of 1988, he
was apparently worried by the special treatment Gorbachev had
shown Margaret Thatcher, and he was clearly in the mood to
establish more fruitful economic relations.   Traveling with the
French delegation were business leaders and bankers who subsequently signed an agreement for cooperation with Soviet authori-
ties.   As a result of the visit, Credit Lyonnais granted US$2 billion
in credits to finance the creation of joint Franco-Soviet enterprises.[12]   On a diplomatic level, the French president expressed
support for Soviet disarmament measures and pledged to endorse
the choice of Moscow as the site of a human-rights conference to be
held in 1991 if the rest of the European Community agreed.[13]

Gorbachev established a special relationship with Margaret
Thatcher, despite the fact that Great Britain expressed deeper reservations toward the Soviet leadership's initiatives than other
European countries.   Thatcher's antagonism showed during Gorbachev's 1989 trip to London, when she chided the Soviets for arms
sales to Libya.   Nevertheless, the British Prime Minister continued
to support the domestic restructuring policies in the Soviet Union,
which perhaps she saw as consistent with her economic ideology.[14]

Relations between the Soviet Union and the Federal Republic of
Germany also improved, despite differences over Berlin and the
division of the two Germanys.   Bonn reacted enthusiastically to the
possibility of negotiations to lighten its military burden in NATO.
The FRG has also responded enthusiastically to the opening of opportunities for economic cooperation with the Soviet Union and all

12. In 1989, France was fourth among the Soviet Union's West European trading
partners.
13. Among European leaders, Margaret Thatcher opposed such a conference (El
País, November 26, 1988).
14. El País, April 7, 1989.

of East Europe.[15]   In addition, the majority of East European countries, with the Soviet Union in the lead, signed the final resolution issued by the Conference on European Security and Cooperation in Vienna, which called for cooperation on issues such as
human rights, the protection of ecosystems, and condemnation of
terrorism.[16]

ASIA

An important part of the new Soviet foreign policy was its approach
to the continent where the other half of its territory lies.   The
Soviet leadership's decision to eliminate short- and medium-range
missiles in the Asian territories was one of several actions to win
the goodwill of the countries in this region.   Perhaps the most
spectacular of these measures, and the one that most clearly
demonstrated Gorbachev's commitment to change, was the withdrawal from Afghanistan.   The Soviet Union's decision to accept a
negotiated settlement to the Afghan conflict dated back to the 1986
negotiations between Pakistan and Afghanistan under the auspices
of the United Nations.   By February 1988, Gorbachev had officially
set a timetable for Soviet troop withdrawal (which began in May),
and the Soviet Union in April signed the Geneva accord, calling
for the withdrawal of the superpowers from Afghanistan.   While
the Afghan opposition organized, the Soviets tried to exert influence to foster the creation of a government of national reconciliation, a formula attempted in other regional conflicts.   Whatever
the ultimate outcome of this approach in the case of Afghanistan,
the last of the Soviet troops returned to Soviet territory on February
15, 1989.[17]   Thanks to the policy of glasnost, the Soviet public was
able to voice its support for withdrawal, as well as to criticize the
decision to invade in the first place.   Opinions are divided as to the
costs, risks, and benefits of the Soviet role in Afghanistan, and
there are even those who claim that they warned the leadership of
the risks and inadvisability of the operation when the invasion

15. *El País*, October 16, 1988.
16. *El País*, January 18, 1988.
17. See the chronology of events in "L'URSS et le Monde" (Dossier).   See also
Problemes Politiques et Sociaux (Documentation Française), no. 605, 1989, p. 44.

was launched in 1979 (Bogomolov 1988).[18] In any case, the majority of the population seems to have applauded the end of the war.

In an attempt to reap the fruits of that policy change, Moscow moved to establish closer ties with Japan, China, and India. Economic interest was again one of the prime motivations behind this rapprochement. Gorbachev's projects for economic reorganization depended greatly on the development of the Soviet Far East. The region's wealth of natural resources makes it ideal for integration into the world of expanding economies of the Asian-Pacific area.

But apart from the general climate of cooperation rather than conflict, the Soviet Union made bilateral concessions to the more important countries in the area. The conflict with Japan over the Kurile Islands, which have been occupied by the Soviet Union since World War II, remained unresolved. The return of these islands (or negotiations to that end) was Tokyo's principal condition for closer economic ties (Perkovich 1987).[19] It could be argued, however, that the greatest obstacle to rapprochement was the close relationship between Tokyo and Washington.

Concessions to China were significant: troop withdrawal from Mongolia; revision of the border between the countries; withdrawal from Afghanistan; and initiation of a settlement of the Cambodian conflict. That these concessions bore fruit could be judged by the normalization of relations between the two countries, reaffirmed by the 1989 Peking summit.[20] Although the differences on the Cambodian question persisted, there was agreement on tolerance of various models of socialism and the need for reform (without questioning the primacy of the Communist Party). In fact, the visit to China exemplified Gorbachev's intent to exercise discretion regarding the domestic problems of other countries, for he refused to express an opinion on the social upheaval in China. As in Cuba (see below), China faced the challenge of implementing political modernization to match its economic modernization. But this would entail a process of glasnost that the Chinese leader-

18. See also other Soviet opinions published in "L'URSS et le Monde," op. cit.

19. See also *El País*, December 22, 1988.

20. At the end of the Soviet visit, the Soviet Union announced its plans to import liquid carbon from China and to build railroad networks and increase trade relations. See *El País*, May 15-18, 1989.

ship clearly refused to accept, as the repression during the summer of 1989 demonstrated.

Soviet policy toward India, unlike that toward China and Japan, did not require major concessions, for friendly relations had existed between the two countries for several decades. However, Gorbachev decided to give more emphasis to Soviet interest in India with a high-level meeting in November 1986 and a treaty increasing trade by 150 percent (Perkovich 1987). India endorsed Soviet withdrawal from Afghanistan, though agreement already existed between Moscow and New Delhi on Pakistan's role in the area. If anything, relations between India and the Soviet Union have become warmer after Gorbachev's official visit to India in late 1988. Besides emphasizing the common views of the two countries on such issues as disarmament and economic cooperation, the visit aimed at formalizing plans for the installation of a nuclear plant with Soviet aid and the peaceful joint exploration of space.[21]

In the Middle East, the Soviet Union demonstrated an interest in seeking peaceful solutions to local conflicts under the auspices of the United Nations. Also noteworthy is the Soviet search for rapprochement with countries in the areas that it formerly considered to be enemies (Israel) or potentially dangerous to its interests (Iran). This rapprochement had the goals of promoting stability in the area and establishing fruitful economic ties.

THE THIRD WORLD IN GENERAL

The new diplomacy influenced the Soviet Union's new attitudes toward the Third World in general. Before Gorbachev, Soviet policy for the Third World followed two lines: (1) the ideological focus on export of socialist revolution as a theoretical model, and (2) the pragmatic focus on rapprochement with regimes on the basis of economic and political interests. During the Brezhnev period, the Soviet leadership adopted more pragmatic attitudes toward countries with which Khrushchev had cultivated ideological links. Ties were established with countries regardless of the political orientation of their governments, and by 1979 there were seventy

21. *Pravda*, November 18-21, 1988.

diplomatic delegations in such diverse countries as Asia, Africa, and Oceania, and economic accords with more than sixty of them. Notions such as an "integrated world economy" and the need for increased trade with these countries began to emerge during this period (Valkenier 1979, 17-33).

The Soviet leadership of the 1970s, however, continued to give favored treatment to the "socialist-oriented" countries and to make policy on the basis of the revolutionary potential of others. Many of these considerations were motivated by geopolitical calculations based on traditional confrontation with the United States. Examples of this include Afghanistan, Angola, and Ethiopia. Still, the end of the Brezhnev period saw the emergence of a more realistic and discriminating analysis of the problems of the underdeveloped world.[22]

Under Gorbachev, there is a greater tendency toward "realism" or "deideologization" with respect to the possibility of socialist change in the Third World. A shift of focus in relations with these countries became a vital component of perestroika. Along with the need to cut military spending to fund Soviet domestic recovery, it was essential to reassess development aid, which represented more than 1 percent of Soviet GNP from 1976-1980 (VI UNCTAD 1987). This aid, motivated by Soviet commitment to countries, usually with a socialist orientation, needed to be restructured, reduced, and made more efficient. At the same time, Soviet attainment of greater international confidence and, above all, closer ties to the United States had to be grounded in more cooperative attitudes toward points of tension, which were located primarily in the Third World. This implied a reduction of commitments toward previously favored allies while establishing closer economic ties with newly industrialized countries.

Speeches and actions of the Gorbachev leadership have been devoted to greater Soviet multilateral development aid and joint solutions to the problems of underdevelopment. On the debt problem, Gorbachev (in his address to the United Nations in December 1988) proposed implementing a moratorium of up to 100 years on

22. See *Países en Vías de Desarrollo, Leyes, Tendencias y Perspectivas* (published also in English as *Developing Countries, Laws, Tendencies and Perspectives*). Moscow: Mysi, 1974. This paper was one of many written by teams of specialists in the Institute for World Economy and International Relations.

debt-service payment for the neediest countries and, in some cases, complete cancellation of the debt. In the case of countries of greater economic viability, the repayment of the debt should be tied to indicators of development. In any case, Gorbachev maintained that the debt and other problems should be resolved in international fora organized under the auspices of the United Nations.[23] This approach differs substantially from the Cuban call for a complete and unconditional moratorium.

In light of the Soviet Union's shift away from aid to its favored allies in the Third World, it is interesting to examine the debate between Soviet specialists organized by the *New Times* journal in December 1988.[24] In this exchange, it was maintained that those countries that pushed industrialization and accumulation following the Soviet example and implemented immediate distribution of income and wealth failed in their attempt to overcome underdevelopment. This failure was attributed to the inefficiency of the public sector, widespread corruption, extreme voluntarism, irrational restriction of the private sector, and authoritarian and antidemocratic political systems. All of these were seen as leading to disillusionment of the population, emergence of black markets, and economic stagnation. Some of the participants in this debate tried to salvage the idea of "socialist orientation" as theoretically valid. But their advice to socialist-oriented countries was that they apply solutions similar to those of glasnost and perestroika: economic reform and democratization. At the end of the 1980s, perestroika was offered as a role model, just as in its heyday Soviet socialism was for the "noncapitalist path."[25]

On the ideological level, Dobrynin presented the new Soviet concepts on liberation struggles to the international community. In an extensive article that appeared in the *International Journal,* he argued that the Soviet Union had not renounced its solidarity with emancipation struggles. However, he wrote, the export of counterrevolution should not be opposed by revolutionary violence but rather by the "primacy of law," that is, "the repudiation of the in-

---

23. Statement by Gorbachev, reproduced in "L'URSS et le Monde," op cit.
24. *New Times (Tiempos Nuevos),* no. 52, December 1988.
25. In this sense, a Soviet expert on Latin America emphasized the fact that, thanks to perestroika, the Soviet model again became attractive to the majority of the left forces. See Harnecker (1988).

terference of any state in the affairs of another." The article also
stressed the primacy of universal values over class in international
relations. Finally, the article accepted the continued existence of
objective differences between exploiters and the exploited and the
inevitability of struggle to establish a just social order. But, he
wrote, it is essential, "before addressing these contradictions, to
win the battle for the survival of humanity" (Dobrynin 1988, 9-15).

In the case of Latin America, the new Soviet foreign policy had
a double meaning. For Cuba, it meant decreased aid and pressure
to adopt perestroika-like political and economic measures. In
Nicaragua's case, petroleum supplies were reduced in 1987, and the
Soviet Union announced in 1989 that it would halt its assistance in
military hardware and arms.[26] Moreover, Soviet interest in contributing to the settlement of regional conflicts implied exerting
pressure on these countries to adopt a more conciliatory disposition
to negotiate with the United States. These pressures may have indeed influenced the concessions that the Sandinista government
has made to its neighbors and the United States since 1987. In
Cuba's case, it is less likely that pressure would have the same effect
(though it may have influenced the negotiated departure of Cuban
forces from Angola). Fidel Castro has proved unwilling to import
free-market practices and western-style democratization. In contrast, Cuba appeared more open to negotiation on the question of bilateral relations with the United States and firmly resolved to
normalize relations with the rest of Latin America. A modus
vivendi between Cuba and the Soviet Union emerged after
Gorbachev's official visit to Havana in April 1989.[27]

For the larger Latin American countries, the new Soviet foreign
policy signified new possibilities for economic cooperation and
diplomatic relations. Those who already had strong trade relations with the Soviet Union, namely Argentina and Brazil, were
more likely to benefit in the short term; but other countries in the
region stood to strengthen their economic ties with Moscow. The
importance that Moscow placed on these countries was evident during Shevardnadze's tour through the region in 1987. In addition
to explaining the changes in Soviet policy to the region's govern-

26. See *El País*, May 12 and 17, 1989.
27. See *El País*, April 6, 1989.

ments and signing economic accords, he announced Gorbachev's forthcoming visit to the continent. President Alfonsín of Argentina traveled to the Soviet Union in October 1986 to reach accord on joint ventures for export production and sale of Argentine agro-industrial technology to the Soviet Union.[28] President Sarney of Brazil visited Moscow in the fall of 1988 to reach final agreement on several joint ventures and the exchange of industrial patents and techniques (principally in the food industry).[29]

This pragmatic trend in foreign policy did not dampen the interest of Soviet Latin American experts in the region's revolutionary struggles. This interest was shown by a debate on the role of the left in the Latin American revolutionary process.[30] Represented in the debate were two broad positions. First, there was the orthodox tendency, which defended traditional dogma on the vanguard of the Communist parties and exorcised the "ultra left wing" as the cause of revolutionary failures. Against this was the liberal current, which recognized the different groups among the left as legitimate representatives of diverse parts of the populace. According to one proponent of this school, divisions in the left corresponded to a critical phase of capitalism in which many of the Latin American countries found themselves. For the liberal current, the problem was not finding legitimate vanguards or a single path to power but rather coordinating the forces espousing different paths to socialism. From this debate, it can be inferred that socialism is no longer viewed as a short- or medium-term stage in society's evolution. That the debate took place indicates the penetration of perestroika even into the area of academic investigation.

CONCLUSION

Of all the structural changes the Soviet Union has undergone since the triumph of the October Revolution, perestroika appears to be the most ambitious and, therefore, the most risk-laden. It is no less than an attempt to modernize the Soviet state and open it to the ex-

---

28. See *América Latina*, no. 4, Moscow, April 1987.
29. *Pravda*, October 19-21, 1988.
30. The journal *América Latina* provided a forum for this discussion, which has taken place in periodic installments since early 1987.

ternal world.   The consequences it would hold for international
relations would be far-reaching.

On one hand, there is the possibility of cooperation in countless
issues on which the previous Soviet position was not very constructive.   On the other hand, there was also an impasse in the reactions of the western world toward the Soviet opening.   It was as if
the old adversaries of the Soviet Union were caught off guard, left
with no answer to the initiatives.   This lack of response on the part
of the West, disguised as distrust of deceptive Soviet tactics, revealed
a lack of understanding of the depth and meaning of the changes
taking place and a dangerous political shortsightedness.   The delay
of a favorable response to the Soviet initiatives threatened the survival of the new approach.   Gorbachev was relatively successful in
consolidating his power, but the moderates and conservatives in
the Soviet Union continued to watch for any miscalculation or mistake.   If socialism is reversible, so is perestroika, though the alternatives might not be very clear.

REFERENCES

Aganbegyan, Abel.   1988.   "New Directions in Soviet Economics."
    New Left Review, no. 1619.
Bertram, Christoph.   1988.   "L'Idée de Maison Europeanne aurait-
    elle vielli?" *Les Nouvelles de Moscou,* no. 25.
Bertrand, Maurice.   1988.   "Ouvertures Sovietiques." *Le Monde Diplo-
    matique,* February.
Bogomolov, O.   1988.   "Quién se equivoco?" *Literaturnaya gazeta,*
    Moscow, March 16.
Dobrynin, Anatoly.   1988.   "La política exterior soviética: principios
    básicos y el nuevo pensamiento." *Revista Internacional* 3.
Gorbachev, Mikhail S.   1986.   *Political Report of the CPSU Central
    Committee to the 27th Party Congress.* Moscow: Novosty.
Harnecker, Martha.   1988.   *Perestroika: La revolución de las esperanzas.*
    Interview with Kiva Maidanik by Martha Harnecker, Hermanos
    Vadell, Venezuela, chapters X and XI.
Hough, Jerry.   1985.   "Could Star Wars Foment a New Russian
    Revolution?" *Washington Post,* January 6.

Hough, Jerry. 1987. "Gorbachev Consolidating Power." *Problems of Communism* 4.

Karlitsky, Boris. 1988. "Perestroika: The Dialectic of Change." *New Left Review*, no. 1619.

Parrot, Bruce. 1988. "Soviet National Security Under Gorbachev." *Problems of Communism*, November–December.

Perkovich, George. 1987. "Moscow Turns East." *The Atlantic.* Boston (December). Quoted in "L'URSS et le Monde" (Dossier), 37-40.

Valkenier, Elizabeth. 1979. "The USSR, the Third World and the Global Economy." *Problems of Communism*, July-August.

VI UNCTAD. 1987. Quoted by I. Dobozi: "East-South Economic Relations." Paper presented at EADI Conference, Amsterdam, September.

9

The New Soviet Foreign Policy and Its Impact on Latin America

Boris Y. Yopo

This paper is a preliminary evaluation of political initiatives taken by the new Soviet administration in its relations with Latin America in the 1980s, particularly in the South American area.[1] A discussion of the strategic political interests of the Soviet Union in the region requires an analysis of the diverse factors that have influenced the formulation of Soviet policy for Latin America. Insofar as the Soviet Union held superpower status and maintained a wide presence in different regions of the world, global factors were frequently decisive in explaining behavior in the area and conditioning the bilateral dynamics of the relations that the Soviet Union established with different Latin American governments (Blasier 1983, 130). The significance and scope of recent Soviet activism in the region was framed, therefore, by the set of priorities and objectives defined by the new program for the Communist Party of the Soviet Union (CPSU) foreign policy, the principal points of which were formally established at the 27th Congress of February 1986.[2]

---

1. There are several works that analyze in detail the history of Soviet-Latin American relations until the ascent of Mikhail Gorbachev. The most relevant are Clissold (1970), Blasier (1983), and Varas (1987a). The economic-commercial dimension of these ties has been examined in depth in works such as those of Berrios (1987) and Evanson (1985).

2. *Soviet News*, no. 5313, London, February 26, 1985, pp. 73-91.

THE NEW DICTATES OF SOVIET FOREIGN POLICY

The report presented by General Secretary Mikhail Gorbachev to
the 1986 Congress made it clear that the new Soviet foreign strategy was aimed principally at seeking a decrease in international
tensions to reduce the defense budget, thereby freeing resources for
the internal economic reorganization already underway.[3] In his
first interview with the western press in September 1985, the new
Soviet leader foresaw that the top priority of his government was to
improve radically the functioning of the internal economy, and
that the success of this objective depended fundamentally on the development of a peaceful and stable relationship with the rival superpower.[4]

Foreign policy thus became more subordinated than before to
the needs of internal transformation. But also, as some Soviet officials have explicitly pointed out, this should not serve in the future
as a compensation for the deficiencies exhibited by the Soviet
Union's internal development. In this respect, Deputy Minister of
Foreign Relations Vladimir Petrovsky said, "Nowadays, the
Leninist concept that the triumph of socialism is demonstrated
solely through our domestic policy has been elevated to official
Soviet state policy." A greater synchronization of the domestic
economy and policy with foreign and defense policy and the clear
preeminence of Soviet "national interests" over other commitments in the formulation and implementation of foreign policy
were the distinct facets of the Soviet Union's new approach to the
international system.[5]

As previously suggested, the Soviets' negative evaluation of the
international context of the 1980s was a necessary antecedent to the
readjustments introduced by the Soviet leadership to its foreign
policy program, including the postulates or premises on which
Soviet security is based. In marked contrast to the optimistic evalu-
ations of the international situation in the 1970s (détente between
the superpowers and rise of the national liberation movements), by
the 26th CPSU Congress in 1981 Secretary General Leonid

3. Ibid., p. 79.
4. *Time,* September 9, 1985, p. 5.
5. "Gorbachev is Forging a New Foreign Policy," *International Herald Tribune,* August
6, 1984, p. 1.

Brezhnev presented a more somber and cautious outlook on the prevailing tendencies in the international scene. Examples pointing to a situation of increasing polarization between East and West in the early 1980s included the nonratification of the SALT II Treaty; the invasion of Afghanistan; the substantial increase in U.S. military spending; NATO's decision to deploy intermediate range missiles in Europe; Washington's renewed threats against Cuba; and the expansion of a series of regional conflicts.

In the report of the 27th CPSU Congress, Gorbachev expressed Soviet sentiments:

> . . . [N]ever in the decades that have gone by since the Second World War has there been such an explosive and complex situation in the world as in the first half of the 1980s. The rightist group that came to power in the United States and its followers in NATO made a sharp turn from détente to a policy of using military force. . . . In view of this, the Central Committee of the CPSU analyzed the nature and dimensions of the threat and defined practical steps to improve the situation.[6]

Implicit in this analysis was the recognition that the policies of the Soviet Union before Gorbachev had been insufficient to contain the "neoglobalist" plans of the Reagan administration (and, paradoxically, on one occasion had the effect of reinforcing the strategy), while the costs of maintaining strategic parity with the United States in the existing climate of tensions and international polarization were rising. These costs markedly restricted prospects for improving living conditions in the Soviet Union and imposed restrictions to domestic development projects. (According to western intelligence reports, the Soviet Union devotes 15 to 18 percent of its gross domestic product to defense).

On the basis of this scenario, the new Soviet leadership decided to reformulate its foreign strategy. Its aim was to reverse the military escalation and zero-sum competition that characterized relations between the superpowers in the 1980s. The central objective in this new period was to create the political conditions in the international system that would enable Soviet interests and security needs to be satisfied and simultaneously achieve a significant reduction of global military spending. This would be possible and necessary, according to Gorbachev and other top leaders, because the world continued to be increasingly interdependent. Gorbachev's view was that the greater volume and sophistication of arms production would not lead to an increment in the security margin of the countries involved in the spiraling arms race. It is in this context that Gorbachev and the Soviet leadership launched their "new vision" of international relations,[7] oriented at generating greater predictability in the relations between the superpowers.[8]

REGIONAL CONFLICTS AND INTERNATIONAL SECURITY

One of the most complex issues affecting relations between the superpowers in the 1980s was the problem of regional conflicts. The Soviets generally opposed interpretations that linked détente between the superpowers to Soviet actions in the Third World, disassociating the two processes. For example, in the early 1970s the Soviets did not renounce détente associated with the ratification of the SALT I Treaty, despite the intensification of U.S. bombing in Vietnam. Soviet military analysts again began to emphasize in the 1980s the risks of a confrontation between the superpowers stemming from the escalation of local or regional conflicts (Katz 1982, 134). Moreover, as early as 1980 several Soviet analysts, including well-known political commentator Alexander Bovin, argued that the effects of unilateral actions in the Third World would be to strengthen forces in the West opposed to a new period of détente. In 1981, Brezhnev proposed to the United States the

7. It is fitting to note that central to this "new vision" is the abandoning of the concept of class struggle as a "guide for action" in international relations. The conservative elements in the Communist Party of the Soviet Union, led by Politburo member Yegor Ligachev, resisted this change, which led to an open polemic with Soviet Foreign Minister Eduard Shevardnadze. The latter, reflecting the outlook of Gorbachev's closest collaborators, emphasized that the common problems facing humanity dictate that the "struggle between systems will no longer be the determinant tendency of the present era" Keller (1988, 5). For a discussion of the implications of this ideological change in the sphere of foreign relations, see Kennan (1988).

8. As for the importance assigned by the Soviet leadership to the factors of predictability or adherence to the "rules of the game" in relation to the United States, see Adomeit (1986). On the recent Soviet foreign policy proposals, see the article "Will the Cold War Fade Away?" *Time*, July 7, 1987, p. 14.

establishment of a code of conduct for the superpowers in the Third World.[9]

Another factor that increased Soviet interest in seeking negotiated settlements to certain regional conflicts was the growing political and financial cost of supporting certain allies or client states in Angola, Vietnam, and Afghanistan. This new approach involved the tacit acceptance that some of these conflicts could not be resolved by military means, and there was risk of such conflicts being prolonged for decades.[10]

Under Gorbachev, there emerged a new strategy for regional security proposals, explicitly linking Third World conflicts and prospects for a stable accommodation with the United States. It is interesting to note the strong influence exerted by some of Gorbachev's chief foreign policy advisers, who had a great deal of experience with relations with the West and were sensitive to the perceptions and effects that Soviet policies generated in the capitalist world. Among these advisers to the Soviet leader were Anatoly Dobrynin, former Soviet ambassador to the United States for twenty years; Alexander Yakovlev, Soviet ambassador to Canada until 1985; and Georgi Arbatov, Director of the Institute for the Study of the United States and Canada (ISKAN) of the Soviet Academy of Sciences. Both Dobrynin and Arbatov stressed the importance of distinguishing between rightists and realists in the "ruling circles" of the West to avoid actions that would bolster the more conservative sectors opposed to a new Soviet–U.S. rapprochement.[11]

9. It is interesting to note that for some western analysts the Brezhnev leadership's proposal for a code of conduct in explosive areas of the Third World was framed within a global logic aimed at establishing a relation based on the two superpowers' condominium of the world. Former President Nixon has pointed out that Brezhnev explicitly proposed the idea of a shared hegemony of control in the international system during the summit meeting held in Washington in June 1973. On this subject, see Slulzberger (1987a, 1987b).

10. In an important 1982 speech, Yuri Andropov warned that "one thing is to proclaim socialism and quite another is to build it," criticizing the difficulties experienced by different regimes with a "socialist orientation" that received aid from the Soviet Union. Three of the principal Soviet concerns in this respect are the internal fragmentation that exists in these countries, their level of political instability, and the growing economic dependence on the Soviet Union. On this last point, see Fukuyama (1986, 1987).

11. *Report on the 27th Congress of the CPSU,* Rand, February 1987.

During the first three years of the new Soviet leadership, Gorbachev launched an intense diplomatic offensive in diverse areas of the Third World, making complex proposals and favoring a collective management of situations that affected regional security. For example, the Soviet leader updated the proposal to establish a code of conduct to regulate the competition of the superpowers in the Third World. During the first summit meeting between Reagan and Gorbachev, held in Geneva in November 1985, the two agreed to formalize regular consultations between the Soviet foreign ministry and the U.S. Department of State over Third World conflicts.

Also noteworthy was the constructive role the Soviet Union played in the preliminary agreement reached by Cuba, Angola, and South Africa to resolve the conflict in Southern Africa. The U.S. Undersecretary of State for African Affairs, Chester Crocker, said the agreement constituted "a case study on joint cooperation of the superpowers in support of solutions to regional conflicts." With the departure of Soviet troops from Afghanistan, the recognition of a neutral and nonaligned status for that country appeared imminent. Former Secretary of State Henry Kissinger judged this step the most significant Soviet foreign policy action since the withdrawal of its troops from Austria thirty years ago. It is important to note that for the Soviet leadership the policy of "national reconciliation" implemented in Afghanistan represented in a certain sense a model that with certain variations could be valid in other countries that experienced civil war.[12]

On the other hand, the Soviet leader presented in July 1987 a global security proposal for Southeast Asia and the Pacific. On this occasion, the Soviet Union proposed specifically to reduce naval operations in the Pacific, especially those involving ships with nuclear arms on board; to limit anti-submarine activities; and to adopt measures of mutual trust, such as the notification of movements of land, amphibious, naval, and air maneuvers. Foreign Minister Shevardnadze also stressed the Soviet Union's signing of the protocols for the Treaty of Rarotonga, which declared the South Pacific a nuclear-free zone (Varas 1987b).

12. "South Africa, Cuba and Angola Sign Namibia Peace Accord," *International Herald Tribune*, December 14, 1988, p.2; see also Kissinger (1987).

One of the most innovative aspects of Soviet security proposals was the decision to strengthen multilateral mechanisms for the prevention and resolution of international conflicts. In an eleven-point program presented by Gorbachev in September 1987, he proposed to create a global international security system, reactivating the role of the U.N. Security Council in the sphere of international security. Among other measures, the Soviet leader proposed reactivating the Military Committee of the U.N., one of the functions of which would be to authorize joint military actions in critical situations. He also called for the following measures: (1) creating a multinational center for the management of conflicts; (2) establishing of a direct line of communication among the permanent members of the Security Council; (3) granting the Council the power to verify peace agreements; (4) increasing the powers of the International Court of Justice and the International Atomic Energy Agency; (5) forming a U.N. committee to investigate acts of international terrorism; and (6) supporting U.N. peacekeeping operations. This last point was a marked turnaround in the Soviet Union's decades-long policy of refusing to support and finance such operations. The Soviet Union demonstrated its commitment to this point by contributing funds to the U.N. peacekeeping forces in Lebanon, repaying its debt of US$197 million for this area of operations.[13]

Soviet concerns for regional security problems would seem based on the premise that the prospects for negotiation between the East and West blocs are growing. But because there was no resolution of the diverse conflicts in the Third World at the close of the 1980s, the process of international détente was unstable.

LATIN AMERICA AND THE NEW SOVIET FOREIGN POLICY

Soviet policy and interests in Latin America are determined not only by local conditions or bilateral dynamics. Also influencing policy would be the global context of relations with the United States and the general strategy of the Soviet Union regarding the

---

13. "Soviet in Shift Backs a More Powerful UN," *International Herald Tribune,* October 9, 1987, pp. 1 and 6; "Look Who's Playing Peacekeeper Now," *U.S. News and World Report,* November 2, 1987, p. 47.

Third World. As a starting point, any analysis should consider that Latin America is the Third World area farthest from and of least importance to the Soviet Union. This was clear in Gorbachev's address to the CPSU Congress in February 1986. When listing the strategic priorities of the Soviet Union, Gorbachev placed them in this order: (1) the defense of land and sea borders; (2) Afghanistan; (3) Europe, Asia, and the Pacific; and (4) certain "hot spots," such as the Mid-East and Southern Africa. Central America was a low priority in this geopolitical scheme, and South America was not even mentioned.[14]

That the Soviet Union has no vital security interests in Latin America (excepting Cuba) would not imply the absence of long-term objectives for the region. In the past, an important interest of Soviet policy for Latin America was to gain diplomatic recognition from the countries of the region. This goal sought to overcome the status of international "pariah" that afflicted the Soviet Union from the beginning of the century until the end of the Cold War period. In this sense, the greater flexibility of postwar alignments permitted Soviet–Latin American ties to expand on the political and economic plane. At the beginning of the 1950s, Soviet relations with Latin America were almost nonexistent, and Soviet links were generally limited to local communist parties. At the end of the 1980s, the Soviet Union maintained full diplomatic relations with nineteen Latin American and Caribbean nations (all the South American countries except Chile and Paraguay). There were more than 10,000 Latin American students attending Soviet and East European universities at the end of the 1980s. From 1960 to 1983, the volume of foreign trade between the CMEA (Council for Mutual Economic Assistance) and Latin American countries multiplied fifteen-fold, rising to US$5.6 billion in 1983.[15]

In this sense it is pertinent to note the importance of Latin America within the context of the Soviet Union's new diplomatic activism. Recent visits by Deputy Foreign Minister Viktor Kompletov to four countries in the region, as well as those by Foreign Minister Eduard Shevardnadze in October 1987 to

---

14. "The Other Superpower: The Soviet Union in Latin America, 1917-1987," *Report on the Americas*, no. 1, NACLA, February 1987.

15. *Soviet Posture in the Western Hemisphere*, Committee on Foreign Affairs, House of Representatives, Washington, 1985.

Argentina, Brazil, and Uruguay (and previously to Mexico), were unprecedented in the history of Soviet–Latin American relations. They provided clear evidence of Soviet interest in strengthening trade and political relations with the countries of the region. At the same time, never had so many high-level Latin American officials visited Moscow as during 1984 to 1988. Those who paid official visits to the Soviet Union included presidents Alfonsín of Argentina, Sanguinetti of Uruguay, and Sarney of Brazil, as well as Mexican Foreign Minister Bernardo Sepúlveda and foreign relations ministers from other Latin American countries.

Complementing these high-level contacts, the Soviets also conducted a "silent diplomacy" to take advantage of the new openings brought by constitutional regimes replacing dictatorships. Indications of the active level of relations include the authorization for Aeroflot flights by Argentina, Bolivia, and Uruguay; the reopening of the Soviet-Uruguayan Cultural Center (the activities of which were suspended in 1975); the renewal and establishment of cultural and scientific accords in Colombia, Mexico, Peru, and Costa Rica; the new consular agreements with Argentina, Brazil, Bolivia, and Costa Rica; and the many economic and trade agreements recently signed with various Latin American states.[16]

To understand the meaning of this renewed Soviet interest in Latin America, one must return to the analysis underlying the present strategy of the Soviet Union in the Third World. A new style of diplomacy emerged under Gorbachev, which as a continuation of domestic glasnost is characterized by an "open" and "direct" dialogue with the diverse leaders who make up world public opinion. The strategy would seek to incorporate the greatest number of government and nongovernment leaders in a crusade for nuclear disarmament and other objectives consistent with the present agenda of Soviet foreign policy.[17] Although relations with the

16. For a more detailed analysis of the extensive network of political and commercial relations recently developed between the Soviet Union and Latin America, see works by Augusto Varas published in the *Anuario de Políticas Exteriores Latinoamericanas* (1985-1988), compiled by the Programa de Seguimiento de las Políticas Exteriores Latinoamericanas (PROSPEL), and edited by GEL, Buenos Aires.

17. One of the effects of this new "public diplomacy" has been the greater "visibility exhibited by Soviet representatives in various Latin American capitals, in contrast to the excessive reserve and hermetism which Soviet diplomatic personnel had traditionally maintained in Latin America" (Greenberger 1988).

United States remained central to the Soviet Union, they no longer had the exclusive character prevailing in the Brezhnev-Gromyko era. In his address to the CPSU Congress, Gorbachev explicitly stated:

> ... [T]he world is much more extensive than the United States ... and in world politics it is not possible to confine oneself to relations with one country, no matter how important it may be ... as we know this only promotes arrogant attitudes.

This view was an attempt to adopt a more multilateral rather than bilateral strategy in dealing with U.S. relations. However, this step presupposes an explicit acceptance of the growing role various new forces would play in the international system. In particular, the Soviet Union would have to adapt to a world of increased fragmentation and diffusion of the centers of influence.[18]

Based on this analysis, relations with the larger countries of Latin America received greater priority in Soviet foreign policy. As early as 1981, Brezhnev referred to Argentina, Brazil, and Mexico as countries destined to play an increasingly important role in world affairs. But it was not until Gorbachev that the Soviet foreign policy staff promoted a more systematic policy of rapprochement, especially with the so-called medium powers of Latin America. Thus, it was no coincidence that Shevardnadze visited Brazil, Mexico, and Argentina during his first two tours to Latin America. Soviet long-range interests in the region would not be found in the convulsed Central American region but rather in Mexico and the large South American countries. In 1987, Gorbachev's top foreign affairs adviser, Alexander Yakovlev, referred to the important role that the newly industrialized countries, such as Brazil, were beginning to play in a multi-polar world. Yakovlev said the new Soviet foreign strategy was characterized by its multi-polarity, taking into account the "objective con-

---

18. An Indian analyst, commenting on the Soviet Union's recent diplomatic initiatives, pointed out that their aim is to promote the broadest possible interclass alliances in an anti-nuclear mobilization. This strategy would politically isolate the United States and create obstacles for its defense programs, especially its Strategic Defense Initiative, thus permitting Moscow to reduce its defense budget without significantly changing basic Soviet security requirements. See Bauerfee (1987).

tradictions" that existed between these countries and the developed capitalist world (Fukuyama 1986, 6-7).

In the 1970s, Soviet analysts already pointed to the growing impact of certain Latin American countries in world affairs. Nevertheless, it was not until ten years later that policies were implemented for the region that reflected this analysis. Two important experts in Third World and Latin American policy, Karen Brutents and Vadim Zagladin, wrote articles in the 1970s arguing that the future course of Latin America would not be decided in small countries with revolutionary regimes (for example, Nicaragua) but rather in the medium-sized powers of the region (see Litwak and MacFarlane 1987, 21-39; Fukuyama 1986).

Gorbachev's new policy for the Third World was in great measure grounded in the analysis of specialists favoring a Soviet policy more oriented toward cultivating ties with "moderate" countries, chosen for their weight on the international scene. In this context, the Mexican foreign minister received a high-level reception during his week-long stay in Moscow in 1987, during which he met personally with Gorbachev. The Libyan foreign minister was also in Moscow at the same time, but his presence went by virtually unnoticed. Gorbachev, in his book *Perestroika: New Thinking for Our Country and the World*, openly praised "the energetic foreign policy of Mexico and Argentina, their responsible position on disarmament and international security, and their contribution to the initiatives of the Group of Six."[19]

SECURITY INTERESTS IN
SOVIET–SOUTH AMERICAN RELATIONS

The Soviet Union's major objectives in South America did not include the promotion of Soviet regimes, but they did include the strengthening of what Soviet analysts called the "independent course and anti-imperialist tendencies" that the foreign policy of Latin American countries began to show at the end of the 1970s. The motivation, of course, was to increase the margin of action for

19. Gorbachev (1987, 220-221). See also "Moscow's Third World Game," *Newsweek*, March 23, 1987, p. 13; "Soviet Stressing Ties to Moderate Nations," *International Herald Tribune*, May 26, 1987, p. 1.

the Soviet Union in the international arena. It should be recalled, for example, that when the United States declared a grain embargo for the Soviet Union in 1980, Argentina and Brazil became the "western reserve" from which the Soviet Union ensured its supplies.[20] It is no coincidence that after the War of the Malvinas, and in the context of more constitution governments, the Soviets perceived improved conditions for initiating rapprochement with Latin American countries. In an extensive article written in 1983 on the effects generated by the war in the South Atlantic, Karen Brutents wrote that the conflict served to promote Latin American unity; undermine anti-Sovietism and anti-communist sentiment in the region; facilitate the reintegration of Cuba into Latin America; demonstrate to the countries of the region that the United States was not a trustworthy ally; and help Latin America better understand "imperialist" interference in Central America.[21]

On the other hand, the Soviet Union had specific strategic interests in Latin America, the most important of which were to ease tensions toward Cuba and maintain a cautious and low-profile policy in Central America. Insofar as the Soviet Union is a naval power, the War of the Malvinas also took on strategic relevance. The Soviets have shown concern in the past for the possibility of a NATO subsidiary in the South Atlantic and have pointed to the Malvinas' special value for "imperialist states, because of their important geographic position on strategic routes linking the Atlantic and Pacific oceans, and because of their proximity to Antarctica" (Brutents 1983).

Viktor Volsky, Director of the Institute of Latin America of the Soviet Academy of Sciences, expressed the Soviet Union's concern regarding the pretensions of the other superpower and NATO in the South Atlantic. After remarking on the economic importance of the southern seas, he pointed out that the Panama Canal was too narrow for the passage of large war ships and was vulnerable to destruction by a single missile, in contrast to the Strait of Magellan, which would not entail such risk. For their part,

20. This episode is discussed in this volume by Carlos M. Vilas in Chapter 6.
21. The Soviet leadership is "realistic," however, in relation to the limitations and obstacles facing the implementation of an "anti-imperialist" policy in Latin America. See Brutents (1983, 131-60).

Brutents and Zagladin stressed the importance of Latin America for U.S. strategic interests because of the reserves and diversity of nonrenewable raw materials and natural resources.[22]

Consolidating political ties with Latin America was, within this set of priorities, the most effective way of advancing the Soviet Union's specific interests in the region without risking destabilization of the complex structure of relations with the United States.[23]   Both Shevardnadze, during his tour through Latin America, and Gorbachev, in his book on perestroika, emphasized caution. Gorbachev (1987) wrote:

> We do not seek to exploit anti–U.S. attitudes and even less to add fuel to that fire, nor are we trying to undermine the traditional links between Latin America and the United States. This would be foolhardy—and we are realists, not rash adventurers.

The Soviet leadership always recognized the influence the United States had in the region, as well as the specific importance the Latin American countries placed on relations with Washington. The quotation above was intended to avoid any ambiguity that could generate unnecessary friction in Latin America, an attempt by the Soviets to calm tensions in the western hemisphere. The leadership of the Soviet Union wished to avoid frictions that would negatively affect ongoing negotiations with the United States on

22. Interview with Viktor Volsky, *La Razón*, Buenos Aires, November 21, 1985; Vadim Zagladin, *FBIS* SOV-84-129/CC-12-13; Yopo (1986); Turrent (1986, 96), p. 96; and Brutents (1983, 132).

23. Soviet leaders have been particularly cautious about their military presence in Latin America, generally proceeding within the limits established during the 1962 Cuban missile crisis and other subsequent "understandings" reached with the United States in 1970 and 1979. Essentially these were "understandings" regarding the Cuban situation, but they do serve as a frame of reference for Soviet actions in the rest of Latin America. They consist of three main points: (1) no introduction of nuclear missiles in the continent; (2) no utilization of Cuban ports (or others) as strategic operations bases; and (3) no modification of the "defensive" characteristics of the Soviet brigade stationed in Cuba. The presence of military advisers would represent the threshold of tolerance acceptable for the United States, although in the case of Central America (Nicaragua), the restrictions seem to be greater in comparison to the South American continent, where the presence of Soviet military advisers in Peru has been tacitly accepted. On this subject, see respective articles in *International Security* 8: 1, Summer 1983, and *Journal of InterAmerican Studies and World Affairs*, February 1985, p. 19.

more essential matters: the arms race and the Strategic Defense
Initiative pursued by Reagan, then downgraded by Bush. In
particular, the Soviets wished to avoid statements that would
strengthen those in the U.S. who "need regional conflicts to exist
in order to continue manipulating the level of confrontation and
falling back on a policy of might and anti-Soviet propaganda"
(Gorbachev 1987).

From the standpoint of Soviet interests, it was more effective to
support Latin American policies that converged or reinforced the
positions of the Soviet Union on the international scene. At the
same time, the Soviets sought "responsible" cooperation with the
United States in areas that affected international security. With
respect to Latin American security, the Soviet Union explicitly
backed measures to mediate the Central American conflicts, specifically the Contadora and Esquipulas agreements.[24] Gorbachev personally informed various Latin American leaders that Moscow
"does not promote nor export socialist revolutions" in Latin
America, and he supported political settlement of the conflicts in
the region.[25] As part of this policy of nonconfrontation, the Soviet

24. Esquipulas I and II were the names given to the meetings of five Central
American presidents that resulted in a general agreement to reduce regional hostilities.
25. It is interesting to note that in this respect, within the framework of the new
vision of international relations, the Soviets seem to be reevaluating the significance and scope of "internationalist solidarity" in the Third World. In reference
to this, Soviet academician Boris Merin commented:

> In the present context all local conflicts tend to turn into regional, and even
> world, conflicts. The nuclear era requires revolutionary forces to adopt an ex-
> tremely sober attitude before making the decision to take up armed struggle . . . to
> overcome the sectarian approach when choosing the forms of struggle by correlat-
> ing it with the global problems of the survival of man, such are the problems fac-
> ing the area's progressive forces today. It is very difficult to resolve this problem
> in Latin America as the majority of the extreme-left organizations refuse to con-
> sider the realities of the nuclear century.

When Alfonsín visited Moscow, among the issues discussed was the Chilean situation. According to the Argentine press, the head of state expressed his concern
over the actions of the Manuel Rodríguez Patriotic Front in Chile. In this sense,
Gorbachev would have agreed "with the need for a gradual transition to democracy
in Chile to be accomplished in the least traumatic manner possible," while
Alfonsín would have assured his Soviet counterpart that Argentina would be opposed
to any formula that would try to exclude the legitimate political groups from national life. On the first point, see the quotation in Perosa (1988, 27). With respect
to the Alfonsín-Gorbachev talks, see *Clarín*, Buenos Aires, October 16-17, 1986.

Union adopted measures to build mutual trust, agreeing to submit information to the United States about safety measures in the nuclear energy plants in Cuba;[26] recognizing the "neutral" status of the Panama Canal, in times of peace as well as war, according to the statements by Soviet ambassador Yuri Dubinin; and maintaining regular consultations with the United States at the foreign ministry and presidential levels on the Central American crisis, a dialogue in which the Soviets made specific proposals for reducing the level of tensions in the zone of conflict.[27]

It is interesting to note, in this respect, the timing of these Soviet announcements, which coincided with the escalation of the Panama crisis and the negotiations associated with Esquipulas II. Both situations presented an opportunity for the Soviet leadership to demonstrate its posture of conciliation and respect for international law. Thus was avoided any exacerbation of tensions that would provide new ammunition for the intransigent right in the United States, which sought to promote the "Soviet threat" in the western hemisphere. Through symbolic gestures, the Soviet Union demonstrated that it did not seek unilateral advantage from regional crisis. And by backing the negotiations proposed by the Latin American countries, the Soviets were able to achieve in an efficient way the objective of rapprochement with diverse Latin American governments, while neutralizing those in the United States who persisted in upholding geopolitical theses from the Cold War era.

On the other hand, one of the most notable aspects defining the new course of Soviet–Latin American relations was the so-called

26. Cable Agencia Tass, May 6, 1987; *International Herald Tribune*, May 26, 1987, p. 1; *La Epoca*, September 23, 1987, p. 3.

27. From the Soviet perspective, this dialogue strengthened their image as a responsible world power with a legitimate role in regional security problems. With respect to policy in Central America, the Soviet Union did not accede to the apparent requests by the guerrillas (FMLN) in El Salvador for shipments of land-air missiles. According to a report from the U.S. Department of Defense, Moscow substantially reduced shipments of military material to Nicaragua, from 18,000 to 13,000 tons in the first nine months of 1988. Further, Gorbachev personally told President Reagan that the Soviet Union would completely suspend heavy arms supplies to Nicaragua if the United States would proceed in the same manner with its allies in Central America and would also suspend military aid to the Nicaraguan Contras. See Gutman (1988); *Soviet Weekly*, August 31, 1985, p. 10; and "Shevardnadze Talks with Shultz," *International Herald Tribune*, March 28, 1988, p. 3.

high-level direct diplomacy.[28] During bilateral meetings between high-level officials, political and security issues occupied the agenda, which attested to Soviet interest in Latin America's participation in matters that transcended merely regional affairs.[29] In a 1986 interview, Soviet Deputy Foreign Minister Viktor Kompletov (1986) explained the factors that lead to reevaluating ties with the region:

> Latin America is a new protagonist in issues of international security (its interest now transcends the merely regional scope); take, for example, the participation of Mexico and Argentina in the Group of Six; the opposition voiced by Latin American countries in the United Nations to nuclear testing and militarization of space; Brazil's proposal, backed by Argentina, to transform the South Atlantic into a peace zone; and the greater Soviet–Latin American cooperation in multilateral organizations.

In this vein, during bilateral meetings Shevardnadze and the foreign ministers of Argentina and Uruguay discussed security issues such as the South Atlantic, Central America, and nuclear disarmament. Argentine Foreign Minister Caputo indicated agreement with the Soviet Union on the issue of regional conflicts, while Shevardnadze expressed his support for Argentina's role in the Group of Six. In the meeting between Shevardnadze and President Sanguinetti of Uruguay, the former agreed to back the latter's claims in the Antarctic. In return, Uruguay endorsed the Soviet position in the United Nations for the demilitarization of outer space. In a joint communiqué during Alfonsín's visit to the Soviet Union, both countries supported the creation of a "peace zone" in the South Atlantic, as well as the dismantling of British military installations in the Malvinas, perceived by the Soviet Union to be an extension of NATO. The July 1986 Soviet–

28. For a detailed analysis of recent Soviet–Latin American presidential meetings, see Perosa (1988).

29. Insofar as Mexico's independent foreign policy initiatives have been favorably received in the Soviet Union, Foreign Minister Sepúlveda's 1987 visit to Moscow was important for learning the Soviet leadership's agenda for Latin America (Cables from AP and Notimex, May 6 and 7, 1987); "Soviets Seek New Links in the Area," *Latin American Regional Reports* (Mexico–Central America), RM-87-06, July 16, 1987, p. 7.

Argentina fishing agreements gave Moscow a presence in the South Atlantic in defiance of the British opposition.[30]

Moreover, the Argentine government endorsed the unilateral moratorium on nuclear testing declared by the Soviet Union and hailed Soviet proposals for completely eliminating nuclear arms by the year 2000. Both sides also agreed on the need to activate U.S.–Soviet negotiations on nuclear and space arms in all international forums.[31] Similar joint statements were issued after Shevardnadze's visit to Brazil at the end of 1987.[32] Indeed, President Sarney's visit to Moscow in October 1988 (the first by a Brazilian head of state), was a sign of the qualitative leap taken in Brazilian–Soviet relations, expressed by an increasing convergence of positions on international security. One analyst commented that "at the same time that the political agenda of Brazil–U.S. relations was being progressively exhausted, a Brazil–Soviet political agenda was gradually being constructed" (Hirst and Segre 1988, 49). Both the organization of protocol during the visit and the substance of the talks demonstrated the importance the Soviet leadership placed on relations with Brazil.[33]

Especially important in political terms was the declaration on the promotion of peace and cooperation signed by the countries. This declaration went beyond the bilateral framework, establishing itself as a model for relations between states with different sociopolitical systems, that is, a model for East-West relations for the 1990s, as President Sarney put it. It was significant that this document was similar to ones the Soviet Union signed with countries with which it had a special relationship, such as India.[34]

In summary, the Soviet Union and the South American constitutional regimes underwent growing rapprochement during the second half of the 1980s, a process facilitated by the changes in the

30. *El Periodista*, no. 160, October 8, 1987, pp. 6-7; *International Herald Tribune*, September 26, 1987, p. 4; *El Día*, Mexico, August 8, 1987, p. 11; *Clarín* (international edition), no. 581, Buenos Aires, February 2, 1986, p. 1.

31. *Declaración Soviético–Argentina*, APN, October 18, 1986, pp. 5-6; *La Nación*, Buenos Aires, October 16, 1986.

32. *Gaceta Mercantil*, October 1, 1987, p. 3; *El Periodista*, ibid.

33. Mikhail Gorbachev, speech at the reception for the Brazilian president, *Soviet News*, October 25, 1988, pp. 1 and 9.

34. "Dai em Moscou a Fronteira do Precoceito," *Veja*, October 26, 1988, pp. 62-66; *Estado de Sao Paolo y Journal do Brasil*, October 19, 1988.

Southern Cone countries and by the effects of glasnost and perestroika in Soviet foreign policy. The result was a broad area of
agreement on political and international security issues, as could
be observed by official declarations, joint statements, and the voting
records in the United Nations.

REFERENCES

Adomeit, Hannes. 1986. *Soviet Crisis Prevention and Management*,
OPS-008, October.

Bauerfee, Jyotirmay. 1987. "Moscow's Alliance with India."
Problems of Communism, January–February.

Berrios, Ruben. 1987. *Soviet–Latin American Economic Relations.*
Occasional Paper 227. Washington, D.C.: Kennan Institute for
Advanced Russian Studies, Wilson Center.

Blasier, Cole. 1983. *The Giant's Rival.* Pittsburgh: University of
Pittsburgh Press.

Brutents, Karen. 1983. "Conflicto en el Atlántico Sur:
Consecuencias y Ensenanzas." *Las Crisis de las Malvinas: Orígenes
y Consecuencias.* Moscow: Academy of Sciences.

Clissold, Stephen, ed. 1970. *Soviet Relations with Latin America.*
Oxford: Oxford University Press.

Evanson, Robert. 1985. "Soviet Political Uses of Trade with Latin
America." *Journal of InterAmerican Studies and World Affairs*, no. 2,
Summer.

Fukuyama, Francis. 1986. *Moscow's Post-Brezhnev Reassessment of the
Third World*, R-3337-USDP, Rand, February.

———. 1987. "Patterns of Soviet Third World Policy." *Problems of
Communism*, October.

Gorbachev, Mikhail S. 1987. *Perestroika: Nuevas Ideas para su País y
el Mundo.* Mexico: Editorial Diana.

Greenberger, Robert. 1988. "Moscow Is Increasing Visibility and
Influence in Latin Democracies." *Wall Street Journal*, April 5.

Gutman, Roy. 1988. "Shevardnadze Talks with Shultz." *International
Herald Tribune*, March 28, 3.

Hirst, Monica, and Magdalena Segre. 1988. "La Política Exterior
de Brazil en Tiempos de Crisis." In *Las Políticas Exteriores de*

América Latina y El Caribe. Ed. Herald Munoz. Buenos Aires: PROSPEL, GEL.

Katz, Mark. 1982. *The Third World in Soviet Military Thought.* London: Croom Helm.

Keller, Bill. 1988. "Kremlin No. 2 Leader Disputes Shevardnadze in Ideological Split." *International Herald Tribune,* August 8, 1988, 5.

Kennan, George. 1988. "The Gorbachev Prospect." *New York Review of Books,* no. 21-22, January 21.

Kissinger, Henry. 1987. "How to Deal with Gorbachev." *Newsweek,* March 2, 20-23.

Kompletov, Viktor. 1986. "Relaciones Unión Soviética–América Latina." *Panorama Latinoamericano,* no. 119, Moscow, Novosty, December.

Litwak, Robert, and Neil MacFarlane. 1987. "Soviet Activism in the Third World." *Survival,* February.

Perosa, Hugo. 1988. "Los Viajes al Máximo Nivel: La Diplomacia Directa como Factor de la Consolidación de las Relaciones de Argentina y Brasil con la Unión Soviética." Paper presented at Las Relaciones América del Sur–Unión Soviética: Perspectivas para los Noventa, an international seminar organized by FLACSO, Buenos Aires, November 15-17.

Slulzberger, C. L. 1987a. "How Brezhnev Offered to Split the World with Nixon." *International Herald Tribune,* July 27.

———. 1987b. *The World and Richard Nixon.* New York: Prentice Hall.

Turrent, Isabel. 1986. "La Unión Soviética en America Latina: El Caso de Brazil." *Foro Internacional,* September.

Varas, Augusto, ed. 1987a. *América Latina y la Union Soviética: Una Nueva Relación.* Buenos Aires: Grupo Editor Latinoamericano.

———. 1987b. *La Perestroika y su Efecto Sobre las Relaciones entre América Latina y la Unión Soviética,* no. 351, FLACSO, September, 19.

Yopo, Boris Y. 1986. *La Unión Soviética y las Crisis Centroamericana,* no. 6, Doc. Trabajo PROSPEL, July.

Part IV

Assessment of Regional Conflicts

10

Nicaragua and the Central American Conflict

Viktor Volsky

The destiny of the Sandinista Revolution was closely intertwined with the regional crisis that arose in Central America in the beginning of the 1980s. The crisis was one manifestation of the intense development of events in Nicaragua and other countries in the region, as well as the result of the United States' brutal reaction to the sociopolitical situation in the region, which quickly changed. The conflicts that arose in relation to Nicaragua were outcomes of the interaction between the internal and interstate contradictions that substantially defined the structure and character of the evolving Central American conflict. Thus, its settlement will be obstructed until relations with Nicaragua are normalized and that country's pressing internal problems are resolved.

The hostile posture toward Nicaragua that arose in the subregion in the first years after the new government took power, to a great extent the result of the United States, left an indelible imprint on Nicaraguan government policies. The strategy of "economic reconstruction and rebirth" was substituted by the strategy of "survival." The objectives of the militarized economy consisted in the maximum use of domestic resources, financial and material, and restrictions on the purchase of imported goods. The first priority became the military defense of the country. To this end, major human material and financial resources were mobilized. Defense spending rose from 20 percent of budgetary spending in 1980 to 50 percent in 1987.

The Sandinistas were able to resist, but they did so by paying a high economic and social price. The direct and indirect material damages inflicted on the country during eight years of military actions totaled more than US$12 billion. More than 50,000 Nicaraguans were victims of the military aggression of the counterrevolutionary forces supported by the United States. Several other negative factors affected the Nicaraguan economy: the trade embargo imposed by the Reagan administration against Nicaragua in May 1985; the cancellation under U.S. pressure of credit facilities (private bank and multilateral); and the unfavorable world market conditions for Nicaraguan products. Moreover, the economy was hampered by the Sandinista government's errors in economic policies and poor management in the early stages of the revolutionary transformation.

As a result, the country found itself in a deep economic and financial crisis. The gross national product decreased by 13 percent from 1984 to 1988; it fell by one-third on a per-capita basis. Hard currency earnings from exports fell by 50 percent, while the balance-of-payments deficit rose to near US$1 billion in 1988. Unprecedented inflation rates swept the economy.

It was clear by 1987 that the government had failed to control the economy and stimulate production growth with state regulatory methods. Financial and economic reforms were implemented in 1988 to strengthen market mechanisms. The Nicaraguan government has outlined three principal goals steps for resolving the crisis: (1) curbing the galloping inflation; (2) achieving maximum growth of production, especially in the agrarian sector; and (3) increasing exports. At the close of January 1989, a package of extraordinary economic measures was announced, consisting of a considerable reduction of state spending, including spending for investments and social needs. There occurred reductions in the broad administrative apparatus, not excepting the Sandinista Popular Army and the Ministry of the Interior. These cuts had the aim of transferring labor to agriculture, where there was a pressing scarcity.

The major condition for the stabilization and recovery of the Nicaraguan economy was the establishment of a lasting peace. Economic growth required reduction of the excessive burden of defense costs, and the redirection of energies and resources to the reconstruction of the war-torn economy. However, the problem of attracting substantial and diversified international aid to activate the economy remained very important. On the political level, and equally necessary, was the unification of Nicaraguans at all levels of society for the reconstruction of the country.

In recognition of the above problems, the government persistently worked toward achieving a "national reconciliation" and sought to guarantee the participation of private business in accomplishing the task of national reconstruction. However, the normalization of the political situation in Nicaragua depends directly on ending the military conflict imposed on the country by the United States. It is a fundamental condition for the reestablishment of national unity within the framework of the pluralist political system.

The strategic defeat of the armed counterrevolution in 1985 and 1986 destroyed the plans of the Contras and the right-wing opposition to win the massive support of the population and to gain control of part of the country for the creation of a provisional government. The signing of the Peace Pact in Esquipulas in August 1987 was a turning point in shifting the confrontation with the counterrevolutionary forces from the military arena to the nonmilitary sphere. An important step toward national reconciliation was the accord signed between the Sandinista government and the Nicaraguan resistance in Sapoa in March 1988. Although the extremist element of the Contras succeeded in breaking off these negotiations on June 9, 1988, in general there was a reduction of the strictly military component of the anti-Sandinista strategy carried out by the right-wing opposition with the support of the United States.

The singularity of the situation in 1988 and 1989 was evident in the United States' de facto recognition of the Contras' strategic defeat. In the new situation, also affected by the Esquipulas pact, the United States has directed its main efforts to politicizing the economic crisis. It is no coincidence that the head of the Nicaraguan Catholic Church, Cardinal Obando y Bravo, in 1989 appealed to the new U.S. president to lift the economic sanctions and normalize relations with Nicaragua.

Momentum was given to the domestic political settlement by the agreements signed in February 1989 in Costa del Sol (El Salvador). Opposition leaders in Nicaragua hailed the event. By signing these agreements, the FSLN demonstrated its commitment to adopt measures leading to national reconciliation and democratization of domestic political life. In accordance with the Salvadoran agreements, the Nicaraguan government freed 1,984 former members of Somoza's National Guard. The government announced general elections for February 1990 under the supervision of international observers, as well as a plan for disarming and relocating 10,000 Contras based in Honduras. Nevertheless, it must be stressed that the allocation by the U.S. government of new aid to the Contras[1] made this plan more difficult to implement. Many bourgeois political leaders who emigrated returned to Nicaragua for the electoral process. It is noteworthy that along with certain political parties, several groups that were part of the armed opposition expressed their interest in obtaining legal status and renounced armed struggle, perhaps in anticipation of the 1990 elections. Indeed, the electoral process provided the foundation for achieving a national settlement.

Achieving national reconciliation, an acceptable settlement from a humanist point of view, depends on favorable external conditions. The settlement of the situation outside of Nicaragua and the resolution of the Central American conflict in general require no small effort from the international community. This was confirmed by the difficulties that beset the Esquipulas talks. At the same time that the countries of the subregion were striving to create a legal basis for resolving the dispute and were implementing practical steps toward this end, the Central American region continued to undergo intensive militarization, and an unmasked pressure was exerted on the participants in the talks.

From the outset, the Soviet Union supported the activities of the Contadora Group and the Esquipulas talks. It was clear that there was no viable alternative to the peaceful settlement of the Central American conflict. Military means were capable only of tangling new knots of contradictions, escalating the conflict to higher levels of opposition. The escalation and the rivalry of the superpowers in extending support—the Soviet Union to the legitimate government and the United States to the Contras—aggravated the conflict and

1. In late 1989, the U.S. Congress, at the initiation of the Bush administration, voted aid to the Contras until February 1990.

made it unpredictably dangerous to international peace. This is why Soviet foreign policy directed its efforts to reducing confrontation in this subregion and supporting national reconciliation in Nicaragua.

Especially important for a political solution within the framework of the Esquipulas agreements was international support. In the opinion of the Soviet Union, the focus of the regional settlement should be to free the still fragile and shaky process from outside pressures, to reject the practice of imposing "development models" no matter how promising they may seem, and to grant all the participants the "right to an option." The practical task was and remains to support the measures of the type approved in the Central American presidents summit of December 1988. The resolution of the Contra problem would undoubtedly aid the normalization of the situation in Nicaragua, and it would also broaden the perspectives for democratization in the country.

International efforts, especially the more active participation of the United Nations and the Organization of American States, could play a positive role in the creation of necessary conditions for a peaceful settlement. The very fact that the secretary generals of these organizations intervened as international guarantors of the Esquipulas process gave additional importance to the 1987 Guatemala agreements. Normalization of the situation could also be furthered by the use of observers from third countries, an issue that has been raised several times by the Central American countries.

Undoubtedly, much also depends on the policies of the superpowers, which bear special responsibility. One cannot speak of "equal responsibility" for the conflict that arose in the 1980s in Nicaragua. The "secret war" the United States waged against Nicaragua in violation of universally accepted norms of international law cannot be equated to the economic and military aid the Soviet Union provided to the government of Nicaragua. Having chosen an extremely narrow political option, the Reagan administration excluded any possibility of a constructive Soviet–U.S. dialogue on Central America. It might be that more favorable conditions for cooperation will prevail under the Bush administration. On what do we think this cooperation should be based? It should be based on the recognition of the high degree of interdependence in the policies of the superpowers in this and other regional conflicts. In turn, this would contribute to taking joint responsibility for reducing to the minimum the military presence in relevant cases and limiting or halting arms shipments.

International efforts would be needed not only to facilitate a peaceful settlement to the Central American conflict; it would be difficult even to consider Nicaragua's economic recovery without international assistance. Broad cooperation unburdened by political restrictions and urgent aid for the wounds inflicted by the war could foster the construction of a new Nicaragua. This would be a big contribution toward transforming Central America from a region of conflict into a zone of peace and cooperation.

11

Superpower Rivalry
in Central America

Francisco Villagran Kramer

As the Central American crisis worsened and spread, the debate over the strategic and geopolitical nature of the region intensified and took on greater urgency. This debate gave rise to the contention that the serious conflicts in the region were fundamentally economic, social, cultural, and political in nature. In other words, they were endogenous and characteristic of Third World societies situated in the zones of influence of a superpower. Structural rigidity, the lack of ideological space, dependency, and the hegemony of a superpower were the salient features. This is the basis of the North-South perspective and the rejection of the thesis that what transpired in Central America was basically an East-West conflict.

As the U.S. and Soviet governments advanced toward greater détente with the establishment of far-reaching accords to reduce and eliminate arms and installations, and as the effects of structural reforms and greater flexibility in the Soviet Union are felt, it can be appreciated with greater clarity and from a better perspective that the origins of the Central American crisis were certainly internal in nature. But as the crisis developed, worsened, and expanded in time and space, it subsumed with an East-West context, taking on an international dimension that could no longer be ignored and becoming an agenda item of superpower summits.[1]

---

1. Among the first analyses of the Central American crisis was that of the Wilson Center in Washington, D.C., published in Feinberg (1982). Among the most recent books dealing with this subject are Leiken and Rubin (1987), Pastor (1987), and Gutman (1988). See also Dominguez Reyes (1988) and Weeks (1986).

It could be argued that it was precisely the superpowers that projected the Central American conflicts into the framework of East-West confrontation. That the Central American crisis is an item of business, though in a veiled manner, on the agendas of their periodic meetings is evidence of the perception of both countries that given its complex and interrelated nature, the crisis will not be resolved by unilateral actions.[2] From a Third World perspective, a peculiar effect becomes evident. It was not the level of confrontation (low- or high-intensity) between the Soviet Union and the United States that most clearly revealed the role that both play in the solution of regional and subregional problems and conflicts, but rather the advances made when the tension between them decreased.

Taking note of this phenomenon makes one more conscious of the important and positive role other powers played, and continue to play, in Central America. These include the members of the European Economic Community (EEC), the Nordic Group, and the Contadora Group and its Support Group. Thus, as the Central American crisis was "internationalized," so too was its solution, as the prosecution of eventual and feasible solutions required international mechanisms and methods. The region's conflicts might be local, but their solution requires international mechanisms and accords.

During periods of détente, the world and regional organizations that promote peaceful solutions to international conflicts offer Third World governments opportunities to explore their own solutions and courses of action. Among the organizations playing this role were the United Nations, the Organization of American States (OAS), the Arab League, and the Organization of African Unity.

2. The four permanent agenda of the superpowers have been arms control, human rights, bilateral relations, and regional conflicts. A later addition was the environment. The May 1989 Moscow meeting between Secretary of State Baker and Foreign Minister Shevardnadze gave priority to regional conflicts, among them Central America. See Oberdorfer (1989). See also commentary on this topic in the *New York Times* and the European press. Central American newspapers highlighted the news that the Soviet Union would halt military assistance to Nicaragua, and that negotiations and diplomacy would be the prevailing notes in U.S. government policy. The developments between the superpowers led the U.N. Secretary General to advise the Central American governments that the "preconditions" placed by certain leaders would not permit progress toward the objectives they were pursuing (*Informes de Prensa*, May 20 and 21, 1989).

These solutions might not satisfy fully the momentary or temporary interests of the superpower involved directly or indirectly in the Third World conflict. Détente in effect reduces the stake of the superpowers in such conflicts. The space opened up to Third World countries, however, can be used advantageously only insofar as the institutional mechanisms for the solution of controversies and conflicts can be effectively utilized.

Although this mediating role was nothing new for the directors and officials of these organizations, it has been new, in more than one sense, for the leaders of Central America. This was confirmed by the series of measures and accords explored and later approved by the governments in the region, specifically during the U.S. election campaign. Once President Bush took office there followed vigorous implementation of perestroika in the Soviet Union, and subsequent Central American agreements fared better. From the end of 1988, there was a better reception in the United Nations for the inter-Central American accords on verification and control of the commitments made at Esquipulas II.[3] These provisions were originally included in the Contadora Act draft, but at that stage they encountered multiple obstacles to their adoption, approval, and execution.

Détente between the two superpowers also gave rise to another phenomenon, that of "cooling off" periods, as in the case of the conflict between the U.S. government and Panama, which involved elements of the Panamanian political opposition. The political space that opened up permitted advances toward guaranteeing the elections scheduled for May 1989, and later a solution to the Panamanian crisis to be sought within the context of democratization and respect of the terms of the international treaties signed by the countries.[4] The handling of the conflict by the OAS in May 1989 clearly demonstrated, on one hand, the determination of the Latin American countries not to allow themselves to be pressured by events and, on the other, to honor the principle of noninterven-

---

3. Esquipulas II was the name given to the August 1989 meeting of five Central American presidents that resulted in a general agreement to reduce regional hostilities.

4. Obviously, this chapter was written before the U.S. invasion of Panama, which violated the U.N. and OAS charters.—(Ed.)

tion in the internal affairs of other states. The precedent of Nicaragua in 1979 evidently played an important role.[5]

Thus, it is useful to explore and analyze the possible political and economic effects of the easing of tensions between the Soviet Union and the United States in the case of certain regions, including Central America, and the options that may be made available to the region.

Within this context I will examine whether: (1) the easing of tensions between the superpowers was accompanied by a reduction in the levels of the conflict in the Central American isthmus; (2) new opportunities and options became available; and (3) alternatives for development would become available to the region. These phenomena and alternatives could not be divorced from hemispheric interest because it was precisely the Latin American regional powers that vigorously contributed to the exploration and advancement of positive solutions for Central America. There are economic and political interests common to all the Latin American countries, such as the foreign debt, and, to a lesser degree, the drug traffic.

THE LINKAGE OF CONFLICTS AND SOLUTIONS

In examining the effects of détente and the easing of tensions between the Soviet Union and the United States, there come to mind conflicts in other regions of the world that have placed the superpowers in situations of confrontation. Examples are Afghanistan, inevitably reminiscent of the tragedies in Vietnam and Kampuchea, as well as conflicts in Africa that are directly related to independence and liberation movements, such as in Angola and Namibia. The common denominator in the conflicts was the direct or strategic interests of both superpowers.

It may sometimes be difficult for Third World countries directly involved in conflicts to accept the intervention of the superpowers in structuring options for solutions to conflicts. Of course, this role of the superpowers implies that the countries involved lack the full

---

5. In 1979, the OAS mediated and managed the exit of Anastacio Somoza from Nicaragua.

capacity to resolve on their own the problems affecting them. This is a reality of the contemporary world that is never denied, but about which no one openly speaks. This is precisely why small countries, such as those in Central America, have perceived that détente opens up important avenues to attaining their legitimate interests, for the large countries have had to reluctantly concede that even small countries have their own legitimate interests.

This is an unequivocally significant advance that is paralleled by another: the recognition by the superpowers that they cannot decide the final outcome of the conflicts affecting small and medium-sized countries in all cases. This change in attitude could be seen best in those countries engaged in prolonged conflicts—for example, those in Central America, which have already experienced a decade of tragedy, during which neither superpower has considered it prudent to impose its own solution. This theme takes us to the techniques of détente linkage and the possible quid pro quo.

POSSIBLE QUID PRO QUO

When situating the Central American conflicts within the model of possible linkages with other conflicts, it should be borne in mind that both superpowers demand a scenario in which compensations are reciprocal. These need not necessarily be equal, but they must be strategically equivalent. The precise nature of these trade-offs is in part determined by domestic political pressures on the superpowers. These could be subtle and sophisticated, responding to ideological and strategic considerations. Thus, there is a direct relation between the conflicts to be resolved and the possible or feasible quid pro quo. A good understanding of the possible trade-offs acceptable to the superpowers would be central for Third World governments in order to find solutions to regional conflicts.

Frequently, of course, governments of Third World countries find themselves pressured by one of the superpowers to assume certain positions with regard to conflicts in their region. As a consequence, they do not always have the autonomy to play a leading role in seeking a solution. The experience in Latin America in this area has been limited but interesting. The region's conflicts

have been precisely the result of the direct intervention of a superpower, in this case the United States, principally in the Caribbean
Basin.[6] The most dramatic example was the missile crisis in Cuba,
which was handled directly by the superpowers. The United States
held only preliminary consultations with Latin American
countries, and the latter never had an opportunity to contribute to a
solution or the establishment of the quid pro quo that resulted.
Twenty years later, the countries participating in the Contadora
process and its Support Group were shown the reservations that the
United States had toward the concerted action of its regional allies.
In particular, it was demonstrated that the United States was neither ready to accept or follow new roads nor move in the direction
of possible trade-offs.

Despite the limited role played by the Central American countries in the 1962 missile crisis, the governments of the region, and
of Latin America in general, gained a clearer perspective on the
importance that superpowers placed on security interests. They
were also able to observe the willingness of the superpowers, on
certain occasions, to seek workable solutions through reasonable
trade-offs. At the end of the 1980s, it appeared that the superpowers
were in a flexible mood with respect to Central America. There
seemed willingness to publicly accept the agreements reached by
the five Central American presidents, or at least to make the
agreements the basis of a solution satisfactory to the superpowers.
The fundamental issue that would determine the success of the
agreement by the governments of the region was whether there
could be found the trade-offs that would satisfy the superpowers.

THE HEMISPHERIC TRADE-OFF

Before exploring how conflicts in different regions are connected,
another area of possible trade-offs should be examined. The problems that existed between the United States and Latin America in
the areas of economic security and hemispheric politics were quite

---

6. The most numerous and sensitive regional conflicts in the American hemisphere have always been those in which the United States was involved. The
Caribbean Basin has been the scene of the highest number of conflicts between
maritime countries. See McFarlane (1987) for a recent focus.

acute and sensitive at the end of the 1980s, including the direct re-lationship of the United States with Latin American interests in Central America. This area is related to only the United States (see Pastor 1988; Hayes 1989; and Church 1984).

I refer not only to hemispheric security—Latin America vis-à-vis the Soviet Union—but also to the hemisphere's own economic and political security with regard to the foreign debt, the drug traffic, and the compliance with Central American peace treaties, particu-larly by Nicaragua. Nicaragua's commitments include internal democratization, national elections in February 1990, and a role in the dismantling and absorption of the Contras. In other words, the response of the United States and Latin America in the event of Nicaragua's noncompliance and/or an intensification of the Salvadoran civil war was central to hemispheric security.

Given this context, one must consider the role of the members of the Contadora Group and its Support Group, particularly the "Big Four" of Latin America—Argentina, Brazil, Mexico, and Vene-zuela. Coincidentally, they were also the countries burdened with the largest external debts; the sum of their external financial obli-gations constituted a potentially explosive problem for the world system. While all of Latin America shares a great interest in the resolution of the debt problem, the problem is most pressing for the Big Four. The problems generated by drug production and traf-ficking are also of great concern in the hemisphere, and they are of particular interest to Bolivia, Colombia, and Peru, affecting their security, freedom of action, and legal authority of the state.

CONSEQUENCES OF U.S.–SOVIET DÉTENTE

In the period between Esquipulas I (1986) and the meeting of the Central American presidents in La Paz, El Salvador (1989), several significant events occurred that had extraordinary implications for the relations between the superpowers. The events can be summa-rized under the general heading of perestroika, which fundamen-tally altered the world scene (Gorbachev 1987; Mandelbaum 1989).

Fruits of this new opening included not only the advances in the reduction and elimination of certain nuclear armaments, but the no less spectacular acceptance of inspection and verification procedures. New meaning was given to the principles of good faith and honoring of commitments, initiating a new chapter in the relations between the superpowers and their respective allies. In this spirit, the Soviet Union proposed in the United Nations that relations between sovereign states be governed by international law. While straightforward enough, this proposal implied that Soviet foreign policy would not be based primarily on Marxist principles, such as class struggle. While these principles were previously accepted by the Soviet Union, never had they been embraced so dramatically.[7]

The process of reforming the economic, social, and political structures in the Soviet Union, with the purpose of establishing a parliamentary-type system, presented a very different image of the country at home and abroad. No doubt Soviet analysts and officials could better comprehend the democratization processes taking place in other areas, as well as the positive role that ideological pluralism and respect of human rights play in Third World countries, as a result of their own political changes.

In the economic sphere, efficiency, productivity, and commerce were no longer viewed strictly along Marxist lines, as the Soviet economic system rapidly opened up and became more flexible. The end of capitalism was no longer treated as imminent or inexorable. As fundamental as these changes have been, it is important not to misread the overall situation as unidirectional shifts away from socialism toward capitalism.

There were also changes in the Soviet Union's view of the economic processes occurring in Third World countries involved in conflicts with the United States. For example, contrary to what one may have read, the Nicaraguan government pursued a mixed economy strategy throughout the 1980s, attempting to coexist with the private sector. The greater ideological flexibility of the Soviet Union under Gorbachev promoted understanding of the policies introduced by the Nicaraguan government under pressure from the United States and regional agreements. The new Soviet flexibility in effect means that it no longer conditions its foreign assistance on particular political and social models of development.

7. Presentation given by the Soviet delegation to the United Nations, Sixth Commission, General Assembly, 1988. See also the chapters by the Soviet academicians in this volume.

There have also been significant changes in the United States, among them the recognition that an overdose of ideology in its foreign policy was counterproductive, especially when it linked ideological, strategic, and other elements in world and regional conflicts. This overdose continued to cloud the vision of those responsible for the formulation, evaluation, and execution of the policies in Central America.[8] It could be possible that the great role in foreign affairs sought by the U.S. Congress could result in more attention being paid to the legitimate interests of the countries in regions where the United States has investments and strategic security interests. With regard to Central America, the efforts of then House Speaker Jim Wright to win the Reagan administration's support of Central American peace proposals proved useful and perhaps crucial. President Bush appeared open-minded toward the Arias plan for regional peace, as well as more flexible on funding the Contras. The "bipartisan" agreement of March 24, 1989, suspended military aid to the Contras on the condition that progress be made toward democratization in Nicaragua, a process whose central event was the national elections of February 1990.

Most extraordinary perhaps was the tacit acceptance by the Bush administration that the Central American crisis was not the province of the United States and the Central American countries alone, but that the Soviet Union should also participate. This recognition took the form of attempts to set limits on Soviet interests in the region, in particular the assertion of the Bush administration that the Soviet Union had no legitimate security interests in Central America, while the United States had many. In other words, Washington rejected equivalence of interests in the region as a basis for negotiation.[9] The United States demanded that the Soviet Union cease its military aid to Nicaragua and pressure the

8. President Reagan's policy for Central America was characterized by strong anti-communist, anti-Soviet rhetoric. The ideological focus was so strong that National Security Adviser Robert MacFarlane declared before Congress during the Irangate hearings that he had not taken certain actions for fear of being labeled a "commie" by members of the Reagan administration.

9. The contents of the compromise agreement were made known in Central America by the United States Information Agency. The information for this chapter is taken from the article appearing in "Logra Bush acuerdo bipartidista sobre Centroamerica," *Publicación de Agencia Centroamericana de Noticias*, no. 104, April 17, 1989. See also Pear (1989).

Sandinista government to honor its commitments to democratization. However, statements by U.S. Secretary of State James Baker
suggested some flexibility. This was indicated in the U.S. declaration that if Contra aid was tied to Nicaragua's compliance with the
Central American agreements, then the Soviet Union should ter-
minate its military assistance to the Sandinista government
(Feldmann 1989). The Soviets expressed their initial reaction at
the April 1989 meeting between Secretary Baker and Soviet
Foreign Minister Eduard Shevardnadze in Vienna. According to
press reports, the latter insisted that the United States halt military
aid to its Central American allies. Baker declared this a "non-
starter position."[10]

It was clear that the positions of the two superpowers were gradually drawing closer. It was unlikely that the U.S. government
would accept the premise of equivalence of interests in Central
America as a basis for negotiations. This did not, however, preclude negotiations to reduce or halt the military aid that the two
countries provided to the Contras and to the Sandinista government. Such a reduction would respond to the increased desire in
Central America for an end to the military aid provided by the superpowers, with the aim of a reduction in the size of the armed
forces in all the countries. The diminution of direct and indirect
military costs would allow human and material resources to be
channeled to economic recovery.

In the subsequent May 1989 meeting between Baker and
Shevardnadze in Moscow, the former evidently sought greater rapprochement with the announcement that the United States in the
future would stress diplomatic and political negotiations vis-à-vis
Nicaragua, anticipating that the Soviet Union would end its military aid to the Sandinista government. Further, both men declared support of both governments for the Esquipulas II accord.

It is important to place these meetings and the progress
achieved within a context of theory and reality. It was known that
the United States did not want a "second Cuba" in Central
America. Thus, the main issue was not Soviet missiles or naval
bases in Nicaragua or El Salvador or shipments of sophisticated

10. "Baker Urges Contra Aid. Sees Testing of Moscow," *Washington Post*, April 13,
1989.

Soviet arms, but rather it was to avert another complicated geopolitical situation such as that engendered by Cuba in the Caribbean, long considered an "American sea." The position might be stated as follows: Cuba is irksome but manageable; two Cubas, intolerable and untenable.

THE PROBLEM OF AFGHANISTAN

Precisely within this climate of détente, during a meeting among the two superpowers in Geneva in April 1988, it was agreed that the Soviet Union would withdraw its troops from Afghanistan and that the United States would not obstruct that withdrawal. During the previous nine years, there had been an increase in covert operations authorized by President Reagan (and approved by Congress subject to certain requirements) to support anti-communist insurrectional forces fighting against Soviet-supported governments, regardless of their proximity to the Soviet Union. It has been argued that U.S. support to the Mujahadeen was directly proportional to that received by the Kabul government from the Soviet Union. Consequently, once the Soviet Union withdrew its troops, U.S. and Pakistani support to the Mujahadeen would presumably end as part of the great power trade-off. This equation rested on the presumption that Afghanistan's pro-Soviet government would suffer a total collapse with Soviet withdrawal, similar to that in South Vietnam when U.S. forces pulled out.

The Soviets completed their withdrawal within the established timetable, but the pro-Soviet government did not fall; the Mujahadeen did not enter victoriously into the capital. Thus, the Soviet withdrawal appeared as a great success, eliminating a source of domestic and international criticism without immediate strategic loss. The U.S. government, however, did not consider itself obliged to end the military and financial support it had provided the insurrection movement via Pakistan.

The Soviet withdrawal from Afghanistan would seem to call for a quid pro quo by the rules of negotiation. Among other options, it could have been linked with Nicaragua (see, for example, Ottoway 1989; Friedman 1989; and Oberdorfer 1989). In both cases, a superpower provided political support and military supplies to combatants in a country in its sphere of influence. The trade-off proved not as simple as it appeared at first sight, because the United States insisted that Nicaragua renounce its alleged policy of exporting revolution, continue the democratization process stipulated in the Central American peace accord, and maintain ideological pluralism with a mixed economy. The result presumably would be to leave the people of Nicaragua and Afghanistan the right to a periodic change of leaders through democratic and free elections. The Soviet Union and Cuba would end their military assistance to Nicaragua, and the United States would halt its military, financial, and political assistance to the Contras and the Mujahadeen. The latter would then be given a significant share of the power in the new government of Afghanistan. The weak link in this scenario was that the Mujahadeen made no immediate progress in asserting its control over Afghanistan. Apparently, the U.S. goal was not merely to obtain the withdrawal of Soviet troops, but also to effect the fall of the Kabul government, which would have brought to power an anti-Soviet regime on the Soviet border. It is possible that this was the quid pro quo that Washington sought but the Mujahadeen could not quickly deliver.

THE UNITED STATES AND CUBA: ANGOLA AND NAMIBIA

During the negotiations involving the United States and Cuba over the withdrawal of Cuban troops from Angola, quite significant progress was made, breaking the impasse over Namibia's independence. One cannot rule out the possibility that Cuba and the United States used this opportunity to exchange views over a range of issues. If this conjecture is true, then there are important conclusions to be drawn by Central American governments, particularly Nicaragua and El Salvador. The possibility of rapprochement between Cuba and the United States (in Angola and Namibia) offered a framework for future negotiations over the Central American and Caribbean region.

Two lessons came out of the negotiations over Angola. First, the United States and Cuba reached agreement in areas of mutual interest. The withdrawal of Cuban troops from Angola and the guarantees for the effective execution of the accords demonstrated that détente between the two superpowers fostered favorable conditions for dealing with sensitive matters. Second, Cuba's relationship with the Soviet Union differed substantially from the rhetoric the United States directs at Central American countries. Neither a proxy nor a tool of the Soviet Union, Cuba had the autonomy to decide in which matters it would pursue direct involvement or disengagement. A thorough understanding of the Angola situation would also consider thirty years of ongoing revolution, which produced both assets and liabilities in Cuba and its political leadership, and the need to reduce the intensity of the confrontation with the United States (see, for example, McNeil 1988).

From a Central American perspective, the media coverage that President Gorbachev's visit to Cuba in March 1989 generated was quite remarkable, particularly the play it received in the United States. For the Latin American countries, and especially for the Central Americans, this occasion revealed the degree of independence the Cuban government enjoyed in its relations with the Soviet Union, as well as Cuba's conviction that perestroika might be beneficial for the Soviet Union, but not for Cuba.

Cuba's relations with the Central American leftist guerrilla movement were quite different from the support that the Soviet Union gave those movements. Gorbachev made it clear that the Soviet Union would not sponsor revolutions in the American hemisphere, but he also said that this did not preclude military aid to Nicaragua. This position revealed the nature of the political and economic relations the Soviet Union sought to establish and expand in the hemisphere.

Nicaragua and Costa Rica were the only two countries of the region that had diplomatic or consular relations with the Soviet Union and Cuba. Both had tried to convince other countries in the region, which reluctantly agreed, of the need to discuss with Cuba its potential role in facilitating and strengthening the regional peace process. Some Central American officials and analysts contend that Cuba sought its own scenario for negotiations, independent of those between the United States and the Soviet Union. The missile crisis would be a frequently cited precedent. The experience of being the object of and not a participant in the negotiations left a lasting imprint on the Cuban regime. The issue, then, was the possible quid pro quo to be established between the United States

and Cuba, or rather between the Central American countries and
Cuba, with the approval of both superpowers. For those Central
American countries faced with Cuba's support to the guerrilla
movements, the quid pro quo could be a reasonably well-defined
framework of economic, commercial, and cultural relations, accompanied by political relations at the diplomatic level. Obviously,
this scheme of relations would put an end to the Cuban support to
the leftist insurrectional movements.

It is essential to bear in mind that the two superpowers always
reserve discretionary areas of decisionmaking (even veto power).
They could take advantage of their roles in the United Nations,
especially in the Security Council, to facilitate or obstruct the accords reached by third countries, until they could establish a satisfactory sphere of action for themselves. The approval and execution
of the measures regarding Namibia's independence were a point
of reference for third countries, including the nonaligned nations.

DÉTENTE AND COOPERATION IN CENTRAL AMERICA

During the period between Esquipulas I (1986) and La Paz (1989), a
feeling grew on the isthmus that the region's governments were
moving decisively in the direction of lasting settlements. Along
with this came a belief that the U.S. government was gradually
putting aside the strongly ideological approach that President
Reagan injected into his country's policies; in other words, there
was a greater degree of flexibility under President Bush. This
would permit different options and solutions to be considered. The
one-track policy of Elliott Abrams (Under Secretary of State for
Hemispheric Affairs in the Reagan administration) that only the
United States could resolve the problems gave way to greater opportunity for concerted action by the Central American governments.[11]

Judging from remarks of presidents Cerezo of Guatemala, Arias
of Costa Rica, and Cristiani of El Salvador, by the end of the 1980s
there was a general perception of greater U.S. willingness to listen

11. Ambassador Frank McNeil (1988) offers an interesting and revealing view on
the manner in which Elliott Abrams conducted U.S. foreign policy in Central
America, and the conflicts that it generated in Washington and the region.

to the points of view of the Central American leaders. At the same time, the Contras and the leftist insurgents in El Salvador appeared to recognize the new conditions. The change in the approach of these groups was evident at meetings held between the Sandinista government and the Contras at Sapoa, and the FMLN and the Salvadoran government in Mexico—extraordinarily important milestones. The participation of the governments in negotiations with each other and with their respective insurgent forces visibly eased tensions in the area.

Parallel to détente at the level of the superpowers and among the Central American governments, there has also been a climate of détente within the U.S. government, which stands to benefit all involved. This is particularly noteworthy in light of the Irangate hearings and the trial of Lt. Col. Oliver North. These revealed that certain groups in the U.S. government were greatly discomfited by the initiatives and resistance offered by certain governments in the area, and they opposed the awarding of the Nobel Peace Prize to President Oscar Arias of Costa Rica.

Another positive factor in the Central American region was the role of the European countries, principally the members of the European Community. Notwithstanding the favorable effects, U.S. opposition to European efforts and presence in the region was made known at a conference in San José, attended by the foreign ministers of Central America, the EEC, and Contadora member countries.[12] The European presence gave the Central American governments the confidence to formulate and adopt initiatives on a regional level, especially when they realized that joint economic and political actions were supported by the EEC and the European political parties with which the Central American governments had active relations through affiliations in the various internationals (Liberal, Christian Democratic, and Social Democratic).

Although the Central American governments sought to negotiate important matters, they all had cards up their sleeves that they drew forth when least expected, sometimes obstructing or delaying

---

12. The French foreign relations minister circulated among the foreign ministers of the Contadora Group and Central America the note that the U.S. secretary of state sent the European ministers expressing opposition to European presence and interest in Central America. It was viewed as one of the most recent testaments to the Monroe Doctrine, as indeed it was.

the implementation of accords. One notable example was the condition periodically raised by Costa Rica and Honduras that Nicaragua drop its suit in the World Court against them. This issue would emerge even in situations in which it appeared that all five governments were moving jointly toward a common goal. The representatives of Costa Rica and Honduras produced this issue at the ultimate hour in late 1989, at the moment of the signing of the request by the five governments presented to the U.N. secretary general for the verification and supervision of the implementation of the Arias Plan. This demand delayed action by the United Nations, as Secretary General Perez de Cuellar later reported. This incident indicates the differences among Central American countries. The central point, however, was that the governments overcame their differences and took steps to honor their commitments.

COMPLIANCE WITH THE
CENTRAL AMERICAN PEACE ACCORDS

Analysis of the different facets of the Central American situation reveals that the focus was not on preventing a "second Cuba" or the presence of Soviet bases or Soviet and Cuban armed contingents. There was no more harping on Cuban and Nicaraguan arms shipments to the Salvadoran guerrillas or to the Guatemalan guerrillas (the latter of considerably less importance and contention). Of course, the United States and the Central American governments have not changed their position on these matters. What occurred was that under the Arias Plan these problems were overcome or resolved through the Esquipulas negotiations, and the Central American conflicts moved from a strictly local level to the international sphere. Verification, supervision, and implementation of the provisions of the Esquipulas accord moved to the United Nations by agreement of the Central American countries and the implicit approval of the two superpowers. The governments of the region took this step when they realized that they could not create the procedures for verification, supervision, and implementation, even with the help of the Contadora Group and its Support Group.

The sequence of events is revealing. First, in Esquipulas II (August 1987) responsibility for the verification of the accord's implementation was given to the International Commission for Verification and Implementation, comprised of the foreign ministers of Central America and the Contadoras, and the secretary generals of the U.N. and the OAS. Later in Alajuela, Costa Rica (January 1988), the Central American presidents agreed that from that point verification would be carried out by an executive commission made up of the foreign ministers of the region. The commission was authorized to enlist the assistance of countries within and outside the region, as well international organizations such as the United Nations.

Subsequently, the possibility of the U.N. assuming the responsibility for verification, supervision, and monitoring of the commitments has been explored. A first step in that direction was taken on November 15, 1988, with the General Assembly's adoption of Resolution No. 43-24, requesting the secretary general to provide broader support to the Central American governments' peace-seeking efforts, particularly through the implementation of the steps necessary for the functioning of the basic verification procedures.

Another important step was taken on November 30, 1988, by the five Central American foreign ministers who were attending the inauguration of the president of Mexico. The five officials signed a petition to the U.N. secretary general, asking him to seek an impartial mechanism for the verification, monitoring, and on-site inspection of the accord's implementation. The U.N. Secretariat was particularly enjoined to assume the delicate task of those provisions related to the termination of aid to insurrectional groups and irregular forces operating in the region.[13]

Once in the arena of the United Nations, it was unlikely that the verification process could be removed from the direct attention of the two superpowers and the other members of the Security Council. The conflicts in Central America thus entered the sphere of multilateral action, for the most part removed from the regional sphere. The most visible effect would be the use of armed forces

13. The Central American leaders identified Canada, Spain, and the Federal Republic of Germany as their choices to carry out their request in conjunction with the OAS secretary general. Moreover, their petition recommended that the body responsible for verification and supervision be given the authority to request, after prior consultation with the executive commission and the consent of the affected country, the participation of the appropriate U.N. agencies, to enforce the adherence of the irregular forces or insurrectional movements to the accords.

under the command of the United Nations. In other words, the Central American countries agreed to enter into the terrain of peace-keeping operations and to accept the accompanying consequences, which means that, according to the powers granted it by the U.N. Charter, the Security Council would have authority over the peace-keeping forces, especially because this type of operation would not be under the command of the local armed forces or the national armies. Their orders would come from the secretary general, who is constrained by the Security Council.

The decision to place the verification of the Central American accords under the domain of the United Nations was not an easy one. For the United States, it obviously implied opening the door to negotiations with the Soviet Union, which might require Washington to alter its position toward Nicaragua and the Contras. For the Soviet Union, it implied moving toward halting its military aid to Nicaragua and seeking guarantees that U.S. military aid to the Contras would cease. There are those who maintain that the change from one U.S. administration to another expedited the Central American decision. Alternatively, it could be argued that it was the climate of détente between the two superpowers that led to the superpowers accepting the role for the U.N.

The Central American presidents postponed their January 1989 meeting to give President Bush the opportunity to acquaint himself with the new developments. Further, they revised their agenda to consider Nicaragua's proposals on the internal democratization process and the voluntary demobilization and relocation of the Contras. During the February 1989 meeting in La Paz, the five presidents reiterated their request for U.N. support, extending it to include not only the verification of security matters, but also the monitoring of Nicaragua's political process, support for the dismantling of the Contras, and regional development assistance.[14]

14. The presidents issued a declaration at the meeting instructing their executive commission to begin immediately the technical meetings to establish the appropriate mechanisms according to the plan previously discussed with the U.N. secretary general. Accordingly, the executive commission asked Secretary General Perez de Cuellar to proceed with the designation of a Technical Group to define, together with Central American heads of state, the guidelines for an on-site verification procedure. The most significant step was Perez de Cuellar's designation of a Technical Group that outlined concrete parameters for the creation of a body of U.N. observers in Central America (ONUCA).

The role of the United Nations in the peace process represented a singular opportunity: it allowed the Central American countries maneuverability in the United Nations and a forum for expressing their views to the two superpowers and other regional powers, including Cuba. This helped, albeit modestly, to build consensus with the two superpowers and to expedite the implementation of the Central American agreements. Moreover, the three countries in the region that do not have relations with the Soviet Union and Cuba were given a forum to deal directly with those countries. Direct contact is an important opportunity that allows representatives of Honduras, El Salvador, and Guatemala to form their own perceptions and opinions of the Soviet Union and Cuba, rather than to view the situation through the lens that the United States has provided them for many years. It will also permit first-hand knowledge of the effects of perestroika.

PARALLEL ACTIONS

In compliance with the peace accords, the countries in the region initiated the domestic measures agreed upon in Esquipulas II: amnesty, ideological and political pluralism, free elections, national reconciliation, and greater respect for human rights. These measures were aimed particularly at Nicaragua and El Salvador, and these governments began negotiations with insurgent forces. Such negotiations were also asked of Guatemala, but none occurred.

Within this framework of theories and realities, the measures taken by the Nicaraguan government in the negotiations with the Contras stand out. There were a number of ways to explain the conciliation shown by the Sandinistas. It may have been the result of pressures exerted by the U.S. government or, alternatively, because of the ideological flexibility of the Sandinista top leadership. It was likely that the state of the national economy influenced the government to make concessions to achieve peace. The fact that the military situation turned decisively against the Contras, perhaps due to the combative resolution of the Nicaraguan people, made these concessions easier to grant. In any event, the Nicaraguan government became convinced that its country should not be isolated from the rest of Central America, and that greater dividends lay in implementing the reintegration of the Contras into Nicaraguan society than in continuing the armed conflict.

In response to the February 1989 accords in El Salvador, the government of Nicaragua took the following unilateral measures:

1. moved forward the national elections for February 25, 1990;
2. invited observers from the United Nations and the OAS to observe all stages of the electoral process, not just the voting;
3. pardoned and released from prison 1,897 former National Guardsmen;
4. consulted with opposition political parties on reforms to the electoral law and legislation guaranteeing freedom of expression;
5. reviewed guarantees of equal access to radio and television for all political parties during the electoral process; and
6. integrated representatives of opposition political parties into the Supreme Electoral Council.

Moreover, Nicaraguan President Daniel Ortega expressed his government's intent to take an active part in the meetings to devise a feasible plan for demobilization and repatriation of the Contras. The steps taken by the Nicaraguan government allowed it to demand in return that the other governments honor the commitments made in El Salvador in February 1989. This effectively disassociated the issue of compliance with the accords from the question of withdrawing the suit against Honduras in the World Court.

The electoral processes in Nicaragua and El Salvador represented important developments. Ortega declared that he would seek reelection, and a large group of opposition parties announced during a meeting with President Cerezo in Guatemala (March–April 1989) that they would participate in the February 1990 election. Thus, the Sandinista government gave clear signs of its willingness to accept the benefits and the risks that accompany democratization.

Similarly, in El Salvador the Social Democrats participated in the electoral process with Dr. Manuel Ungo as the presidential candidate. For its part, the FMLN agreed to participate if the elections were postponed for six months. The government refused, and the March 1989 election was won by ARENA, an extreme right-

wing party with a group within its leadership linked to grave violations of human rights.   The results of these elections certainly
were hailed by the right and the extreme right in the rest of
Central America, principally in Guatemala and Honduras.   It was
widely believed, however, that the possibility of negotiations with
the left had not been eliminated in El Salvador.   Influencing this
optimism was the growing trend in the United States to make
economic and military assistance to El Salvador contingent on efforts to negotiate a settlement of the ten-year-old civil war.   Not
only did President Cristiani inherit the commitment to negotiate,
but indications were that the United States (at least Congress)
would pressure him to do so.   A year after the presidential election,
however, no significant progress toward negotiations was made.

The emergence of the Social Democratic Convergence on El
Salvador's political scene increased the prospects for realistic political negotiations.   Also significant were the FMLN's declarations
during Cristiani's visit to the United States that it favored a negotiated settlement.   The context for negotiations, however, dramatically changed with the major insurgent offensive in October 1989,
though the longer-term impact remained unclear.   In this context
of intensified civil war, the presence of U.N. observers in sensitive
points—the so-called pockets—along the Salvadoran–Honduras border could improve prospects for peace, if nothing else, by obstructing the alleged Nicaraguan arms traffic to the Salvadoran rebels
through Honduras.   Also, the demobilization of the Contras in
Honduras and Nicaragua would mean the loss of an arms market
for the Salvadoran guerrillas.   The result will be undoubtedly the
containment of the Salvadoran conflict.

THE ECONOMIC CONSEQUENCES OF PEACE
AND OPTIONS FOR DEVELOPMENT

Ten years of conflict and adverse economic conditions debilitated
the economies of the region, impairing the system of economic integration, once a source of pride.   War and threat of war diverted
resources, for all the countries in the region built up their armed
forces, markedly increasing public spending on security.   The national budgets bear witness to the sacrifices made to keep the

armed forces functioning at the level deemed necessary by the military in each country. The national budgets were further burdened by rising population, compounded by the return of political and economic refugees to their homelands. Thus, the progressive reduction and disarmament of armed forces agreed upon by the five governments would have a significant economic impact on the region's countries.

The creation of a climate of mutual trust between armies and governments,[15] and between the respective power structures in these countries, would be necessary. The close relationship between the military aid provided by the superpowers and pressure exerted by the national armies to maintain their present levels of organization and force showed the interrelationship between the political effects of détente and the power structure of each country.

While military expenditure rose and social needs increased, the region confronted an acute foreign debt problem and reduced export volume.[16] Nicaragua and Costa Rica were the most debt burdened, followed by Guatemala. Tragically, Central America's debt was not considered sufficiently important to be addressed by the Baker and Brady plans, with the possible exception of Costa Rica. Future political stability requires that the foreign debt problem of all these small countries be resolved. Traditional and nontraditional exports did not grow in the 1980s at rates sufficient to earn the hard currency necessary to maintain their level of imports and service their foreign debts. With the possible exception of Costa Rica, the countries of the region were virtually permanent candidates for support measures by the International Monetary Fund and other lending agencies (see IRELA 1989).

On the positive side, the Caribbean Basin Initiative (CBI) initially seemed to make a wider range of export alternatives possible. Expectations were also raised by the joint cooperation programs being developed by the European Economic Community in conjunction with the Central American countries and Panama. Both the

15. I refer to what is known as a confidence-building measure for the armies and governments of the region, and the different branches of the real power structure in Central America. See, for example, Tanner (1988) and Child (1986).

16. The Consejo Superior Universitario de C.A., the Ford Foundation, the Secretariat of the Central American Common Market, and the Universidad de San Carlos published important studies on the region's foreign debt and structural adjustment programs. See Kramer (1989).

CBI and EEC programs to promote exports offered in principle encouraging prospects. A third source of international aid was the U.N. Development Program's regional development package, proposed in 1988 but still in search of funding in 1990.

Within this spectrum of hardships and options for economic cooperation, attention turned to the "economic consequences of peace" (to use the title of Lord Keynes' famous pamphlet written after World War I). What peace brings to Central America would be closely linked to détente. In 1990, there were signs that the priorities of the United States in granting foreign assistance had shifted toward Central Europe. Peace will have economic and political costs, which require realistic examination, particularly the recognition that it will not automatically bring prosperity.

Central to recovery would be rejuvenating the Central American Common Market (CACM). Despite the conflicts among the members of CACM, a degree of economic cooperation continued throughout the 1980s. Arrangements for a regional payments system, in national currencies without conversion to U.S. dollars, were seriously discussed. At the same time, there was pressure from the outside for the economies to shift away from integration to more open trading policies with the rest of the world (see World Bank 1989).

Because of the ideological and political weight that the business sector had in all the countries except Nicaragua, there was a tendency to lose sight of the structural rigidity and the social injustices inherent in the national economic systems, which were part of the cause of the armed conflicts. If these could not be overcome, the same cycle of instability and war would be repeated. The common goal of the region should be to establish peace and promote development with social justice, peacefully if possible. The European governments, including the Nordic Group, showed a clearer understanding of this problem, though to some extent the U.S. government took note. There was no sign, however, of a return to the philosophy and approach of the Alliance for Progress. One hopes that with détente the discussion of the structural problems that plague the countries of the region could be freed from the strong ideological approach of the past. If discussions of social injustice were no longer taboo, ideological pluralism could flower. Strengthening political pluralism, as called for by the Esquipulas II accords, would gradually permit the Central American countries to overcome the causes of instability undermining development and peaceful coexistence.

REFERENCES

Child, Jack. 1986. "A Confidence-Building Approach to Resolving Central American Conflicts." In *Conflict in Central America: Approaches to Peace and Security*. London: C. Hurst & Co.

Church, Frank. 1984. "We Must Learn to Live with Revolutions— If the U.S. Can Befriend China, It Can Accept Nicaragua." *Washington Post*, March 11.

Dale Hayes, Margaret. 1989. "The U.S. and Latin America: A Lost Decade." *Foreign Affairs*, Winter.

Dominguez Reyes, Edme. 1988. *The Soviet Union and Central America: Views and Policies: 1979–1987*; and *Soviet and Cuban Policy Towards Nicaragua: 1979–1987*. 8th Nordic Research Conference on Latin America, Stockholm, July.

Feinberg, Richard E., ed. 1982. *Central America—Dimensions of the Crisis*. New York: Holmes & Meir.

Feldmann, Linda. 1989. "U.S.–Soviet Relations: U.S. Presses Moscow to End Military Aid to Nicaragua." *Christian Science Monitor*, April 18.

Friedman, Thomas L. 1989. "Baker's Statement on Soviet Aid to Nicaragua May Reflect a Deep and Subtle Pragmatism." *New York Times*, April 18.

Gorbachev, Mikhail S. 1987. *Perestroika: New Thinking for Our Country and the World*. New York: Harper & Row.

Gutman, Roy. 1988. *Banana Diplomacy*. New York: Simon & Schuster.

IRELA. 1989. *Western European Development Cooperation with Central America;* the Randford Report; and *Las perspectivas de cooperación y acciónes conjuntas en C.A., entre el PNUD, LA CEE, y sus estados miembros*. Madrid: IRELA.

Leiken, Robert, and Barry Rubin. 1987. *A Central American Crisis Reading*. New York: Summit.

Mandelbaum, Michael. 1989. "Ending the Cold War." *Foreign Affairs* 68, 2, Spring.

McFarlane, Neil. 1987. "The Superpowers and Latin American Conflict." In *Regional Cooperation for Development and the Peaceful Settlement of Disputes in Latin America.* Ed. Jack Child. IPA Report, no. 26, Boston.

McNeil, Frank. 1988. *War and Peace in Central America.* New York: Scribners & Sons.

Oberdorfer, Dan. 1989. "Soviets Indicate Intent to Relax their Posture in Central America," and "Baker Pursues Reengagement with Soviets." *Washington Post,* May 14.

Ottoway, David B. 1989. "Diplomatic Confrontation Looms on Regional Issues—Superpowers Lack Rules for Dissolving Disputes Over Aid in Nicaraguan, Afghan Conflicts." *Washington Post,* April 16.

Pastor, Robert A. 1987. *Condemned to Repetition.* Princeton, N.J.: Princeton University Press.

——. 1988. "Securing a Democratic Hemisphere." *Foreign Policy,* no. 73, Winter 1988-1989.

Pear, Robert. 1989. "Bush's Trade Behind the Transformation of Central American Policy." *New York Times,* April 16.

Tanner, Fred. 1988. *From Europe to Central America: Regional Cooperation and Peace Processes.* IRELA Working Paper, no. 15. Madrid: IRELA.

Weeks, John F. 1986. "An Interpretation of the Central American Crisis." *Latin American Research Review* 21, 3.

World Bank. 1989. *Trade Liberalization and Economic Integration in Central America.* Washington, D.C.: World Bank, March 10.

12

Superpower Rivalry
in Africa

Colin Legum

The Soviet Union's challenge to the western powers in the Third World, first pursued through the Cominform (then called Comintern) in the 1920s, had its inspiration in Trotsky's stress on world revolution. With the fall of Trotsky, state interests took priority over world revolution. The fostering of revolution, however, was not altogether abandoned for situations likely to undermine western hegemony without damaging Moscow's particular interests. The aims of the Cominform were threefold: (1) to implement the fight against imperialism (that is, against western capitalism); (2) to encourage the spread of revolutionary ideas and movements in the colonies and elsewhere; and (3) to support communist parties worldwide. However, the Stalinist policy of putting state interests first led to serious contradictions within the Cominform, eventually disillusioning prominent colonial Marxist leaders such as George Padmore of the West Indies, Solly Sachs, and H. M. Basner of South Africa (see Padmore 1956; James 1938).

By the mid-1930s, anti-colonial leaders saw the Cominform as an instrument of Soviet interests, which hastened its disintegration. At the outbreak of World War II, the only Cominform influence in Africa was limited to communist parties in Egypt, Sudan, and South Africa, and a tenuous alliance with the Rassemblement Democratique Africain (RDA) in French West Africa. Further, quarrels between the Cominform and anti-Stalinist elements (for example, in the Fourth International) divided and weakened the anti-colonial movements.

Two developments during World War II gave new encouragement to Moscow.   First, the Red Army's considerable military
achievements created a wave of sympathy in the colonies, as well as
a greater interest in "socialist achievements."   Second, the upsurge
of anti-colonial liberation movements produced a political climate
seemingly favorable to the Soviet Union as a champion against
western colonialism.   It appeared that by the end of the war the
Soviets would be in position to forge effective alliances with the liberation movements and undermine western influence.   In this
context, support for national liberation struggles became a cornerstone of Moscow's foreign policy.

World War II destroyed West European hegemony over much
of the globe; the Soviet Union emerged from the war as a new
world power and the United States as the dominant leader in the
West.   Until the accession of Mikhail Gorbachev, Africa was seen
by the Soviet Union and the United States as a key continent in determining the new balance of world power.   Along with the
Middle East, Southeast Asia, and the Indian sub-continent, Africa
became an important arena in the rivalry between the superpowers.   Aside from Cuba and, much more marginally, Nicaragua, the
United States faced no serious threat in Latin and Central
America.

During World War II, the anti-colonial tradition of the U.S.
public found strong expression in the policies of the Roosevelt administration, which produced considerable tension and disagree-
ment between the United States and the European colonial powers.
The Dutch were angered by Roosevelt's stand on Indonesia, the
French by U.S. policy toward Indochina, and the Belgians by demands for early independence of the Congo (now Zaire).   Further,
the Portuguese resistance to abandoning Angola, Mozambique,
Guinea-Bissau, Cape Verde, and Timor was adamant; and the
British were in no mood to yield on India and the rest of the empire.

The postwar Labour government in Britain, however, set in motion the decolonization of its empire, which forced the French under de Gaulle to follow suit.   On the other hand, Spain, Portugal,
and Belgium sought to maintain their colonies in the face of pressures to the contrary.   The relatively peaceful way in which the
British transformed their empire into a new Commonwealth of

Nations, and the success of the French in meeting the demands for independence in Sub-Saharan Africa (though not without major violence in Indochina and Algeria), substantially reduced the anti-western feelings of the colonial liberation movements. After initial reluctance, Spain and Belgium yielded to decolonization so suddenly and drastically in the case of the Congo that briefly an opportunity for Soviet influence appeared. But it was the obdurate refusal of the Portuguese to follow suit that created real opportunities for the Soviet Union, especially in Angola and Mozambique.

Western interest in Africa, the perception of which is now shared by Americans and West Europeans, is twofold: (1) to retain influence (political, economic, and military) in the former colonies, and (2) to deny opportunities to the Soviet Union to expand its influence. Up until the end of the 1980s, these objectives had been achieved, though the fate of South Africa still hangs in the balance. The only other African countries seen as failures of western policy are Ethiopia, Angola, and Mozambique (though increasingly less so in the last case). In Ethiopia, the western powers vested their hopes and interests in the survival of Emperor Haile Selassie long after it had become clear that his days were numbered.

As befits its role as a challenging superpower, the Soviet Union has sought to expand its influence and military capability globally. Under Stalin, Khrushchev, and Brezhnev, Moscow's consistent policies were to seek to undermine western interests, to expand Soviet influence in winning political allies, to improve its role as a trading nation, and, above all, to strengthen its strategic position, especially as an emerging naval power. There is no evidence that the Soviet Union ever worked from a master plan to achieve these objectives. Its policies bear all the hallmarks of opportunism, in the strict sense of grabbing at opportunities as they presented themselves.[1] Nevertheless, Soviet policy has been remarkably consistent in several major respects. First, it has given undeviating support to national liberation movements operating against governments regarded as belonging to the "imperialist camp." Related to this policy, it has given strong political and diplomatic support, as well

---

1. For a more detailed discussion of Soviet Policy in Africa, see Nation and Kauppie (1984); Albright (1980); and Korbonski and Fukuyama (1987).

as military and some economic aid, to governments and move-ments identified as struggling against "imperialism," even when such protagonists did not profess to be supporters of Marxism or the Soviet Union. In this respect, it has remained true to the original role it cast for itself as leading the struggle against "imperialism."

Second, whenever opportunities presented themselves, the Soviet Union sought to secure naval and air facilities from its clients. Examples of military installations acquired were the naval base in Alexandria under Nasser, naval and air facilities in Somalia, and naval facilities in Ethiopia.

By the late 1950s, the Soviet Union pursued another goal in Africa: undermining Chinese influence in Africa. This rivalry was exemplified in three particular cases. Despite his anti-com-munism, the tyrannical Idi Amin enjoyed the support of Moscow. This Soviet policy was dictated by Moscow's need for a foothold in East Africa to counterbalance what it saw as the influence of the Chinese in Uganda's neighbor, Tanzania. In the same vein, in Central Africa Moscow gave its military support to the Zimbabwe African People's Union (ZAPU), led by the anti-communist Joshua Nkomo. Preference went to ZAPU over the Zimbabwe African National Union (ZANU), led by self-proclaimed Marxist-Leninist Robert Mugabe, because ZANU received Chinese military aid. Also, the Soviet Union's initial involvement in Angola was due in part to Chinese support for opposition movements. Subsequently, of course, it was drawn into the struggle by a strong Cuban initiative.

Moscow has been inconsistent in applying its policy of support for national liberation movements, as shown by its policy shifts on Ethiopia and Somalia. It supported the Eritrean People's Libera-tion Front when it began its struggle against Haile Selassie and when Soviet military facilities were functioning in Somalia. When it suited Moscow's interest to switch its alliance from Somalia to the military regime of Mengistu Haile Mariam in Ethiopia, the Eritreans found themselves facing an Ethiopian mili-tary armed by the Soviets.[2] However, Moscow's consistent support for the African National Congress (ANC) of South Africa has en-abled it, with the help of the Communist Party of South Africa, to become involved in a major way in the liberation struggle against

2. For a discussion on Soviet policy in Eritrea, see Legum et al. (1986).

apartheid. This influence, together with its alliance with the Movimento Popular de Libertacao de Angola (MPLA) government in Angola, has ensured a major role for Moscow in the affairs of Southern Africa.

It was surprising that the Soviet Union was unable to exploit more successfully the seemingly golden opportunities presented by the collapse of colonialism in Africa and the Middle East. Several explanations account for this failure. First, the Soviet Union failed to develop any lasting alliance with national liberation movements because the appeal of nationalism was much stronger than that of Marxism. The two ideologies were often in conflict over issues such as the characteristics of the anti-colonial movements and support for nonalignment. While willing to accept Soviet support, leaders of liberation struggles almost uniformly rejected moving into the "Soviet camp." So long as it suited their nationalist interests, they accepted Soviet military and political support, but once they achieved the immediate aim of liberation from alien rule, the next priority was to consolidate their independence by turning to those best able to provide them with opportunities for trade and economic and technical aid. Although not always even-handed in their application of nonalignment policies, African leaders for the most part refused to become entangled in struggles between the major powers. The outstanding exception has been Ethiopia, which will be discussed in greater detail below.

Second, the Soviet Union lacked the economic resources (or at least the willingness to commit what they possessed) to meet the needs of their putative allies. The Soviets certainly have been lavish in supplying military aid—a commodity that they do not lack. But their import needs and the present international economic order are unfavorable to the development of substantial trade between the Soviet Union and most Third World countries. Except for Cuba, Vietnam, and, to a lesser extent, Ethiopia, Moscow and its COMECON[3] partners have been unwilling to divert major economic resources to African countries. Indeed, as shown in the case of Angola, Moscow has in recent years openly advocated the need for African countries to develop their trade with the West. Because of the colonial heritage and other reasons, Soviet technical aid

---

3. COMECON is the trading bloc of the East European countries.

proved inappropriate to African needs, forcing even pro-Soviet governments to seek western aid.

Third, the Marxist (or, more accurately, the so-called Marxist) regimes in Africa have been broken reeds with the exception, so far, of Ethiopia. Because of the civil war that prevailed since Angola's independence and the support given to the UNITA[4] by South Africa and the United States, the MPLA lacked the opportunity to implement its Marxist policies. No structured Marxist party was created in the country, and effective power lies with the army. The MPLA government's hold on power remained so tenuous, it was forced to accept the mediation of Washington over foreign troop withdrawals from its territory, despite the American refusal to grant it diplomatic recognition. The ambiguous nature of the regime was shown by the fact that while its military support came from the Soviet bloc and Cuba, its economic ties were almost exclusively with the West. Across the continent in Mozambique, the influence of Marxism was much greater. However, by the late 1980s, that government sought and obtained the economic and political patronage of the West.

The other so-called Marxist regimes—Guinea-Bissau, Benin, and the Congo—have been high in Marxist rhetoric and low in performance. The latter two survived mainly on French economic aid and gave up any pretensions of being Marxist (as has Guinea-Bissau). The "scientific socialism" of Siad Barre's regime in Somalia remained at an aspirational level only as long as the Soviet Union fulfilled its role as the nation's armorer. Despite the official attachment to Marxism of the unified ZANU-Patriotic Front in Zimbabwe, President Mugabe has followed a careful, pragmatic course so as not to upset the basic economic structures he inherited at independence. And by the end of the 1980s, he further liberalized his economic policies to encourage foreign investment.

Thus, with the exception of Ethiopia, the first four decades of independence clearly demonstrated two basic realities: (1) "scientific socialism" has held little attraction for the first two generations of independent African leaders, and (2) the continent's trade and other economic ties seem indissolubly tied to the West. In the ab-

---

4. The MPLA government encountered armed opposition from UNITA (in English, Movement for the Total Independence of Angola), led by Jones Savimbi.

sence of real progress toward South-South links or radical changes in the existing international economic order, trade dependence on the West would be unlikely to change. The critical economic crisis through which Africa passed after the mid-1970s further strengthened the continent's ties with the West.

Two other developments helped strengthen western influence in Africa: (1) after the death of Mao, China's role in the Third World declined, and (2) new policies emerged in the Soviet Union that had a direct and important impact on Africa.

In summary, Soviet policies in Africa failed to produce any of the major goals originally envisaged (though the situations in Ethiopia and South Africa offered possibilities for gains in the 1990s). Marxism as a state ideology fell on stony ground in Africa, and western influence was not eroded as a result of decolonization. The relationship between Africa and the West remained characterized by strongly ambivalent feelings due to disputes over South Africa, the failure to alleviate the continent's heavy foreign indebtedness, and the lack of economic aid to sustain growth. As in the Soviet bloc and China in the 1980s, the impetus toward democratic multi-parliamentary government and economic liberalization grew significantly in Africa, a change from the post-independence climate that favored single-party states and domestic economies characterized by parastatals. The parastatals, despite their promise to establish national control over the economies, resulted in a form of state capitalism rather than socialism. Further, they produced intolerable and inefficient bureaucracies that, with some exceptions, served to obstruct rather than promote economic growth.

CUBA'S ROLE IN AFRICA

In many African eyes, Cuba gained more respect than that achieved by the Soviet Union, thanks to its role in Angola, where it stopped the advance of the South African army at the crucial battle of Cueto Cuanavale in 1988. Robert Pastor (1983) summed up the policies of Havana as follows:

> Cuba is a small country with a big country's foreign policy. No other developing nation maintains more diplomatic missions, intelligence operatives, and military advisors and troops abroad

than does Cuba, not even the oil-producing states that can afford
it. The gap between its internal resources and its external capa-
bilities is filled by the Soviet Union, not because of altruism, but
because the Soviets are assured that what the Cubans do abroad
will serve their purpose.

However, it is a mistake to treat Fidel Castro as a mere instrument
of Soviet foreign policy. Certainly Cuba's expeditionary force of
14,000 troops was crucial to the defeat of the Somali army by
Ethiopia during 1975-1976, and thus to Soviet support of the
Mengistu government. But Castro refused to deploy Cuban troops
against the Eritreans, leaving the Soviets with the thankless and
onerous task of putting down their rebellion. Having earlier supported the Eritrean cause, Castro was unwilling to fight it in the
interests of the Soviet-Ethiopian alliance, a considerably more
principled position than that taken by Moscow.

In Angola, the Cubans drew the Soviets into the conflict at a
time when Moscow remained undecided on whether to intervene
(see Legum 1976). Havana rather than Moscow dictated the military tactics in Angola, and Castro openly criticized Soviet military
advisers after the disastrous campaign against UNITA in 1987.
Cuba, not the Soviet Union, joined negotiations with Angola and
South Africa on the American initiative to withdraw foreign troops
and implement independence for Namibia (based on U.N. Security
Council Resolution 435). The Soviet Union remained on the side-
lines of the negotiations, with its role confined to urging the
Angolans to pursue negotiations. It is moot whether Moscow in
fact exercised any serious influence on Cuba in the negotiating process. The withdrawal of Cuban troops under the agreement reached
between Luanda and Pretoria would end its effective military presence in Africa. With Cuba's ailing economy and Castro's opposition to glasnost, further intervention in Africa was unlikely.
Nevertheless, Castro's influence as a respected figure in the nonaligned movement remained substantial at the end of the 1980s.

THE SOVIET UNION AND ETHIOPIA

Ethiopia represented the most important success of the Soviet Union
in helping to build up a genuinely revolutionary Marxist party in

Africa. By 1975 the Soviets learned from their expensive mistakes in Africa not to place their confidence in a military of a bourgeois-nationalist regime. To ensure a durable ally, it was necessary to create a committed vanguard party schooled in Marxism-Leninism. To this end, the Soviets used their military aid program to persuade Mengistu to convert his military regime into a Marxist party. At the same time, they trained a vanguard elite to run the new party, then showed great patience and persistence in bringing the Workers' Party of Ethiopia to fruition.

The Soviet interest in building up a potentially durable alliance with Ethiopia was to secure naval facilities in the Red Sea. This ambition, the quest for "blue sea ports," had been cherished by Russian leaders since the seventeenth century. The desire for naval facilities in the Red Sea became more urgent with the build-up of the new Soviet navy under Admiral of the Fleet V. Gorshkov, who stressed the threat posed to the Soviet Union by American nuclear-armed submarines in the North Indian Ocean. Gorshkov played a significant role in Moscow's decision to switch its alliance from Somalia to Ethiopia (see Legum and Lee 1977, 1978).

The Soviet-supported revolution in Ethiopia failed to develop fully only because of opposition by the Eritrean People's Liberation Front (EPLF) and the Tigrayen People's Liberation Front (TPLF). Their resistance encouraged other regions in the country to launch armed struggles against the regime in Addis Ababa. Notwithstanding the efforts of over 220,000 Ethiopian soldiers, Soviet military supplies, and Warsaw Pact military advisers, the EPLF not only survived, but in 1988 it destroyed a third of the Ethiopian army at the battle of Afabit. At the same time, the TPLF controlled upwards of 80 percent of the province of Tigray.

Mengistu, who described the Soviet Union as "the leader of the world's progressive forces,"[5] proved himself to be a faithful student of Moscow's teaching. Nevertheless, he has stubbornly refused to accept Soviet advice on the need to find a political settlement with the Eritreans, Tigrayans, and the other dissident regional movements. This is an example in which the strong nationalist sentiments of a client state made it resistant to foreign advice, even from a vital ally. With the Ethiopian revolution reaching a stale-

5. See *Africa Contemporary Record*, 1978-79, New York.

mate, and with Gorbachev's commitment to negotiating regional conflicts, the future relationship between Moscow and Addis Ababa remains uncertain—particularly after the recent attempt by elements in the army to overthrow Mengistu.

THE SOVIET ROLE IN SOUTH AFRICA

Moscow's role in South Africa and Namibia has been confined principally to support for the liberation struggles and strong diplomatic support for the international campaign against apartheid, including backing for mandatory sanctions and moves to isolate South Africa in the world community. Its two favored liberation movements are the ANC, which has an alliance with the Communist Party of South Africa, and the South-West African People's Organization of Namibia (SWAPO). When the ANC decided to establish a military wing, Umkhonto we Sizwo, to launch an armed struggle against the Pretoria regime, Moscow pledged its full support and provided military aid and training. Because the ANC failed in its persistent attempts to win support from the West (other than Sweden and some of the other Nordic countries), its ties with Moscow became increasingly close. The ANC never ceased trying to win western support, however, and its sense of nationalism remained stronger than its attachment to Marxism.

During the Brezhnev period, Moscow began to lose heart in the efficacy of an armed struggle against the formidable military fortress of South Africa. Through secret diplomacy, it encouraged political negotiations as a more hopeful way of ending apartheid. Under Gorbachev, the opposition to armed struggle was made public, much to the displeasure of the ANC. The ANC saw armed struggle as necessary to compel Pretoria to accept a new democratic constitution and the liquidation of the apartheid system.

In his 1987 book *Perestroika: New Thinking for Our Country and the World*, Gorbachev wrote:

> The Soviet Union has no special interest in Southern Africa. We want only one thing: countries in the region must at last have the chance to settle their development issues, their home and foreign affairs, independently, in peace and stability.

When Mozambique's President Joaquim Chissano visited Moscow in August 1987, Gorbachev told him that the Soviet Union's policy was not directed toward obtaining a unilateral advantage in Southern Africa, and that future aid would concentrate on humanitarian and economic projects rather than on the supply of military weapons. Perhaps even more significant, he went on to say: "The Soviet Union does not support the argument of 'the worse, the better,'" and expressed the belief that while the collapse of apartheid was inevitable, he favored a political solution to the region's problems. Opposition to revolutionary violence was made explicit by Soviet Deputy Foreign Minister Anatola Adamishin, who said that the Soviet Union wanted to avoid "suffering and bloody death in South Africa. . . . We think we have a common interest with America in stability in the region, and that, sometimes, we can take useful steps with the Americans."[6]

SOVIET NEW THINKING

The license provided by perestroika has enabled Soviet officials to speak out and reveal doubts about past Soviet policies in Africa. Boris Assoyan (1987), former Moscow diplomat in Lesotho, wrote:

> If you imagine revolution as a . . . short and spontaneous outbreak of revolutionary force, then such a revolution [in South Africa], under prevailing conditions, is scarcely possible. . . . In the South African context, a revolution can take place only over a relatively long period of revolutionary struggle, international pressure and complicated diplomatic and political maneuvers.

Quoting Lenin, he said that it was a mistake to think that the revolutionary classes always have sufficient power to manage the overthrow. Even more stark was the view expressed by Victor Goncharev, a Deputy Director of the Moscow Institute of African Studies, who said it would take at least ten years for black South Africans to achieve their liberation, and from 25 to 100 years to

---

6. This statement was made in an interview with the BBC in December 1987, in the midst of the preliminary negotiations with U.S. Assistant Secretary for African Affairs Dr. Chester Crocker, which led to the agreements over Angola and Namibia.

bring about a "socialist revolution."[7] The new Soviet line, however, does not rule out other forceful measures, such as sanctions.

How much has Soviet policy toward South Africa changed under Gorbachev? Clearly, the open repudiation of armed struggle marks a significant change of policy. But Goncharev and others argue that the fundamentals of Soviet policy have not changed, because the region had never been seen as an arena for superpower rivalry.[8]

Vladimir I. Tikhomirov, Research Coordinator at the Moscow Institute for African Studies, explained that Soviets saw armed struggle as temporary, as an attempt to reach a negotiated settlement. Tikhomirov (1989) wrote:

> What needs to be taken into account is that any armed struggle has its own limits, and that it is inadmissible to allow organized resistance to the oppression of the Pretoria authorities to degenerate into runaway terrorism. Besides, the Soviet Union does not believe that a large-scale civil war in South Africa—and still worse if it breaks out on a nationalist or ethnic basis, the possibility of which cannot be ruled out—would be the best way of solving the problems confronting that long-suffering country.

Yu. Yukalov, the head of the Soviet Foreign Ministry's Department of African Countries, confirmed this explanation of Moscow's position on armed struggle.[9]   Overall, Gorbachev's policy of perestroika would seem to send a mixed message of support for socialist movements in the Third World.[10]

7. Interview with Victor Goncharev in *Work in Progress*, Johannesburg, June 1987.

8. Ibid. Goncharev went on to say, "There may be changes and differences of approach to these problems; to behave more realistically, more flexibly, with every side participating in the resolution of the conflicts."

9. Yukalov said, "We never elevated the armed struggle into an absolute. In settling acute conflict situations, we call on all sides to rely upon the strength of politics, rather than on the force of arms" (*Izvestiya*, December 30, 1988).

10. Addressing this question, Tikhomirov (1989) explains: "The Soviet Union holds that the situation in Southern Africa requires in the first place the necessity to comply strictly with the principle of freedom of social choice for every nation in the region. In practical terms, this means that while the Soviet Union had given, and continues to give, broad support to the countries that have opted for socialism, it also commits itself to respect the choice that has been made, or will be made, by other states as long as it is a free and democratic choice." In support of this view, he quotes Gorbachev's statement to the Zambian president, Kenneth Kuanda, in November 1987: "The Soviet Union supports the right of every nation independently to choose ways and forms of its development" (*Izvestiya*, November 28, 1988).

THE END OF SUPERPOWER RIVALRY IN AFRICA?

At the end of the 1980s, it was perhaps possible to envisage that Africa would cease to be an arena for rivalry between the United States and its western allies on one side, and the Soviet bloc on the other. But it was much too early to draw firm conclusions. Rivalries persisted. Gorbachev had not agreed to American and British proposals to end the regional conflicts in the Horn of Africa along the same lines as those followed in the negotiations over Angola and Namibia. This difference in response could have been because the Soviet Union was in a stronger position in Ethiopia than in Angola, or because of Soviet strategic interest in the Red Sea. A more optimistic interpretation is that Gorbachev needed more time to prepare the ground in Ethiopia for a super-power initiative. In another unresolved source of tension, the Soviet Union gave no sign of being willing to end its substantial arms sales to Col. Gaddafi of Libya, despite strong American de-mands that it should do so. Even in Angola, a negotiated settle-ment left considerable potential for conflict. The Soviet Union re-mained pledged to continue supplying the MPLA government with arms, while the United States was similarly committed to military assistance for UNITA. On the positive side, the superpowers success-fully cooperated to settle the issues of foreign troops in Angola and independence of Namibia.

While the United States welcomed and encouraged the thawing of the formerly permafrost relationship in Africa, Washington's suspicions remained. Even the successful collaboration over Angola and Namibia has yet to dispel such suspicions, though it has helped somewhat to lessen them. Two major tests remain before there can be any certainty that the era of superpower rivalry in Africa has finally ended: (1) Soviet willingness to cooperate in resolving the acute conflicts in the Horn of Africa, and (2) American will-ingness to involve the Soviet Union in promoting political negotia-tions in South Africa. While Gorbachev remained silent over fu-ture Soviet policy in Ethiopia, he was explicit in defining a possible Soviet role in Southern Africa:

> The efforts to defuse conflict situations in the world call for in-novative approaches and a new political thinking that is based on realities and takes into account the interests of all the sides.

This approach has been reflected, in part, in the proposals for a national reconciliation in Afghanistan, and a political settlement can undoubtedly be applied to the problems of Southern Africa. If guarantees are needed for a political decision to be arrived at, such guarantees could be contemplated by the United Nations, through the permanent members of the Security Council. As to the Soviet Union, it is prepared to play its positive role in this process.[11]

REFERENCES

Albright, David E., ed. 1980. *Africa and International Communism.* Bloomington: Indiana University Press.

Assoyan, Boris. 1987. *Literaturnaya gazeta,* Moscow, October 7.

Gorbachev, Mikhail S. 1987. *Perestroika: New Thinking for Our Country and the World."* New York: Harper & Row.

James, C. L. R. 1938. *The Black Jacobins.* London: Secker & Warburg.

Korbonski, Andrzej, and Francis Fukuyama, eds. 1987. *The Soviet Union and the Third World.* Ithaca, N.Y.: Cornell University Press.

Legum, Colin. 1976. *After Angola: The Coming War in Africa.* London: Rex Collings.

Legum, Colin, et al. 1986. *La Horne de L'Afrique.* Paris: L'Harmattan.

Legum, Colin, and Bill Lee. 1977. *Conflict in the Horn of Africa.* London: Rex Collings.

———. 1978. *Continuing Conflict in the Horn of Africa.* London: Rex Collings.

Nation, R. Craig, and Mark V. Kauppie, eds. 1984. *The Soviet Impact in Africa.* Toronto: Lexington Books.

Padmore, George F. 1956. *Pan-Africanism or Communism.* London: Dobson.

Pastor, Robert. 1983. "Cuba and the Soviet Union: Does Cuba Act Alone?" In *The New Cuban Presence in the Caribbean Basin.* Ed. Barry B. Levine. Boulder, Colo.: Westview Press.

Tikhomirov, V. I. 1989. "Soviet Policy in Southern Africa." In *African Contemporary Record,* 1988-89, Africana, New York.

11. *Izvestiya,* November 28, 1988.

13

Superpower Rivalry in Asia

Sharam Chubin

In the 1980s change in many aspects of international relations, both cumulative and simultaneous, triggered a profound transformation of the structure of international relations that has existed since 1945. Most conspicuous were changes within China and the Soviet Union, which have regional as well as global importance. Further, there was the rising economic power of Japan, Germany, and the newly industrializing countries (NICs). Economic rivalries strained existing security arrangements and might do so even more in the future. While political alliances and nuclear weapons stabilized Europe, much of the rest of the world experienced conflicts of varying intensity and duration after World War II. Superpower rivalry in the Third World was most pronounced. A remarkable shift in Soviet political thinking affected all aspects of that country's politics, including values and definitions of security, and became the principal catalyst in superpower relations. If applied to arms control and other areas, these changes could lead to a modification if not dissolution of existing alliance structures.

Such change would constitute a major new factor in international relations, with implications for superpower competition in all regions. The impact on international security (that is, for the international community), on East-West rivalry in the Third World (specifically in Latin America and Asia), and on conflicts in these areas was not clear. The answers to these in part depend on the answers to the questions we shall address: What impact did superpower rivalry have? What impact would diminishing this rivalry have? And what impact would actual cooperation have on international security and Third World conflicts?

THE SOVIET UNION AND EURASIA

It is instructive to compare the role of the United States in Latin America to Soviet behavior in Asia. The similarity lies in the sense of *amour propre* that great powers traditionally show toward their neighbors, and their claims to unspecified but usually paramount or even exclusive rights in a specific zone. This attitude manifested itself in military expeditions against neighbors, gunboat diplomacy, covert and not so covert activity, annexation (or purchase) of territory, and the proclamation of "doctrines" (as various as Monroe's and Brezhnev's) warning both outside powers and local actors about the limits to the great powers' tolerance. The difference between Latin America and Asia is perhaps more instructive. The major difference is that the United States is a maritime state, unchallenged by any proximate or equivalent power in the hemisphere. Its claims to unchallenged dominance in the region, however strident, reflect a palpable reality. Its unattractive "big stick" policy has been sporadic and mixed with genuinely good ties with its neighbors; one need only note the Rush-Bagot agreement of 1817 as an exemplary model of frontier arrangements.

The Soviet situation is different. It is a vast power whose borders encompass two continents. If its past claims in the name of security were met, it would effectively dominate the two continents. Even without geopolitical rhetoric, it would be very difficult to imagine that such a massive power in the center of Eurasia, defining its security in terms of all its neighbors' military weakness, is comparable to the American situation in the West. Acquiescence in the hegemonic power of the Soviet Union would have entailed a very different postwar Europe than the one that was constructed with considerable difficulty.

While Soviet attitudes toward its southern neighbors were domineering and chauvinist (racist and great power), they were not so very dissimilar from those of the United States. The main difference is that while the United States remains a potential haven for the discontented Latins and Hispanics of the New Continent, there was no rush to migrate north from the Islamic states on the Soviet periphery.

Another important difference, more accentuated now than in the immediate postwar period, is that Soviet Union cannot expect—in normal times—general acquiescence to its claims to being the paramount power in Eurasia. Quite apart from the fact that this would be inherently destabilizing for the international system (in a way that indulgence of an equivalent U.S. claim is not), unlike the United States, it is bounded in Europe and Asia by significant great and medium powers—Germany (as it is only too well aware) and China, and also Japan and India further behind. Its situation and the geopolitical balances are more complicated than those of the United States in the western hemisphere.

The attitudes of Soviet leaders about their country's borders in the past two generations were determined by a sense of vulnerability combined with ambition as much as by ideology. Vulnerability arose from extensive and far-flung borders with seven neighbors stretching from the Barents Sea to the Sea of Okhotsk. However, Soviet domination of its immediate neighbors in the name of security could not be tolerated by other powers because it would have entailed effective domination of Eurasia. The Soviet definition of security until the very recent past (and especially under Stalin) was indistinguishable from dominance. By demanding parity or "equal security" against all potential rivals—of which there were several because of Soviet behavior—the Soviets sought a dominant position in Eurasia that was bound to be contested by other world powers.

Soviet definitions of "security" until recently were primarily political/military in content, implying Soviet dominance or control of its neighbors. The corollary of this approach defined neutral states as potential threats and states aligned with its principal rival as actual ones. Because of the Cold War, relations between the United States and the Soviet Union in the Third World tended to be seen as being zero sum. In practical terms, this meant that Soviet policy attempted to increase its control—or, failing that, influence—throughout Asia and to diminish that of the United States or its allies. To counter encirclement, the Soviet Union promoted and supported anti-colonial movements and later encouraged nationalist moves that targeted western interests. If the Soviet aim was to be the dominant state in Eurasia, this could not be achieved without driving the United States from the continent. Both politically and strategically the exclusion, removal, or diminution of the U.S. presence involved weakening the CENTO and SEATO pacts, for example, and restricting deployment of SAC forces around the periphery of the Soviet Union.[1] The Soviet rationale was thus clear: to weaken and eliminate U.S. political presence in the region and to remove military infrastructure to extend Soviet influence.

However, Soviet policy was more complicated than this statement of aims, because it had to rely on local conditions, preferences, and opportunities. Even the modest postwar demand for the right to have "friendly" states on its borders appeared to be a euphemism for satellites or puppets rather than a "reasonable" reference to a buffer state. In large part because of specific Soviet acts in East Europe, Azerbaijan, and elsewhere, Norway, Turkey, and Iran were driven into alliance with the United States. Soviet policy aimed at weakening these states' ties with its rival, using local rivalries for its own ends and strengthening its own links with important states or states with potential nuisance value. This required involvement in Asian regional politics as an arms supplier (India, the Arab states versus Israel, Iraq versus Iran) and as a supporter of decolonization.

Soviet policy was in general "opportunistic," in that it reacted to, rather than guided, events, and it was characterized by no coherent grand strategy other than the weakening of the United States and the increase of Soviet power and influence. Coherence was a luxury an ambitious power could ill afford in the tangle of regional animosities and cross-cutting alignments, particularly if one felt constrained by maintaining ideological consistency. Soviet policy in Asia became akin to juggling several balls in the air at the same time, a virtuoso performance requiring agility and dexterity as well as commitment. The alternatives—not to play at all or to play with fewer balls—were unthinkable for a global communist power. Fewer commitments would have increased Soviet vulnerability, re-

---

1. These initials stand for the Central Treaty Organization, the Southeast Asia Treaty Organization, and the Strategic Air Command, respectively. The latter, made up of bombers with nuclear warheads, was particularly important before the proliferation of U.S. intercontinental ballistic missiles.

ducing the overall effect while inflating the stakes. As long as the Soviet Union maintained a definition of security tantamount to its own dominance, incompatible with the presence of a countervailing power on the Eurasian periphery, it was bound to see in each regional conflict opportunities to extend its interests and reduce those of its putative foe. Support for anti-western forces was thus seen as inherent in Soviet interests (Cuba, Iran), just as later a similar attitude took place regarding China (Vietnam and India, for example). Soviet decisions were ad hoc: whether to support the Arabs in 1973, not to do anything vis-à-vis China in 1978, or to increase support (and later invade) Afghanistan. Nevertheless, there was in each a strategic rationale that came from a definition of security that made them in some sense inevitable.

In response to Soviet policy in Asia, the United States insisted on its right to protect its air and maritime access to Eurasia and to block Soviet preponderance. To accomplish this, the United States sought local allies and access to bases. An aspect of this response was the generally skeptical view of indigenous movements that destabilized areas of strategic importance (for example, the Persian Gulf). Afghanistan caused a turning point in Soviet policy, one that reflected concern about strategic encirclement (the United States and China) as well as great-power hubris and opportunism. New developments transformed the East-West conflict in the 1970s. The recognition by the United States of limits to military power, the increasing autonomy of Third World conflicts, and the attendant energy crisis demonstrated the advent of new security concerns. These, along with the Sino-Vietnamese War, all were signs of new trends changing the East-West zero-sum game. But it was not until Gorbachev demonstrated a recognition of this in concrete that the old order passed.

Nuclear weapons stabilized Europe and made possible lesser wars in the "peripheries." It is also true that the nuclear dimension—nuclear powers involved in unstable regions—also imparted a degree of caution, instilling restraint and prudence in the Third World. Furthermore, the existence of two superpowers—a bipolar system—was itself a factor for stability. Kenneth Waltz argued that this made the balance more stable, the calculability of power much easier, and the essential balance of power much less sensitive to changes in alignment or accretions of military power.[2]

If the nuclear-superpower dimension lurked in the background instilling caution, it also made "victory" impossible or difficult. If wars could not have decisive results because of political restraints, then nuclear weapons could be said to have "decelerated history," in Raymond Aron's phrase. Superpower competition in Third World wars tended to raise the spectre of confrontation flowing from miscalculation or escalation. It also relegated local states into clients and proxies, rendering them more "irresponsible" for being able to manipulate the superpowers. Local conflicts took on the characteristics of the broader East-West competition and became polarized, with their stakes exaggerated and their costs consequently amplified.

The stakes of individual conflicts were inflated by acute East-West competition in part because the Third World was seen not only as the arena for competition, but also as the judge of the historic competition between the two different systems. As these local entanglements yielded lower payoffs and threatened détente and domestic economic growth, the Soviet Union redefined its approach to security. By stressing diplomacy and openness and reducing its claims on its neighbors, it also reduced the risks stemming from an alliance of putative enemies, such as China, NATO, and Japan.

SOVIET POLICY AND CONFLICTS IN ASIA

The U.S.–Soviet rivalry in Asia has been the product of geopolitical factors, and also it can be attributed to the claims of special rights and extensive interests made by the Soviet Union. While the rivalry inherent between a maritime and continental power could not disappear, the reduction of Soviet claims made possible relations that were not zero-sum. Reducing the ideological component of relations between the superpowers would make their competition less virulent. Competition would be more focused and less extensive, with core interests like defense of the homeland predominant. There would be less inclination to intervene in conflicts

2. For a discussion of this, see Chubin, Adelphi Paper No. 237, 1987.

and to take on new commitments. Emphasis on regional actors may come to be a hallmark of superpower policy in the Third World, but it is unlikely to be a high priority. The shift in Soviet thinking epitomized by the peace offensives in Europe and Asia in the late 1980s unfroze other alignments, facilitating contacts between India and China, North and South Korea, Indonesia and China, and Thailand, Vietnam, and Kampuchea. The diversification of Soviet relations—one day Oman, another perhaps Israel and Saudi Arabia—suggested a more conventional diplomacy.

The Gorbachev reforms were unlikely to be rejected in favor of a return to Stalinism. Once released, these forces could not be neatly contained. In international relations too much was invested in changing Soviet commitments and image to allow a quick or tactical return to the past. In some respects the nonmilitary costs (diplomatic and political) loomed much larger as a constraint on a Soviet reversal of policy than did the strictly military. However, in the euphoria of the late 1980s, it was necessary to identify areas of special sensitivity.

If the outer empire of the Soviet Union was a sensitive area, so too was the inner empire. The Islamic and Asian parts of the Soviet Union increased in importance in the 1980s, not only because of the revival of Islam on the Soviet periphery (and of religion in the Soviet Union), but also because the southern republics were the major source of labor to meet increased demand. The continued spread of local nationalism, intense during 1988-1989, required some accommodation, particularly in the Muslim republics of the Transcaucasus and Central Asia. Any interference in the Islamic question by an outside power would provoke a strong Soviet reaction. Soviet policy focused on meeting the nationalist demands (where possible) domestically and neutralizing its external allies. The latter involved establishing links with border countries broadening diplomatic relations to acquire leverage where possible in strategic areas (arms supplies, transit trade).

Internationally, two areas of uncertainty remain problematical. First, there was the role of accident and chance, the unplanned event creating opportunity to gain advantage. The Soviet Union, like other states, could not know in advance what its reaction would be to particular events, so much would depend on the specific contexts. Regional instability would persist for some time, and attempts to reduce or mitigate them would be worthwhile to reduce the possibility of superpower confrontation.

A second area of concern stemmed from change within the Soviet Union. The expansion of political rights and nationalist expectations could lead to a backlash in the event of economic failure and/or civil strife threatening the integrity of the state. Political instability and economic deterioration could encourage elements within the Soviet government to pursue an aggressive foreign policy as a substitute for reform. Historically, there are few cases where great powers accepted decline gracefully without a military defeat.

Assuming that the prospect was for a less activist, more discriminating Soviet policy in Asia, not abandoning allies but reducing commitments and avoiding new ones, the international context would change for the United States. Without the Soviet Union as a threat, Washington would be less able to devote major resources to Third World interventions. With the exception of Israel and perhaps Central America, there would be little domestic consensus for U.S. involvement. Further, pressure for U.S. allies to share the defense burden in Asia would increase as tensions declined. For example, with the United States deprived of the Soviet enemy, economic competition with Japan would not be offset by that country's role as a military ally. A diminished threat from the Soviet Union would eventually make countervailing presence in East Asia less urgent. At the same time, considerations of regional/political balance and diplomacy would make Asian countries anxious to retain the U.S. presence in Asia for the foreseeable future. In Northeast and East Asia the Soviet Union's economic weakness will limit its role as a major player.

THE PROSPECTS FOR REGIONAL CONFLICTS

Superpower rivalry has distorted regional conflicts, militarized them, given them prominence, and made them more intractable, but rarely has it been the cause or source of the conflict itself. The superpowers used military and economic aid to extend influence with Israel, Cuba, and Vietnam, and to force a United Nations role in Angola. But even for conflicts in which they were directly involved (such as Afghanistan), superpower agreement was not sufficient by itself or a necessary precondition for comprehensive settlement.

Over the last forty years, the majority of Third World conflicts started as civil wars: Kampuchea, Angola, Afghanistan, Nicaragua, El Salvador, the Horn of Africa, Lebanon, Sri Lanka, and Sudan. The wars of the 1950s and 1960s, in Korea, Vietnam, and between Pakistan and India, were similar. Many since 1945 were wars of decolonization and independence, or from the consequences, anomalies, and ambiguities of the colonial experience in respect to national borders. Wars for independence ("national liberation") and decolonization were stoked by the Soviet Union and China.[3] These were followed by wars for unification. The "cleaning up" operations of the Indonesian government in East Timor and elsewhere—Bangladesh and India, and Iraq and the Kurds—are typical of this phase. Less frequent and clearly of local origin were the wars between states, including China and Vietnam, the Sino-Soviet border clash of 1969, and the Iran-Iraq war.

Whether interstate wars would replace the intrastate variety would depend in part on the international environment and on the utility, costs, and alternatives of resorting to force. Superpower restraint in arms supplies and in manipulating local antagonisms would be helpful in not exacerbating existing tensions. Also contributing to reduced tensions in Asia would be the improvement in relations between China and the Soviet Union. The presence of several loci of power in Asia (the Soviet Union, China, Japan, India, the NICs, and U.S. offshore presence) suggests that polarization is a thing of the past. Regional conflicts that remain geographically self-contained, though regrettable, would not constitute a threat to international stability. Against these optimistic considerations run others. As regions become more autonomous from the superpowers, indigenous balances may become harder to maintain, with the consequent emergence of new powers such as India in South Asia. These states may be more prone in a permissive regional environment to undertake unilateral interventions (for example, the Maldives and Sri Lanka). In other areas, such as Southern Africa and the Levant, there have been similar instances

---

3. The same point is made for Africa by Colin Legum in Chapter 12 of this volume.

of interventionary forces from local states (South Africa, Israel, and Syria).

There is some question as to whether the greater restraint by the superpowers would be copied by governments in the developing world. Views about the utility and costs of force and alternatives to it are not always compatible. In addition to differences in historical experience and concrete conditions, the differences arise from the structure of political institutions in these countries in which political accountability is limited. Furthermore, the nationalism that swept nineteenth-century Europe only recently reached many Third World countries, and there is a close relationship between war and nationalism. If nationalism persists or is irresponsibly cultivated, it can be a force for more interstate conflicts. (Israel and Iraq provided examples of this in the 1980s.)

Even without access to aid from superpowers, the means for supplying conflicts remained abundant. The growth in Third World arms suppliers not only made military commerce more competitive and more difficult to control, but it also provided the buyer arms appropriate to its needs rather than hand-me-downs from the inventories of the superpowers. Faith in regional institutions had to contend with the reality that it is often in these very institutions that regional schisms are the most pronounced.

THE SUPERPOWER AND REGIONAL CONFLICTS: FROM COMPETITION TO MANAGEMENT

As the international system approached the end of the millennium, it was in rapid transition from the familiar one dominant since the end of World War II, which characterized the nuclear era. Less clear was where the transition would lead and how much and which parts of the existing structure would remain. On certain assumptions it is possible to explore the prospects for regional conflicts and potential superpower roles.

First, however much other things may change, the existing basic structure of international relations would persist. With states competing for scarce resources and ready to use force as an ultimate instrument, and with no superior agency able to stop them, wars will remain a possibility, and prudent states thus should plan accordingly. Second, domestic political processes will remain autonomous. International relations will remain subject to political considerations not purely derivative of economic processes. Third, great powers will remain a distinctive class of state not merely by virtue of superior power, but by reason of the scope of their interests. Superpower competition will persist, though more carefully circumscribed, and will take the form of what might be called "competitive cooperation." Fourth, the end of the Cold War may see a decline in the cohesion of alliances and a diminution of concern for some areas of the world. Superpowers' retrenchment and the associated devolution of responsibility would not be without risks. Regional conflicts arise not from the cognitive or bureaucratic failures of superpowers, but from the difference of interests of local parties. These groups have their own calculations and expectations about force and find outside assistance because of other rivalries not directly associated with their own. Unique characteristics of the superpowers make it desirable to keep them involved constructively in the management of regional conflicts. The trick will be to avoid isolationism, unlimited competition, or great-power directorate over international affairs.

Despite the handicap of the potentially escalatory nature of their participation, the superpowers remain unique in certain positive respects. A global perspective is the most obvious of these assets, for many key issues transcend regional politics and regional solutions. Global standards and norms are required where issues concern nuclear and chemical weapons, ballistic missile proliferation, terrorism, or military interventions by Third World states. Were international norms to be breached and thresholds (moral or military) frequently contravened in regional conflicts, it is difficult to imagine that the restraints operating in superpower relations could continue unimpaired. The crossing of such thresholds as the threat or use of nuclear or chemical weapons would render regional conflicts vulnerable to superpower intervention.

If, as we have argued, it is desirable to keep the superpowers involved in regional conflicts in constructive ways and discourage their (excessive) retrenchment in order to offset regional hegemones and provide a global perspective, it is necessary to consider how feasible effective intervention might it be. There are three sets of contributions that the superpowers could in theory make: (1)

those relating to their own relations; (2) those relating to global issues; and (3) those contributing to regional stability.

The first category could include bilateral actions between the United States and the Soviet Union to reduce suspicions, such as verification and inspection. Other possible moves would be reduction of military budgets, modifications of offensive doctrines, and norms of conduct in specified regional conflicts. The second category could include cooperation in a number of "restraint regimes," for example, on the transfer of sensitive materials or technology, or bilateral and multilateral agreements on how to deal with terrorism. The third category could cover the cooperation spectrum from active to passive, unilateral to bilateral, and tacit to formal. For example, an agreement not to intervene in certain crises, thus decoupling regional from global issues, could be specific in a "hands-off" agreement that was bilateral and reciprocal. Agreement to act rather than *not* to act is also possible. The traditional "sphere of influence," an acknowledgment of respective interests, had the advantage of reducing misunderstandings and providing the two parties with a relatively free hand within a specified area.

A variant of the sphere of influence would be the attempt to provide assurance to a great power by guaranteeing a local state, leading to a buffer of countries. Another version of this approach is the neutralization of a contested state, such as Laos in the early 1960s. Finally, there is the possibility of joint enforcement action, envisaged in the U.N. Charter, Chapter 7, and threatened in the Security Council by the permanent members in the passage of the "preliminary" Resolution SC. 598 in July 1987. The risk of a tyranny of superpower management is limited by the practical difficulties of keeping restive peoples subjugated for very long.

None of these is a pattern of interaction, and potential types of cooperation are inevitable, but there appear to be few substitutes for superpower cooperation in dealing with some categories of problems. It would therefore be regrettable if superpower relations were to advance only in the limited sphere of bilateral relations without encompassing areas further afield, where in the present era of détente they could make a very useful and even unique contribution.

Part V

Are There Avenues
of Cooperation?

14

Economic Interdependence and Superpower Policy in the Third World

V. B. Benevolensky

Until recently, ideology and issues of military policy have dominated the approaches to Third World problems. Economic assistance was extended to less developed countries mainly within the context of competition between the two major social systems.

Policy changes now under way in the Soviet Union are due to the recognition that our world is multidimensional and interdependent. Interdependence on a global scale was recognized first in the nuclear sphere. This is a case of negative, destructive interdependence. The same is true for ecological interdependence: the hazards of global pollution make people all over the world one community. But there are cases of positive, constructive interdependence. The most obvious instance is economic interdependence. Economic partners always benefit from relations they engage in, at least to some degree. Even in cases of a most pronounced asymmetry of economic interdependence, the display of economic pressure is perceived to be more bearable by the weaker party than attempts to use political or military force. One might add that economic influence usually turns out to be more lasting and dependable than purely political or military influence.

The importance of economic leverage as a foreign policy instrument increased during the last ten to fifteen years as the political potential of military force diminished. This shift was due not only to the nuclear deadlock, but also to the apparent inefficiency of military means to resolve regional conflicts. Therefore, there is good reason to anticipate further increases in the prominence of economic factors of superpower strategy in the Third World.

It follows that the basis for the substitution of economic for more aggressive foreign policy instruments (diplomacy, military force, or paramilitary operations) in the process of superpower competition in the Third World is provided by the growth of economic interdependence of a majority of countries of the modern world. One possible way to quantify the growth of economic interdependence is to compare the rates of growth of international economic relations with the rates of growth of the world industrial output. From 1970 to 1987, industrial output, in real terms, of the developed countries increased 59 percent, while the volume of imports rose 115 percent and exports 131 percent.[1] For the developing countries, industrial output and imports rose even more (89 and 125 percent, respectively), but exports by much less, only 39 percent.[2] This growth of global economic interdependence has been manifested by the synchronization of the world business cycle since the 1973-1975 recession.

The growing involvement with the world economy is not just a characteristic of small countries or countries lacking self-sufficiency in important resources (energy, materials, and financial resources). Even economic giants with a strong resource base, like the United States, have engaged in world trade to an increasing degree. The share of foreign trade in U.S. GNP increased from 8 percent in 1970 to 15 percent in 1987.[3] At the same time, total foreign assets in the U.S. economy grew tenfold in the fifteen years after 1970, reaching $1060 billion in 1985.[4] We can conclude that the integration of the U.S. economy into the world economy has reached a qualitatively new level.

The Soviet Union is also concerned with closer integration into the world market. Further economic isolation from the world economy would have a negative effect not only for its internal economic and social development, but also for its position in international political relations, and thus for its status as a great power. Of

---

1. *"Prilozhenie k zhurnalu MEMO,"* IMEMO Institute, 1987-1988.
2. Ibid.
3. *Statistical Abstract of the United States,* 1988.
4. *Survey of Current Business,* June 1987, p. 40.

course, the Soviet Union still has a long way to go to reach a level of integration into the world economy typical of the industrialized countries.   On a policy level, however, there is already a firm understanding of the necessity to do so.

The existence of interdependence does not simply imply that such relations are strictly symmetrical.   The typical situation is quite the opposite.   But asymmetrical interdependence does not imply instability.   Interdependence is a relation, the disengagement from which negatively affects all partners involved in the relation. From this characteristic it follows that if a broad system of interdependency is considered, asymmetries in some elements of the system (bilateral or multilateral) could render the entire system more stable.   An analysis of the asymmetries uniting the modern world into a whole could highlight some of the strategic interests of the participants of international relations, as well as the influence of partners on each other's policies.   Such an analysis with respect to economic interdependence can highlight the opportunities to substitute economic foreign policy leverages for the use of political and military force in international relations, which would be a great step toward humanizing international policy, to the creation of a nonviolent world.   This is especially important for superpower policy in the Third World.   Of particular importance are four aspects of asymmetrical interdependence: financial, scientific, technological, and food security.   Each provides insight into interdependence, with different opportunities for U.S. foreign policy.

INTERDEPENDENCE IN THE FINANCIAL SPHERE

The interdependence in the financial sphere is clearly asymmetrical.   Developments in U.S. financial markets determine the climate of international finance, not the other way around.[5]   The dollar still is the most important reserve currency, and the United

5. Foreign financial assets amounted to only 5.6 percent of the U.S. total. The outflow of private direct investment during 1980 to 1985 was no more than 2.1 percent of U.S. private fixed nonresidential investment, and the inflow of foreign direct investment a negative 4.8 percent. The total volume of foreign direct investment in the United States in 1985 only reached 3.4 percent of the volume of assets of U.S. nonfinancial corporations (*Statistical Abstract of the United States*, 1987, pp. 417, 475, 512, 777; and *Survey of Current Business*, June 1987, p. 40).

States still holds the prominent position in the major international economic organizations. Counteraction to unilateral U.S. measures in the financial markets is a difficult and costly affair because it requires joint action by the majority of other western countries and Japan, which is not easily achieved. Under such circumstances, financial instruments have a great potential as tools of U.S. foreign policy. Financial pressure is particularly effective against industrialized countries having an "open" financial system and countries of the Third World heavily dependent on foreign financial sources. In this context, one should not overstate the problems of the large U.S. foreign debt and the current-account balance. U.S. financial markets remain quite immune to external shocks. By the use of protectionist measures, the U.S. government could rather quickly solve the problem of the trade and current-account imbalance, though such a remedy would run counter to U.S economic and political interests.

INTERDEPENDENCE IN THE
SCIENCE AND TECHNOLOGY SPHERE

The second most important instance of interdependence is in the sphere of science and technology. As for international finance, the United States holds here a powerful position. Aside from the Soviet Union, only the United States has a resource base permitting research and development that covers all the range of science and technology. But at the same time, other countries have been successful in developing and applying a whole range of modern technologies that challenge the formerly undisputed leadership of the United States. Among these countries are not only those of West Europe and Japan, but also the newly industrializing countries (NICs, the so-called Tigers of Asia). Concentrating effort and resources on a limited number of priorities in technology, taking advantage of a relatively cheap labor, and seizing on organizational improvements in the diffusion stage of the innovative process enabled those countries to achieve important positions in the world economy. Thus, the technological interdependence has a much more symmetric character than the financial.

The American market for advanced technology is strongly in

terdependent with world markets (see tables 14-1 and 14-2). From a more symmetric interdependence in science and technology there follows a well-grounded self-interest for cooperation with countries possessing important achievements in this field. At the same time, the U.S. government faces constraints in using access to modern technology as an instrument of political pressure. For example, problems of adherence to COCOM rules by the NICs now are being solved by the United States through negotiations. Unilateral approaches, including some instances of sanctions by the United States in the early 1980s, proved to be unsuccessful. To achieve its policy targets, the United States has to take into account the legitimate interests of trading partners. With respect to its main allies, the United States has made quite important concessions, such as allowing participation in Strategic Defense Initiative contracts and access of foreign capital to American high-tech industries.

Nevertheless, the United States retains the potential to turn technology interdependence into political influence. The technology gap has narrowed mainly at the lower edge of the high-tech spectrum. An example of this is the U.S. robotics market: the average price of industrial imports in 1986 was $38,000 a unit, while the average price of all robots sold in the American market amounted to $71,000.[6] These figures suggest that American producers sold in their domestic markets the more sophisticated machinery, relying on imports for the comparatively "low-technology" equivalents. The loss of the competitive edge in consumer electronics and personal computers is offset by the domination in world software markets, the development of artificial intelligence, and other fields of crucial importance for further technological development.

INTERDEPENDENCE IN THE
ENERGY AND RAW MATERIAL SPHERE

The interdependence in the sphere of energy and raw materials is another factor affecting U.S. policy in the Third World. Structural shifts in the American economy since the energy crisis of the

---

6. *U.S. Industrial Outlook*, 1988, pp. 23-5, 23-6.

1970s had a great impact on energy consumption patterns. Total energy consumption per dollar of GNP (in constant prices) decreased 27 percent over the period 1971-1987, and oil and gas consumption fell 39 percent.[7] Conservation measures and the growth of high-tech industries that are low in use of energy and materials weakened the dependence of the U.S. economy on raw materials imports, though this dependence was not eliminated. The United States also took steps to diversify its energy imports, shifting toward the more stable areas of the Third World, including South America. At the same time, strategic stocks of oil and other important resources have been increased. These developments have enhanced the immunity of the U.S. economy and U.S. policy to possible oil shocks or similar attempts to exercise political influence.

INTERDEPENDENCE IN THE FOOD EXPORTS SPHERE

Food exports should also be analyzed within the context of American foreign policy in the Third World. The United States is a major producer of food and animal feed. The U.S. share of the world production of soy beans exceeds 50 percent, comes close to 50 percent for corn, 15 percent for wheat, and 16 percent for meat.[8] The dependence of countries on food imports from the United States can easily be translated into political influence.

World economic interdependence has gone so far that economic leverages have gained much in importance as policy instruments. It seems reasonable to anticipate that in its future policy in the Third World the United States could opt to substitute economic measures for the more traditional foreign policy measures. This does not mean U.S. policy in the Third World is going to become

7. Ibid., p. 10-6. The decline was similar for major metals: consumption per constant dollar of GNP of lead fell 34 percent, copper fell 26 percent, and cement fell 36 percent during the same period (*Statistical Abstract of the United States*, 1988, pp. 407, 667-71).

8. *Statistical Abstract of the United States*, 1987, p. 641. American exports of corn in the 1980s wefe in excess of 60 percent of total world exports of this commodity. The figures for wheat were 30 to 40 percent, and for rice 17 percent. Approximately 40 percent of American agricultural exports went to Asia (one-half to Japan), another 15 percent to Latin America, and 25 percent to West Europe (ibid., p. 640).

Table 14-1. Imports of Selected High-Tech Products
as Percent of U.S. Consumption

	1972	1980	1987
Metal-Cutting Tools	8.0	22.5	50.9
Metal-Forming Tools	6.0	17.1	29.4
NC Machining Centers	NA	20.8	66.1[a]
Robotics	NA	NA	33.3[a]
Electronic Computing Equipment	0.0	6.2	31.5
Electronic Components	6.2	17.5	23.1

Source: U.S. Industrial Outlook, 1988.

a. Data are for 1986.

Table 14-2. Exports of Selected High-Tech Products
as Percent of U.S. Production

	1972	1980	1987
Metal-Cutting Tools	15.1	13.7	21.6
Metal-Forming Tools	18.4	24.3	22.0
NC Machining Centers	NA	13.8	10.2[a]
Electronic Computing Equipment	21.3	29.5	36.3
Electronic Components	11.6	19.2	19.2

Source: U.S. Industrial Outlook, 1988.

a. Data are for 1986.

a factor of proliferation of nonviolence and of an all-embracing harmony. But a shift toward economic instruments could have a positive effect on international relations. The relatively decreasing strategic importance of energy and raw materials, along with a marked rise in prominence of technology and financial resources, would seem to favor more superpower tolerance to social and political developments in the Third World.

15

Socialist Countries and Development Assistance

Jozef M. van Brabant

There are probably three aspects of the programmed notes to this session that either do not at all apply to the socialist countries[1] or that fit the specifics of these countries only rather awkwardly. For one, there is hardly any private development assistance emanating from these countries. Also, these countries as a group would probably and the Soviet Union would certainly contest that the level of their official development assistance (ODA) has shrunken in recent years, say during two decades since the early 1970s. Whether the third remaining pointer, namely official and private development finance, is applicable to the centrally planned economies (CPEs),[2] the Soviet Union in the first instance, is debatable. But I shall zero in on that aspect of the question as well as on whether there are presently better chances for multilateralizing the development assistance of the CPEs than there have been since the initial efforts in that respect were first formulated in the mid-1950s.

The vast bulk of the bilateral as well as multilateral development assistance provided by the CPEs, with the Soviet Union in the lead, has not been development finance in the proper sense. As is well known, nearly all of this assistance has been tied two-ways per

1. In this group I include the traditional components of the world socialist economic system, including Albania, China, Cuba, East Europe, Laos, Mongolia, North Korea, the Soviet Union, Vietnam, and Yugoslavia.
2. Matters are rather fluid in defining this group. In the context of the United Nations, this group includes all socialist countries as defined but Cuba, Laos, and Yugoslavia. I shall be referring chiefly to the European members of the group.

donor-recipient country. Some efforts have been channeled into multilateralizing assistance from the donors' end of the equation. But even that has encountered serious problems. Regarding the first aspect, of some relevance are the facilities created at the level of the Council for Mutual Economic Assistance (CMEA)[3] and some of its affiliated international economic organizations, the two CMEA banks (the International Bank for Economic Cooperation [IBEC] and the International Investment Bank [IIB]) in the first instance. With respect to multilateralizing the recipient side, an interesting footnote—but no more than that—can be constructed around the recent efforts of Czechoslovakia to trade off its dubious holdings of financial assets in developing countries at far below par value through various kinds of switch operations.

When all is said and done, however, the key channels through which East Europe's[4] development assistance is channeled are bilateral trade and payment agreements (BTPAs), cooperation agreements hammered out at the multilateral level with the CMEA and some of its agencies by at least eight[5] developing countries proper,[6] and the potential impact of the Soviet new thinking, especially in foreign policy matters, for measurably improving

3. This organization consists of full members, one associate member (Yugoslavia), cooperants (eight developing countries and Finland), and observers (other socialist countries, developing countries, and representatives from international organizations). In what follows, I shall confine myself largely to the active European members of the CMEA as defined below. I shall eschew the alternative, admittedly more euphonic, Comecon because of its political overtones (coined as it was in parallel to Comintern and Cominform) and its incompleteness as an acronym in any case, for it omits the "assistance" in CMEA.

4. East Europe is here defined as comprising Bulgaria, Czechoslovakia, the German Democratic Republic (GDR), Hungary, Poland, and Romania. At times I shall use the concept also to include the Soviet Union when the context makes it clear that I have this wider geographical notion in mind. East Europe and the Soviet Union constitute the active European members of the CMEA. Albania is formally still a full CMEA member, though it ceased active participation in 1961.

5. Afghanistan, Angola, Ethiopia, Iraq, Mexico, Mozambique, Nicaragua, and Democratic Yemen (since early 1990 again Yemen) have special cooperative status, as does Finland, with the CMEA as a result of having signed bilateral cooperation agreements.

6. In what follows, I shall denote the nonsocialist developing countries as developing countries proper. I do not, of course, wish to elevate the developing country CMEA members (Cuba, Mongolia, and Vietnam) or other developing countries that belong in the socialist camp (Albania, China, Laos, North Korea, and Yugoslavia) to a status that does not even remotely reflect their economic potential.

Soviet participation in global development assistance efforts.

In this connection, it is important to recall that development assistance in the CPE or CMEA context is traditionally defined differently from the concepts underlying international conventions. In reports submitted to international agencies, for instance, the CPEs include the assistance efforts extended to socialist countries that by virtue of their low level of economic development benefit from special regimes in settling trade and finance. This is not really different in approach from the practices of market-economy donors. But, because the latter extend little aid to the developing country CPEs, and certainly not in the particular format in which this manifests itself in the case of European CMEA donors, it is advisable to differentiate the two at least conceptually. The CPEs use a concept of development assistance that is far more inclusive than is customary in international deliberations, as discussed below.

Inasmuch as the theme of the session is development assistance proper, that is, the nonsocialist developing countries or Third World as traditionally understood, it will be useful to separate the developing country CPEs from the orthodox market-type developing countries. Regarding the first, I shall refer chiefly to the situation of the three developing country CMEA members (Cuba, Mongolia, and Vietnam).[7] This is warranted if only because these countries have enjoyed a special cooperation regime, and the vast bulk of the claimed development assistance from CPEs is undertaken for the benefit of these three countries. In addition, it may be useful to look at whether the eight cooperant developing countries have apparently benefited from their special status with the CMEA.[8]

7. Note that Mongolia became a full CMEA member in 1962, Cuba in 1972, and Vietnam in 1978. Moreover, whereas Mongolia has been a socialist country from the beginning of the world socialist system and Vietnam (North Vietnam until 1975) became a member after it gained independence in 1954, Cuba joined that rank only after the Cuban revolution turned decisively in the direction of the socialist countries around 1962. These distinctions will be mostly ignored in what follows, however.

8. Note that the agreements with these developing countries have been signed over a protracted period of time, essentially between 1973 and 1987. I shall ignore this particular dating, as the "special" relationship may have already existed, albeit in a somewhat less formal format, prior to the signing of the agreement. This certainly was the case for the agreements with, for example, Afghanistan, Angola, Iraq, Mozambique, Democratic Yemen, and perhaps others. Nonetheless, it may be useful to bear this particular feature in mind in analyzing the data.

Section I presents some background information on the recent trade relations between the European CMEA members and the developing countries, with the latter disaggregated into four conventional regions (Africa, Far East, Latin America, and Middle East here set equal to Western Asia). Section II does likewise for the recent evolution of trade relations between the European CPEs and the developing country CMEA members. It also examines whether one can detect a special status for the eight developing country cooperants from the trade statistics. Inferences from the statistical overview for recent trends in development assistance that can be drawn from trade developments are presented in Section III. I shall examine there as well some trends and features of official resource transfers claimed by or attributed to European CMEA members. Section IV sketches recent new thinking in the CMEA, which is bound to be very important to the developing country CMEA members. Section V looks at some of the instruments through which development assistance has been channeled within the CMEA and how this may be affected by ongoing CMEA reform. The new thinking, particularly in the Soviet Union, relative to international economic organizations and the country's perceived new responsibilities for maintaining a predictable, reliable, and stable global trading and financial environment, is set forth in Section VI. The implications of the ongoing perestroika and still evolving new thinking for fusing development assistance efforts of developed countries as such concludes the original paper. A brief postscript points out seminal developments in East Europe since mid-1989, when this paper was finalized.

I. TRADE DEVELOPMENTS WITH THE THIRD WORLD

Rhetoric to the contrary, trade between the European CPEs and the Third World, as defined here, has always been marginal, rather unstable, heavily concentrated on a few developing countries, and dominated by quite traditional forms of exchange. If anything, recent developments in the global economy and the adjustment problems encountered by the European CPEs have contributed to compressing that trade further, well below levels observed in the 1970s.

Table 15-1 summarizes recent export and import trends based on

Table 15-1. Share of Third World in CMEA Trade

	Exports		Imports	
	Reported Total	Sum Bilateral	Reported Total	Sum Bilateral
East Europe Seven				
1970	10.64	7.66	7.58	7.24
1975	10.89	7.70	8.20	7.47
1980	12.26	8.14	10.93	9.86
1982	14.69	9.41	10.33	9.58
1984	13.15	7.92	10.15	9.31
1986	12.71	6.75	8.26	6.67
1987	12.58	6.87	7.73	6.26
1988	12.41	6.45	8.13	6.82
1989	12.13	n.a.[a]	9.27	n.a.
East Europe Six				
1970	6.91	6.19	5.51	5.04
1975	8.86	7.41	6.01	4.78
1980	10.76	8.59	10.52	8.80
1982	13.13	10.22	8.73	7.45
1984	11.53	8.64	8.77	7.25
1986	11.05	7.61	8.79	5.45
1987	10.22	7.22	7.62	4.52
1988	10.00	6.41	8.02	5.19
1989	8.65	n.a.	8.64	n.a.

Source: Official trade data of the CMEA members.

a. n.a. — not available.

trade data evaluated at current dollar exchange rates and prices.[9] Excepting the spurt of trade expansion in the early 1980s, emanating from the deliberately forced export drive, particularly on the part of East Europe, the share of the developing countries in both exports and imports of East Europe and the Soviet Union, identified in Table 15-1 as "East Europe Seven," has remained modest, barely hovering over 10 percent. Note that the share of developing countries in the exports of the European CMEA members expanded dramatically in 1982-1984, due to an export spurt by the CPEs involved, the availability of convertible currency funds on the part of oil-exporting developing countries, and the contemporary sluggish demand for imports from CPEs in West European markets.

It also needs to be noted here that there has been a sharp deterioration in the statistical reporting of trade. This is particularly pronounced on the export side. Thus, whereas in the early 1970s roughly 70 percent of exports were identified by partner country, in the early 1980s this declined to less than half. The precise reasons are unknown, but one can conjecture that exports of arms and trade with countries, including Israel and South Africa, that tend to be "inconvenient" partners, particularly to Soviet policymakers, are probably responsible for this state of affairs.

There is a similar bulge in the pattern of import shares in the early 1980s. Two points must be made here. First, the identified developing countries of origin comprise a larger percentage of reported import totals than is the case for the exports of the European CPEs. However, there has been a steady deterioration in that respect in recent years. Furthermore, the share on the export side has traditionally substantially exceeded that of imports, particularly in the case of the Soviet Union. This suggests positive imbalances, which offer prima facie evidence of the transfer of real resources to developing countries. Another interesting contrast is that for East Europe the trade shares have been much more stable than for the

---

9. It is important to underline this. Inasmuch as the vast bulk of trade among the socialist countries is cleared at so-called transferable ruble prices (TRPs) that are in principle patterned after average world market prices but with a considerable lag, trends measured in dollars can be quite different from trends measured in rubles. Similarly, trends measured in constant ruble or dollar prices may sharply deviate from comparable trends measured in current ruble or dollar prices. For details on the price regime, see Brabant (1987b).

Soviet Union and ʼhat the export and import shares are more equally distributed. This point will be important in considering the transfer of development assistance.

The deterioration in the gap between reported group totals and the sums of reported countries of origin and destination in the case of East Europe proper stems largely from the serious lacunae in foreign trade data published by the GDR since about 1975, including its decision to report since 1975 only bilateral trade turnover data.[10] The same holds for Romania since 1986, when the foreign trade reporting suddenly collapsed into virtually no details at all on bilateral flows. Both circumstances preclude applying some of our quantitative measures to the European CMEA members, for it is quite difficult to disaggregate trade turnover data for relatively small flows; the GDR does not even publish trade turnover statistics for many developing countries. In what follows, I have made rough estimates for the missing Romanian data, but it proved too cumbersome to attempt to do the same for the GDR.

The European CMEA has distributed its merchandising efforts in developing countries, especially in exports, in particular in countries of Africa, Asia, and the Middle East, whereas Latin America (excluding Cuba) has traditionally received less emphasis. The data shown in Table 15-2 illustrate these points. It is difficult to distill any useful trends from this information, however. The shares of the Asian countries in the total exports and imports of the European CPEs remained fairly stable in the 1980s. On the whole, however, there has been a good deal of reshuffling partners and trade values. This is more the case for East Europe than for the Eastern group combined, suggesting that the Soviet Union has been a relatively more stable (and reliable?) trading partner than many of the East European countries.

II. THE SOCIALIST AND COOPERANT CMEA MEMBERS

Because this is not the place to examine in detail various empirical problems endemic to trade data published by CPEs, particularly

---

10. In various less-than-official statistical reports, the GDR makes available export and import data for selected countries and most regional groups.

those applying to bilateral trade statistics with developing countries, I shall discuss here only a few details regarding the participation of these countries in European CMEA members' trade.

As shown in Table 15-3, trade of the European CPEs with the three developing country CMEA partners has remained marginal for East Europe proper, but not for the Soviet Union. Thus, the share for East Europe has been on the order of about 1 percent of both exports and imports. But it is much higher in the case of the Soviet Union. For the European CPEs combined, the three developing country members account for about 5 to 6 percent of exports and 4 percent of imports. This suggests that the share of these three countries in the trade of the Soviet Union is substantial, on the order of 7 to 9 percent for exports and around 6 to 8 percent for imports in recent years. Also interesting is that the share of these countries has steadily increased, but only in the case of the Soviet Union and, in recent years, East European imports. This offers prima facie evidence that East Europe has been reducing its net transfer of ODA to the developing CMEA members. Nonetheless, for most years the share of these countries in the exports of the European CMEA members exceeds the share of imports, suggesting that the European partners may be running an export surplus. But this gap is evidently more substantial for the Soviet Union than for East Europe in most observation years. Whether this can be identified with ODA will be taken up in the next section.

Though small, the data suggest that the three developing country CMEA members have found an expanding market in East Europe and the Soviet Union. It takes some leap of imagination to identify this with and attribute it to their becoming CMEA members. The data suggest, however, that membership has not harmed the intragroup trade prospects of these countries. Can the same be said of the eight cooperants?

Table 15-3 also exhibits the share of these eight developing countries in the trade of the European CMEA members (excluding the GDR).[11] There is no doubt that the eight countries account for a rather unstable share of both the exports and the imports of the

11. Because for several of these countries no data can be estimated for the period since 1975, I have simply omitted the GDR computations. This is regrettable, as the share of the GDR in CMEA trade with the eight countries was rather substantial in the 1960s and early 1970s.

European CMEA members. Whereas prior to the first cooperant agreement, which was signed in 1973, trade with these countries accounted for less than 1 percent of the exports and imports of the European CPEs, by the early 1980s this share had more than doubled, with some spectacular export surge in the years during which particularly East Europe pushed its exports. There has been some gain also on the import side, but to a far smaller degree than is evident for the export side. This by itself suggests the presence of export surpluses. These are evident for both the Soviet Union and East Europe. A good look at them in the next section will therefore be useful.

In summary, there would appear to be some prima facie evidence that developing countries that maintain some formal relationship with the CMEA have derived benefits in terms of acquiring a larger position in the exports of European CPEs and perhaps also in the transfer of assistance or credits. But there is simply not enough information available to evaluate whether these developments can be attributed to these countries having become associated with the CMEA. I would guess that some formalized form of association with the CMEA certainly has not harmed the trading prospects of these countries.

III. TRANSFER OF ECONOMIC ASSISTANCE

Development assistance can take on many different forms. In the case of the CPEs, however, there is a strict limit, as most assistance is provided directly through net exports of goods and services. If the assistance proceeds in the form of merchandise trade and related services, disbursements can be tracked on a net basis by looking at cumulative imbalances on merchandise account. But this cannot, of course, help to distinguish the particular kind of development assistance provided. Nor can this way of proceeding lead to exact quantification with any high degree of precision. The imbalance may in fact be supported, for example, by short-term supplier credits that must be reversed relatively quickly. This almost certainly applies here too. However, if imbalances run consistently in one direction or are not reversed during a protracted period of time, it would appear safe to assume they originally stemmed from

Table 15-2. Share of Third World Groups in CMEA Trade

(As Percentage of Sum Bilateral Flows)

	Africa	Middle East	Asia	Latin America
	East Europe Seven Exports			
1970	39.45	33.97	20.39	6.19
1975	30.81	40.23	19.65	9.31
1980	28.71	43.90	23.09	4.30
1982	27.22	47.68	20.26	4.84
1984	30.49	35.42	27.04	7.06
1986	28.12	29.21	28.89	13.78
1987	28.19	30.42	31.53	9.86
1988	26.02	31.33	33.94	8.71
	East Europe Seven Imports			
1970	36.31	13.50	35.41	14.78
1975	31.24	24.05	21.16	23.55
1980	22.41	29.23	23.51	24.85
1982	25.25	24.28	27.28	23.20
1984	27.77	27.92	23.59	20.71
1986	31.44	18.20	31.34	18.99
1987	20.71	24.07	32.25	22.94
1988	21.21	28.43	28.61	21.71
	East Europe Six Exports			
1970	31.67	34.12	21.92	12.29
1975	31.77	41.60	15.90	10.73
1980	33.29	49.09	11.90	5.72
1982	30.37	55.12	9.39	5.11
1984	33.71	47.63	10.67	7.99
1986	31.88	36.64	13.18	18.31
1987	33.89	39.15	15.14	11.82
1988	30.66	40.72	18.08	10.54
	East Europe Six Imports			
1970	27.73	17.26	28.74	26.27
1975	35.10	25.66	19.27	19.96
1980	24.27	46.00	9.92	19.81
1982	22.99	47.75	12.79	16.46
1984	30.16	38.56	11.89	19.38
1986	28.96	19.70	19.02	32.22
1987	19.43	22.05	22.92	35.49
1988	16.35	27.62	23.10	32.83

Source: Official trade data of the CMEA members.

Table 15-3. Trade Shares of Selected Developing Countries

| | With CMEA3[a] | | | | With CMEA8[b] | | | |
| | EE7 | | EE6 | | EE6[c] | | EE5[d] | |
	Ex.	Im.	Ex.	Im.	Ex.	Im.	Ex.	Im.
1960	1.90	1.75	0.90	0.66	0.60	0.24	0.36	0.10
1965	3.66	2.90	1.24	1.17	0.64	0.53	0.33	0.67
1970	4.20	2.62	1.50	1.07	0.70	0.16	0.57	0.04
1975	3.59	2.99	1.17	0.76	1.18	0.81	1.94	0.33
1980	4.02	2.73	1.30	0.73	1.60	1.59	1.22	1.83
1982	4.70	3.40	1.46	1.01	2.75	0.60	2.72	0.58
1984	4.67	3.75	1.41	1.21	1.93	0.90	1.68	0.24
1986	5.67	4.39	1.14	1.00	2.08	0.81	1.77	0.54
1987	5.83	4.67	1.14	1.13	1.93	1.19	1.51	0.42
1988	5.72	4.45	1.04	0.82	1.77	1.56	1.17	1.03
1989	5.55	4.25	0.83	0.92	1.25	1.02	n.a.[e]	n.a.

Source: Based on official foreign trade data.

a. CMEA3 is Cuba, Mongolia, and Vietnam.
b. CMEA8 refers to the eight cooperants.
c. EE6 means EE plus the Soviet Union.
d. EE5 means East Europe without the GDR.
e. n.a. — not available.

long-term capital transfers, possibly grants in aid.

In this connection, it is important to clarify the nature of development assistance provided by the CPEs. First, it needs to be recalled that the CPEs have consistently refused to subscribe for themselves to international measures on resource transfers, such as indicative targets set in the course of UNCTAD deliberations or in successive versions of the International Development Strategy that the United Nations has slated periodically, beginning with the decade of the 1960s. Their rationale has been explained on the ground that the CPEs disclaim any responsibility for the economic plight of the developing world (UNCTAD 1976; United Nations 1983). The latter state is indeed squarely attributed to the colonial and neocolonial policies of developed market economies and their organs, including the multi- or transnational corporations and banks. By definition, their Marxist-Leninist calling inhibits them from engaging in so-called unequal exchange.[12] This being so, there is no reason, except socialist solidarity and international commitment, for the CPEs to feel compelled to earmark development assistance according to internationally agreed-upon criteria.

That is not, however, to say that the CPEs do not contribute to economic development of the Third World. Rather than engaging in many forms of development assistance that are quite common in the case of market economies, they often go for the unconventional. Perhaps key is a twofold bias, namely an ideological and developmental one. Ideologically, the CPEs have particular preferences for which developing countries merit their support. This also partly determines the form in which the latter is transferred. Such bias is not unknown in the development efforts of other countries either, of course. Nonetheless, the CPEs usually focus their development assistance nearly exclusively on countries with a left-wing leaning and a sizable state sector, particularly in industry. Developmentally, until recently CPEs have unambiguously favored rapid industrialization solidly anchored to, if perhaps not necessarily paced by, a strong state sector. Rather than championing broad-based development objectives, as often resorted to by market economies, CPEs tend to concentrate their resources in spe-

---

12. This is a complex Marxist category rooted in the labor theory of value and how Marx used this to explain social phenomena. For details, see Brabant (1987b, 18-27).

cific forms and earmark them for well-specified purposes that often have a solid political "accommodation" as bedrock. Furthermore, much of their assistance is provided in real terms, that is, tied on both transfer and repatriation ends.

If the transfer of development assistance proceeds, however, through direct provision of services (such as scholarships for students from developing countries attending institutions of higher learning in CPEs, or East European technicians assisting with the construction of a certain project in developing countries), it is much harder to track the development assistance services provided.

In what follows, I shall look at three different sets of data to get a "feel," however impressionistic and inaccurate, for what may have been happening with the CPEs' development assistance. I look first at merchandise trade imbalances on a cumulative basis. The second set compiles the ODA data that four CPEs have been providing to international organizations more or less regularly since the early 1980s. Finally, I take a brief look at trends shown by independent compilations of development assistance disbursements.

Cumulative Trade Imbalances

Inasmuch as one does not possess a clear guide to the volumes and magnitudes of development assistance, the independent observer has to resort to various second-best measurement techniques. One is the presence and subsistence of trade imbalances. Because we do not really know when trade with developing countries as a whole or with subregional components thereof was in equilibrium, cumulating successive trade imbalances, beginning from an arbitrary base year, necessarily provides only a very coarse gauge—at best an exceedingly indirect illustration—of development assistance granted by the European CPEs. Even so, it may be instructive to look at the cumulative imbalances since 1960. Table 15-4 shows such cumulative imbalances with various groups of developing countries.

As can be gleaned from Table 15-4, the European CPEs have been running a considerable surplus with developing countries over the years, though they started the 1960s with a small deficit. Not surprisingly, this surplus has been chiefly due to the Soviet Union. From a deficit in the early 1960s, its cumulative surplus, with 1959 set equal to balance, has expanded from US$1.1 billion in 1965 to over US$268 billion over the period as a whole, including 1989. By contrast, East Europe's started from US$56 million in 1960 and ended in 1989 with a sizable cumulative surplus of US$28.3 billion. With a few exceptions in the mid-1970s, there has been a consistent increase in this surplus. Such considerable surpluses suggest that there has been capital transfer from the European CPEs to the developing countries.

It is to be noted that this surplus cannot easily be disaggregated among the various developing country partners, owing to the unidentified bilateral flows particularly in the trade of the Soviet Union. In fact, taking the sums of the identified flows, the Soviet Union has been running a considerable deficit with the developing countries as a whole and every subregional group, except the Middle East. Likewise for East Europe, in which the surplus is almost exclusively with the Middle East but also with Africa. Trade with Southeast Asia tends to be roughly balanced and that with Latin America in considerable deficit. To the degree that the disaggregations are identifying the bulk of trade, there is little doubt that East Europe's surplus with Africa and the Middle East has been growing steadily. In the case of the Soviet Union, however, the surplus with the Middle East has been stagnating since about 1982.

Regarding the three developing country CMEA members, there is little doubt that the European partners have run sizable and growing cumulative imbalances. Whereas in 1960 this amounted to about US$17 million, this figure had multiplied by 2,000 in 1987. The real value of these transfers, of course, has eroded over the years as a result of upward price drift. But the data exhibited in Table 15-4 suggest nonetheless a substantial real increase in ODA over the period examined. Note that by far the larger part of this expansion in ODA levels has been footed by the Soviet Union. Its share in total cumulative surpluses in 1989 reached 88 percent, whereas in 1965 it had been 65 percent—in 1960 the Soviet Union actually was in deficit. It is also worth noting that East Europe's surplus expanded very rapidly until the early 1980s, when it con-

Table 15-4. Cumulative Merchandise Trade Imbalances
(In Million Current Dollars)

	With CMEA3[a]			With CMEA8[b]			With All DEs[c]		
	EE7	USSR	EE6[d]	EE6	USSR	EE5[e]	EE7	USSR	EE6
1960	17	-1	18	50	30	20	-141	-197	56
1965	1053	682	171	370	315	55	1520	1136	384
1970	4095	3226	668	991	652	389	5430	3939	1491
1975	7096	5991	904	1543	606	988	12189	8737	3452
1980	12436	10117	2119	2514	3176	-662	30780	24863	5917
1982	17838	14854	2783	9629	6847	2782	44110	30890	13220
1984	23244	19603	3440	13811	8465	5845	58739	39559	19180
1986	27603	23758	3644	18106	10633	7473	71912	48524	23388
1987	30454	26568	3685	19658	11305	8353	82121	56438	25683
1988	33355	29231	3922	20212	11676	8586	91233	63387	27846
1989	35628	31526	3901	20646	12025	8620	96674	68366	28307

Source: Data derived from official trade statistics, assuming that first imbalance occurred in 1960.

a. CMEA3 is Cuba, Mongolia, and Vietnam.
b. CMEA8 refers to the eight cooperants.
c. DEs means all nonsocialist developing countries.
d. EE6 means EE5 plus the Soviet Union.
e. EE5 means East Europe without the GDR.

tinued to rise but at a much slower pace than the surplus maintained or tolerated by the Soviet Union.

Finally, with respect to the eight cooperants, the surplus has risen also, and more rapidly than for all developing countries, particularly since the mid-1970s. This has been especially true for the Soviet Union, as East Europe reversed some of its imbalances around 1980 and has held them fairly level since 1985. Since then, however, it has markedly increased its apparent exposure in the eight countries of special interest. In fact, it bears to stress that the Soviet share of the surpluses, though substantial, accounts for around 60 percent of the total surplus in the mid-1980s, but it had been much more substantial in earlier years (85 percent in 1970, for example).

Official Development Assistance

Since the early 1980s, the Soviet Union and three East European countries (Bulgaria, Czechoslovakia, and the GDR) have been submitting on a more or less regular basis information on their development assistance efforts to international organizations, usually within the U.N. system. The definition used by these countries, while not fully detailed, admittedly differs palpably from what is now more or less standard in reports released by members of the Development Assistance Committee (DAC) of the Organisation for Economic Co-operation and Development (OECD).

In this connection, it is useful to remember that there is no mutually accepted and internationally agreed definition of ODA, for example, in the U.N. In some contrast, DAC members, which provide the bulk of the resources transferred to developing countries, determine their ODA according to common norms. The most recent ones were adopted in 1972. In the DAC's definition, ODA comprises resources transferred to developing countries, possibly through multilateral institutions, by official agencies, including state and local governments or by their executive organs, that meet two tests. First, the transaction is administered for the promotion of economic development and raising the welfare levels of developing countries. Second, it is concessional in character, with a grant element of at least 25 percent (OECD 1983, 169).

It would seem that the CPE calculations include a much wider form of transfers. They include loans with a grant element of not less than 25 percent and outright grants, as for DAC data. The CPEs do grant loans at low interest rates and with long maturities that have a significant grant element embedded. Thus, loans are accorded at annual interest rates of up to 4 percent for a duration of ten to fifteen years, and even longer, sometimes with considerable grace periods. This is well below half of standard interest charges common in international capital markets since the 1970s. On the other hand, such commitments can only be utilized in the donor country for goods and services that the latter is able and willing to earmark for development assistance purposes.

In addition to "regular ODA," CPE statistics include the concealed subsidies in the payment for the services of specialists abroad, training of individuals from developing countries, transfer of equipment and technological know-how to developing countries, and in the sphere of foreign trade (including price subsidies and favorable maritime transport tariffs).[13] For example, if prices charged to developing countries are inferior or superior to "recognized" world prices, the aggregate difference is treated as ODA; when no price is charged, as in the case of student exchanges or technical assistance embodied by sending specialists to developing countries on a temporary basis, the efforts are evaluated in accordance with international criteria, presumably utilizing costing procedures of U.N. organs (UNESCO's in particular).

Table 15-5 lists the official data that the four countries enumerated above have submitted to various U.N. organs since the early 1980s. I have tabulated only the percentages of ODA relative to some national aggregate[14] that CPEs claim to have engaged in. Absolute values are sometimes also submitted, but it is inherently difficult to convert local currency values to dollar magnitudes for technical reasons that need not detain us here.[15]

---

13. See TD/B/949 and TD/B/C.3/186, supplement no. 2, para. 231.

14. It is not crystal clear what these countries mean when they report "national income." I suspect that most are referring to NMP, unless a separate distinction is made between alternative national aggregates, as in the case of the GDR for 1987 shown in Table 15-5.

15. For theoretical and empirical details, see Brabant (1985a, 1985b, and 1987a, chap. 6).

According to the claimed ODA magnitudes, all countries have been providing at or better than the international norm of 0.7 percent of official ODA relative to GDP set for the Second Development Decade declared by the United Nations for the 1970s.[16] There has also been a sharp increase in the level of assistance provided by the Soviet Union, from 0.9 percent of net material product (NMP) in 1976 to 1.3 percent in 1980 and about 1.5 percent in the mid-1980s. The rise has also been pronounced for Czechoslovakia, inching up from 0.74 percent in 1982 to over 1 percent in 1986. In the case of the GDR, there has also been a rise but a much more muted one than is evident for Czechoslovakia and the Soviet Union; there was actually a sharp drop in 1988. The data for Bulgaria are incomplete, but the available numbers suggest that Bulgaria also has been raising the level of its assistance, relative to its aggregate output.

Apart from the fact that the definition of these data is at serious odds with the conventions applied in some international organizations, the magnitudes listed in Table 15-5 are also distorted by two peculiar measurement factors. First, the CPEs adhere to a different system of national accounting, which tends to overstate the relative importance of recorded assistance because GDP is roughly 18 to 26 percent higher than the corresponding NMP magnitude.[17] Furthermore, assistance data include the important transfers made by the CPEs, especially the Soviet Union, to Cuba and Vietnam in furtherance of political and military objectives around the globe. Much of that aid is for direct or indirect military purposes and should therefore not really be included in measuring development assistance efforts proper.

Disbursements Measured by the OECD

Because of the very palpable weaknesses of the official data briefly discussed above, it will be useful to look at alternative measure-

16. That also had in addition a private component amounting to 0.3 percent of GDP. But this could not possibly apply to CPEs, inasmuch as there is inherently little private development assistance raised in these countries.

17. The difference stems from the omission of value-added in the so-called non-material sectors from NMP and amortization, both of which are included in the SNA-type national accounting.

Table 15-5. Official Development Assistance of Some CPEs
(In Percent of NMP or GDP)

	Bulgaria	Czechoslovakia[a]	GDR[a]	USSR
1976-81	0.79			
1976				0.9
1976-80				1.0
1980				1.3
1981-85		0.89	0.78	1.3
1981			0.79	1.3
1982		0.74	0.78	1.3
1983		0.78	0.79	1.2
1984		0.90	0.82	1.4
1985	0.88[b]	0.91	0.86	1.5
1986	1.23	1.08	0.89	
1987			0.87[c]	1.4
1988			0.64[b]	

Source: Based on a great variety of data submissions in published documents of UNCTAD, ECOSOC, and the General Assembly of the United Nations. Further details are available on request.

a.   Percentages relative to "national income." I presume this means NMP, but I am not sure.
b.   Relative to GNP.
c.   0.7 percent of GNP.

ments of commitments or disbursements. Unfortunately, these data are very cumbersome to collect as reports on individual instances of development assistance and, certainly in the case of commitments, are at times self-serving. CPEs do not engage in open discussions about the details of the accounting of development assistance; of course, they look askance at or outrightly disapprove of independent inquiries into their development assistance efforts and performance.

Regarding commitments since the mid-1960s, the United Nations has compiled from daily press reports values of multi- and bilateral commitments.[18] The accuracy and comprehensiveness of these data are, however, contingent on what is disclosed in the daily and periodical press of the CPEs. Trends over time are therefore influenced by shifts in reporting techniques and indeed in the recording diligence on the part of U.N. civil servants.

OECD has over the years made a serious effort to measure disbursements of ODA by the European CPEs according to its definitions and to revise these estimates on a nearly continuous basis as new information is collected. These data are undoubtedly biased for a number of reasons. For one, the OECD's estimation procedures depend importantly on what can be gleaned from the press and the information that recipient countries may be willing to disclose. Also, DAC measurements essentially ignore a number of nonmarket transfer mechanisms that would not normally be tolerated in trade by developed market economies. Thus, the aggregate value of assistance provided in the forms of price supports such as those arranged for Cuban sugar and nickel, of concessionary maritime transport tariffs, of concessionary prices such as for Soviet petroleum, of easy payment terms for technical assistance, of training of students from developing countries free of charge, and so on, is largely ignored in DAC estimation procedures.

Nonetheless, the data thus gathered are of interest for two reasons: (1) they provide quantitative information on resource flows that are not normally released by the CPEs themselves, and (2)

18. These used to be published in quite some detail in *Statistical Yearbook of the United Nations.* Because of the serious erosion in disclosures by the CPEs since the early 1980s and an apparent decline in the degree of interest exhibited by the collection supervisors, this information has recently been divulged in the above source only in very aggregative form, if at all.

OECD staff attempt to compile those aggregates according to criteria that are accepted in the international accounting of development assistance, even though they admittedly ignore nonconventional forms of resource transfers that may well dominate in the assistance that CPEs provide (Dobozi 1988, 326-49).

A summary of key aggregates of these efforts is provided in Table 15-6. There are several interesting features to be noted. For one, the multilateral assistance provided is negligible—well below 1 percent of the estimated total. In addition, the vast bulk of the assistance is extended by the Soviet Union, and the major increment in ODA has been in recent years forthcoming overwhelmingly on account of the Soviet Union: Whereas the Soviet Union accounted for 80 percent of total ODA extended by the European CPEs in 1970, its share in the 1980s has consistently risen to 90 percent in the most recent year for which data are available. Furthermore, this increment has been quite pronounced in bilateral aid to other CMEA countries, which account for over 70 percent of total recorded disbursements in the mid-1980s.

Of course, the percentage of disbursements to GDP/GNP estimated by OECD amounts to only about one-fourth to one-fifth of the levels that the CPEs claim for themselves. Taking into account that these estimates are understatements even under the best circumstances (that is, if all information was available) due to ignoring the disproportionate weight of nonconventional forms of resource transfer, the CPEs' record—particularly the Soviet Union's efforts—in global resource transfer is by no means a bad one. It is certainly below the highly performing donors, such as the Netherlands and the Nordic countries among the developed market economies and several of the oil exporters of the Middle East among the capital-rich developing countries. But it compares more or less favorably to the relative amount of development assistance recorded in recent years for most other developed market economies.

IV. CMEA REFORM AND DEVELOPMENT ASSISTANCE

If the data are rather disturbing, even on matters of principle it is far from clear where the CPEs stand with respect to development assistance as an object of policy commitment. Prior to the crystal-lization of the reform sentiment in the CMEA countries, the main direction for the further development of the institutional frame-work for East-South economic relations was the extension of the scope and diversification of the forms of economic ties under long-term cooperation agreements. More emphasis could be placed on giving expanding scope to the structural adjustment process on a mutually beneficial basis, taking into account the comparative ad-vantages as well as industrial development perspectives and the huge potential for production cooperation. That means also that the applied forms of economic relations must be as flexible as possible to adjust the economic relations to the often difficult and specific economic problems of developing countries and to the changing economic environment. This process could be fostered by improv-ing and enlarging the activities of intergovernmental mixed commissions.

Intergovernmental mixed commissions exist at the bilateral as well as multilateral level. The latter form either a harmonious part of the CMEA infrastructure, as in the case of the non-European members, or they have been glued to the CMEA framework in some fashion, as would appear to have been the case with the vast majority of the agreements that regulate the cooperant status of eight developing countries and Finland. From the review in Section II, it should be obvious that, though these commissions for cooperant countries have not apparently exerted a very substantial impact on reciprocal trade, they would appear to have been useful just the same. Neither do they appear to have very substantially af-fected the level of development assistance provided, as measured by cumulative imbalances in Section III. However, the assumption of some CMEA association may have facilitated the toleration by the European CPEs of these persistent and systematic imbalances.

As regards the relationship between the European and other CMEA members, there have been several developments in the last few years. Because of their potentially ominous implications for fraternal development assistance, it will prove useful to look in somewhat greater detail at the particular case of these countries. The debate on how best to integrate developing CPEs into the CMEA framework has been a long, drawn-out one; it has not so far been concluded. It did receive a measurable change, though, as a

Table 15-6. ODA Disbursements by European CMEA
(In Million Dollars)

	1970	1975	1980	1983	1984	1985	1986	1987	1988
Bilateral									
CMEA DCs	715	1310	1862	2514	2560	2631	3086	3662	3427
Other CPEs	174	95	661	639	469	553	688	586	590
Other DCs	476	607	825	833	832	857	1230	1022	871
Scholarships	42	71	200	270	275	300	310	330	330
Multilateral	6	10	14	9	26	13	14	18	24
Total	1004	1502	2827	3478	3402	3618	4639	5006	4692
Soviet Union	798	1264	2313	3046	2891	3064	4118	4485	4212
East Europe	206	238	514	432	511	554	521	521	480
Percent GNP	n.a.[a]	0.14	0.17	0.21	0.21	n.a.	n.a.	n.a.	n.a.

Source: OECD (1983, 1984, 1985, and 1988).

Note: OECD data vary in definition and presentation over time. I have tried to use the most recently available series (1988 edition of the DAC report), but not all series are covered for all years shown.

a. n.a. — not available.

result of the new Soviet approach to economizing and fostering socialist economic integration (SEI). This was an important topic on the agenda of the second economic summit of the 1980s, which took place in November 1986. No doubt was left about its importance during the two subsequent Council Sessions, of which the 43rd in October 1987 in Moscow was the most important.

There was apparently widespread agreement in Moscow—though the assent in some cases was rather reluctant—to rechart assistance policies to the developing country CMEA partners. All of these countries, admittedly with some reluctance, agreed that past economic and technical development assistance efforts on the part of European CMEA members had not been as effective as they should have been and as the member countries desire to attain. Disenchantment was evident for both recipient and donor. The donor countries agreed to work out a dovetailed multilateral approach to assisting the less developed CMEA partners in such a way that their joint effort would measurably improve the benefits to be gained by the recipients as well as the donors in the medium to long run. This effort is to emanate soon in a medium- to long-term coordinated program for providing economic assistance in a coherent fashion to the three non-European CMEA members.

Although many details are still lacking, the preparation of this special development assistance program has apparently been moving forward at a satisfactory pace, as noted at subsequent CMEA meetings. Even so, this was said to be primarily in the area of involving these peripheral CPEs more closely in SEI, particularly production specialization and cooperation, at the 44th Session, which was held in Prague in July 1988. A third economic summit was to have convened in late March 1989 in Prague, but it was postponed in view of major disagreements on where to go with SEI. There is little doubt, though, that economic assistance efforts figure prominently among the long list of agreements.

Three separate drafts of comprehensive economic cooperation with each of the non-European members were presented in Prague. Once harmonized into a coherent stance on technical and economic assistance, it will become part and parcel of the new SEI strategy that the CMEA members have been elaborating since about 1986. The basic objective is to integrate these countries more fully into the CMEA, including through concrete agreements on production cooperation and specialization, scientific-technological cooperation on more than a gratuitous basis, and further commercialization of their economic interactions with the CMEA. Some forms of assistance to the non-European countries will continue to be provided by the developed membership on a gratuitous basis, however. The programs also contain relatively extensive lists of specific projects to be commissioned.[19] But the donor countries have already made it clear that a number of those projects "require clarification as regards construction deadlines, assessments of the economic expediency of the individual projects, and measures to ensure that they produce returns as soon as possible."[20] Further details are lacking, however. The occasional commentary that one finds in the East European specialized literature since then suggests that negotiations on how best to finalize the program for the developing CMEA members have been by no means easy.

V. INSTRUMENTS FOR MULTILATERALIZING ASSISTANCE

The reasons behind the overwhelmingly bilateral character of development assistance provided by the CPEs are multiple (Zevin 1988, 350-67). Apart from the undeniable dependence of ODA on foreign policy considerations, which tend to be country specific, there are many technical economic aspects that inhibit multilateralizing trade and payments of the CPEs, not only in relations with developing countries. Among the many and diverse factors, key are inconvertibility of the CMEA members' currencies; their habitual preference for BTPAs because they dovetail more easily with the central planning framework; and inability of the CPEs to arrive at some form of multilateralism in their intragroup trade—hence the difficulty of extending whatever clearing arrangements they have innovated in the CMEA context to developing countries or, for that matter, other third parties.

19. At the Prague Session, the Bulgarian Prime Minister, Georgi Atanasov, reported that Bulgaria would be prepared to participate in ". . . 71 of the total 178 actions envisaged in the specific comprehensive programs" (Rabotnichekso delo, July 6, 1988, p. 6).
20. From Soviet Prime Minister Ryzhkov's speech at the Prague Session of the CMEA, as reported in Pravda, July 6, 1988, p. 4.

In this connection, it is important to touch briefly upon several instruments put in place by the European CPEs in efforts to enhance their multilateral cooperation with developing countries. At the CMEA level, these countries have instituted three sets of instruments to enhance relations with developing countries, in addition to the commercial policy frameworks provided by the mixed commissions briefly discussed in Section II. Even a cursory examination of why they have not so far borne any but nominal fruit provides clues of the potential that remains to be exploited.

Perhaps yielding the least amount of assistance proper, but a form of ODA nonetheless, is potentially embodied in the set of provisions that enables third parties, including developing countries, in principle to avail themselves of the transferable ruble clearing arrangements within the context of the IBEC (see Brabant 1978, 77-105). Put briefly, these provisions[21] permit countries that are not CMEA members to avail themselves of the clearing and settlement credit facilities of the IBEC on very advantageous terms. Of course, as usual within the CMEA, these provisions can be taken advantage of only to the degree that the CPE partner running a surplus with developing countries is willing to have that offset against another CPE's deficit with a similar developing country or group of developing countries. Because the conditions for offsetting imbalances of opposite sign are not very good, this facility so far has not been utilized to any noticeable degree.

Similar provisions were put in place for developing countries in the case of the IIB. Particularly, the European CMEA members committed themselves in April 1973 to the formation of a capital fund amounting to TR 1 billion (at the official exchange rate prevailing at this time, about $1.6 billion), of which 5 percent would be in convertible currency. This capital fund, which went into operation in 1974, would be available for the "financing" of medium- to long-term development projects in which CPEs and developing countries would engage. The capital fund was duly constituted, but the first installment of TR 25 million was contributed only in 1975; the proportion of convertible currency has never been disclosed, and it was probably zero. The amount of money earmarked

---

21. The third updated version was issued in 1976 (as discussed in Brabant 1978) and to my knowledge is still applicable today.

for the fund increased very slowly at best. It reached TR 32.8 million at the end of 1985 (Brabant 1987a, 352) and TR 35.2 million at the end of 1988.[22] This is well below what had originally been slated. Nikolay V. Faddeev (1974, 320), then CMEA Secretary, declared that the members had committed themselves in April 1973 to contribute TR 100 million by the end of 1976. This negative feature did not come about because of a reneging on the commitment. Rather, it stemmed from acknowledging explicitly that without the willingness of the individual CPEs to deliver goods and services for earmarked development projects, a loan extended by the IIB from that special fund to a particular developing country would remain without real consequence.

Finally, at the CMEA level the members decided to create a stipend fund to enable students, academics, and professionals from developing countries to study formally or engage in development training in one of the CMEA member countries. I am not sure to what extent this fund has been utilized. If it has, it is simply because one or more of the contributing CMEA members has been willing to earmark special loan currency allocations in support of personnel from developing countries and denominate that "from CMEA stipend fund."

The three preceding examples illustrate that, even with the requisite political goodwill, earmarking funds for development from individual CPEs or the CPEs as a group is an extraordinarily difficult exercise, particularly when commitments are not tied in the national trade plan directly to real goods and services earmarked for delivery as development assistance. This derives in good measure from the peculiar trade and payments regimes, anchored in some sense to inconvertibility of the currencies of these countries individually and of their collective currency.

Inasmuch, as a convertible currency is unlikely to emerge in the near future,[23] initiatives designed to increase development assistance of CPEs and to base them more and more on multilateral criteria have to be grounded ever more tightly on measures taken in the real sphere. The first is decidedly easier to engineer than the

22. I suspect that the increases are nominal accrued interest on unutilized balance rather than incremental contributions to the initial funding of TR 25 million.
23. I do not have space to clarify this here. I have expressed my views on the many intricate issues involved in Brabant (1987c, 1988, and 1989).

second, as it is a direct function of the political will of the CPEs. Measures that can be dovetailed in the real sphere are to a large extent conditioned by the key institutional, organizational, and behavioral features of these countries, and no easy, generally applicable solution appears to be in sight.

One of the key traditional inhibitions to more buoyant trade cooperation has been the incompatibility between the ex ante BTPAs that CPEs insist upon and the market character of the more dynamic of the developing countries, particularly the so-called NICs (newly industrializing countries).

VI. NEW THINKING AND DEVELOPMENT ASSISTANCE

Soon after Gorbachev's ascent to the political apex of the Soviet Union, he ordered a comprehensive review of Soviet relations with developing countries, socialist as well as other. To the best of my knowledge, the outcome of that review thus far has not been publicly disclosed. But major markers can be discerned from recent Soviet policy statements and behavior, including in international forums.

For one, the Soviet Union has been insisting on relative disengagement of support for revolutionary causes and national liberation movements. Gorbachev's visit to Cuba in early April 1989 provided a vivid illustration of this new stance. Second, the Soviet Union has demonstrated its clout in support of resolving a number of regional conflicts (as in Afghanistan, Angola-Namibia, and Kampuchea, to name but a few) that sapped a substantial amount of resources that the Soviet Union could afford—if that is the proper term in this context—to transfer on an unrequitable basis. There is also evidence that the Soviet Union and other CPEs are now insisting upon attaining greater economic efficiency of development assistance. This new thinking is unmistakable in three respects.

First, as briefly commented upon in Section IV, the Soviet Union has been instrumental in reviewing the position of the non-European CMEA members and cooperants, in inducing them (particularly Cuba in Angola and Nicaragua, and Vietnam in Kampuchea) to eschew revolutionary and national liberation causes, in obtaining from them a commitment to contain requests for assistance, and in gaining their concurrence on basing economic cooperation in principle increasingly on commercial terms; or at the very least on the basis of economic efficiency considerations (Kachanov 1989). Clearly, the non-European members are likely to obtain less aid, particularly for other than humanitarian requests, such as in the case of natural calamities, and to be invited to utilize the amounts obtained increasingly in support of propping up mutually beneficial trade relations.

Second, in its new attitude toward multilateral cooperation from within the framework provided by the United Nations, the Soviet Union has been aiming at gaining a common stance among the key members of the United Nations on a number of issues, including on what is required to ensure a greater degree of economic security for developing countries. Its signing of the Integrated Programme of Commodities (IPC) and the Common Fund are symptomatic. Although the financial sacrifices made to render the IPC instruments operational are certainly not negligible, the gains that the Soviet Union expects to obtain by utilizing the Fund may well reduce requests for bilateral emergency assistance by developing countries. Likewise, in its more forthcoming attitude to multilateral assistance efforts, including UNICEF and UNDP, to name only the more conspicuous of the organizations that have benefited from new funding, the Soviet Union has paid more than lip service to the economic, humanitarian, and social causes without exacting any direct ideological or political commitment or concession.

Finally, the Soviet Union has made it crystal clear that, if it were to join the Washington financial institutions, particularly the International Monetary Fund and the World Bank, it would take a more active part in providing development assistance on a multilateral basis. But it would not mainly do so simply for altruistic motives. It has a genuine interest in fostering economic development by supporting projects that will result in a firmer basis for reciprocal trade and cooperation policies.

In spite of the ambivalent attitude of CPEs toward development finance and especially extending development assistance on concessionary terms from the North to the South, the Soviet Union has apparently decided to be more forthcoming in its development efforts. It has already done so through the multilateral agencies of the United Nations, including UNICEF, UNDP, and the related technical assistance programs. It has apparently also decided to foster such multilateralization if and when it is admitted into the Washington financial institutions. This is quite a change in attitude, for the Soviet Union and its allies for a long time decided to shun many multilateral development assistance agencies on the ground that they are simply masks for the neocolonial policies that big contributors thus seek to prolong (Brabant 1990a, chaps. 3 and 5).

With perestroika, a marked shift in positions on development issues appears to be slowly emerging. This is not just a tactical move that may be connected with the Soviet Union's desire to be recognized as an important partner in international economic relations, even though it cannot yet support such claims on the basis of the volume of its own trade and financial flows. This has become evident in the reexamination of the traditional relationship of the developing country CPEs in the CMEA as examined earlier. It has also been the subject of protracted debates on the diplomatic relationships of the Soviet Union with the various developing economies. Finally, it has slowly been giving rise to a new position toward the Washington multilateral financial institutions more generally.

According to a recent clarification of the Soviet position made by Ivan D. Ivanov,[24] any Soviet participation in the World Bank would be based on a careful examination of the balance of merits and disadvantages. As regards participation in the Fund, Soviet membership would be sought, if at all, as a prelude to accession to the World Bank. Among the latter's merits, he counted the potential advantages that Soviet exporters could derive from the ability to bid singly or in tripartite arrangements with developed and developing market economies on Bank-financed projects in the Third World, and thus gather new experience in markets that will be vital to the coveted expansion of Soviet exports of manufactures in the years to come. In other words, by this route the Soviet economy could explore new export avenues and gain a firmer position in world markets for manufactures.

24. I am quoting here from notes I took from a position statement given by Ivan D. Ivanov on the occasion of the workshop on "The Future of the United Nations in an Interdependent World" in Moscow on September 8, 1988.

Another benefit he considered to consist in the human capital stock of the Bank, particularly the technical and professional qualifications of its staff in evaluating the technical and economic merits of development projects. He also deemed the Bank staff to embody a unique repository of knowledge on the international investment climate from which the Soviet Union through its participation could be guided by, if not instructed about, long-term financial markets. As to the disadvantages, the Soviet Union would, of course, have to contribute to the Bank's budget, proceed through the gauntlet of the Fund before it could be admitted into the Bank, multilateralize some of its development assistance, and provide that in convertible currency. He saw no great obstacle in allocating part of the financial resources earmarked for development purposes through the multilateral agencies. As an illustration he cited Soviet observership in the Asian Development Bank since April 1987 as an expression of the Soviet leadership's desire to learn about and apply more multilateral financial development policies.

I have the impression from a number of commentaries, as already noted, that the Soviet Union would be in favor of entrusting greater responsibilities for development finance to multilateral agencies, not just the World Bank and its affiliates or regional counterparts. It is clear that key Soviet reform participants subscribe to the notion that the needs of the low-income countries can still be met only through large transfers on concessionary terms, including through program lending. The needs of the more advanced developing countries would appear to call for different responses that are rooted more in the multiple commercial aspects of long-term development finance.

Where precisely the other European CMEA members at the present juncture stand on development assistance is not known. One may surmise, though, that the countries (including Hungary, Poland, and Romania) that have been going through a protracted, in some cases a wrenching, adjustment phase are unlikely to be prepared to step up their development assistance soon, if they can be found willing to maintain the levels observed in the 1980s at all. This attitude is crystallizing not because these countries have decided to skirt their global responsibilities. Their current economic situation is chiefly responsible for the fact that they are temporarily not in a position to heed their moral and other obligations in a responsible manner. Others, including Bulgaria, Czechoslovakia, and the GDR, are probably following the lead provided by the Soviet Union. In this way, they can avoid having to take publicly an affirmative stance that may be embarrassing and yet afford to review their assistance policies and increasingly base them on commercial considerations.

It bears to stress that from the perspective of the developing countries, the most hopeful sign of perestroika in the Soviet Union and its CMEA allies is not the potential for increased resource transfers as traditionally understood. In fact, though there may be a reasonable expansion in the multilateral component of the resource transfer, it is unlikely to be generated in such a way that it will measurably raise overall assistance on concessionary terms; a temporary stagnation or even decline is more likely in the short to medium run.

Much more important, in my view, is the potential impact of economic reforms in the European CMEA members on the trade prospects of the developing countries, not just those that have traditionally entertained considerable commercial ties with the CPEs. If the CPEs are seriously considering undertaking structural changes in their economies that will enhance the degree to which these countries exploit their comparative advantage based on relative economic scarcities, a potentially vast market for goods and services from the developing countries may open up in the East. Given the prevailing constraints on the balance of payments of both the CPEs and the developing countries, which are bound to linger on into the foreseeable future, such commercial opportunities are unlikely to come to fruition unless all parties involved can design imaginative schemes to accommodate significant changes in the level and commodity composition of trade without measurably exacerbating imbalances on current account.

Whether these increased trade opportunities need to be accommodated through habitual BTPAs or through some form of multilateral countertrade is something worth pondering. Compensatory trade measures usher in constraints on the arena for profitable commercial relations that are likely to restrain trade below levels desirable and feasible in a multilateral trading world. Inasmuch as the latter does not exist and is not likely to be restored very soon, however, there would appear to be considerable economic legitimacy in exploring ways and means of enhancing trading relations, including through countertrade measures. In this, two aspects are very important. Such bilateralization should not be utilized as an excuse to encroach upon the existing room for multilateral trade. Instead, it should lead to trade expansion. Also, provisions should be enacted in such a way that measures can be envisaged that wean the partners from the genuine technical need for engaging in countertrading.

Such technical accommodation to structural adjustment in the CPEs and their trade has not yet occurred, as the data discussed in Section I illustrate. But it is something that is not out of the realm of the possible. It certainly would signal a desirable shift in traditional attitudes of CPEs toward not only the developing world as such, but also toward the potential benefits of engaging in international competition, even if initially only in a highly constrained format.

Such a rise in trade is feasible. It bears to stress that East-South commercial relations have suffered from a number of factors. Some have to do with history. Others derive from political adversity or even commercial constraints (Perczynski 1988, 309-25). Initially, of course, East-South relations were constrained because of inexperience, inasmuch as these countries had never been involved in colonialism and had therefore largely ignored the potential of trade in that direction. When the developing countries obtained their political independence, their economic relations with the metropolitan countries were, of course, strongest, and so was the battleground for maintaining other influences from the mother country—in economics, society, politics, and culture—over the former dependency. Socialist ideology in the CPEs and its communist emanation in practice did not at all help to expedite matters.

Perhaps most spectacular has been the absence of the so-called NICs, particularly the more dynamic Southeast Asian developing countries. They have not so far conquered the European CPE markets for a number of reasons. Some are political, such as the knotty questions revolving around the future of Hong Kong, the status of South Korea, or how best to treat Taiwan. Others have to do with the unquestionable market-oriented approach fostered by the macroeconomic, export-oriented policies of these countries. Such methods are not terribly popular—or effective for that matter—in CPEs. But several European CMEA members, including the Soviet Union, have already expressed interest in participating in the trade of the most dynamic NICs. The Soviet Union, for one, has invited some of these countries, including South Korea, to participate in joint ventures and free trade zones. The first concrete results are presently emerging. With some imagination on the part of these dynamic countries, especially when it comes to the financing of these economic relations, a buoyant level of trade and economic cooperation is within reach.

On the economic front, in many ways the development experience of the bulk of the East European CPEs, barring Czechoslovakia and the GDR, and the developing countries on a medium level of economic development has been very similar. The dash for industrialization, disengagement from the overwhelmingly agricultural base, and diversification of production and consumption structures all worked in the same direction and tended by design to inhibit fruitful trade.

There is hope that a greater measure of economic complementarity between East and South can be identified and instituted. The "objective" factors are there, but they need to be given room to exert upward pressure on sustainable commercial levels through imaginative trading and other institutional shifts in both East and South. Because both East and South are being compelled to explore a more diversified geographical pattern of commercial relations, the opportunities for lifting reciprocal trade levels are in principle very good. This is important for developing countries, if only because they will have to explore new markets, especially in the event that import demand in developed market economies remains constrained by sluggish growth or by protective measures that place barriers in the way of supplies from the South reaching developed markets. Furthermore, the East needs to diversify its sources of supply of critical raw materials and fuels because of constraints from within the CMEA. It also needs to diversify its export markets if it is to make headway with the exportation of manufactures on a medium level of technological sophistication. Finally, both East and South share a common interest in improving international economic security by exploring ways and means of rolling back protective measures and commercial policies that are not conducive to profitable international economic relations.

POSTSCRIPT

When I prepared this article for publication in July 1989, little did I suspect that three broad seminal changes would soon come to the fore in the European CMEA and exert a critical impact on the potential for cooperation between East and South. One was embodied in the sequence of political revolutions in East Europe proper in late 1989 and early 1990, and the desire of these countries to move over to a market-economy setting as soon as feasible. This could not but change the character of relations with developing countries, calling for less politically motivated, more "businesslike" transactions. Of course, the dissolution of the GDR on October 3, 1990, and its full submergence into the Federal Republic of Germany created its own structural shift in East-South relations. The second was the complete collapse of the CMEA in early 1990, something that will only formally be acknowledged in early November 1990, when the organization will be reconstituted under a different name as a weak regional economic secretariat. Perhaps more important than the change in the regional organization has been the dissolution of the TR trade and payments regimes. They will disappear altogether on January 1, 1991. Any of the constants of East-South relations accommodated through the mechanisms of the CMEA are now on the scrapheap of history. Finally, the utter disruption of normal economic and other relations conducted at the union level in the Soviet Union was then being entertained only as a remote possibility. At the time of writing, it was certainly not yet the prevailing reality that it is today.

These changes in the European CMEA have ushered in very important consequences for developing countries. Some exert an overwhelmingly negative impact on trade and economic relations with the South. Others provide new opportunities for mutually advantageous trade and financial relations on a much larger scale, certainly in the medium term, than I intimate in Section VI. The latter beneficial impacts of the sociopolitical revolutions and economic mutations in East Europe will in the first instance challenge the more dynamic of the developing countries. Some imaginative arrangements, as suggested in Section VI, would favorably place these countries with a view to capitalizing on a substantial share of the business that is bound to emanate from the marketization of East Europe. On the other hand, the most detrimental repercussions of the still ongoing economic and political changes in East Europe and the Soviet Union are crystallizing in particular for the developing countries that had earlier enjoyed preferential trade and related cooperation with the European CMEA. These include, in the first instance, the three developing country members of the CMEA. All plans for reviving mutual cooperation and integrating these countries more firmly into the CMEA framework discussed from late 1986 until late 1989 are now completely off. But also the left-wing developing countries in particular among the eight cooperants of the CMEA stand to lose considerably from the mutations in the European CMEA area.

The negative implications are materializing in various concrete forms. First and foremost is the renunciation of the vast bulk of the traditional development assistance engaged in by East Europe and the sharp downward adjustment of ODA levels in whatever form earlier provided by the Soviet Union. These are not just changes taking place in the conceptual approach to providing development assistance. They have already manifested themselves in the abrupt abandonment of some construction, engineering, and educational projects. These tremendous external shocks have been jolting in particular the three countries that have traditionally benefited from the lion's share of the European CMEA's bilateral and multilateral development assistance. Especially Cuba and Vietnam are now confronted with sharply reduced assistance levels. Not only is this manifesting itself in terms of ODA as traditionally defined. Also the trade and payments frameworks of the CMEA in general and the European members individually are being adjusted to reflect "world market" conditions. The demise of the TR regime entails basing trade henceforth on current world market prices and settling accounts in convertible currency. Furthermore, worker remittances and other forms of labor mobility, which earlier provided some form of ODA to many developing countries, are being sharply scaled down and will soon (at the latest when current contracts expire) be discontinued altogether. Earlier efforts to bolster scientific and technological cooperation between East and South have collapsed, and not only because of the disappearance of the GDR.

Whether the favored developing countries will in the future be able to enjoy some preferential status in the markets of the former European CMEA is not at all an easy question to answer. Several of these countries, especially the former CMEA members and cooperants, should be in a position to capitalize on their traditional relations with East Europe and the Soviet Union. Knowledge of markets and partners, for now, constitutes a comparative advantage. Given the urge and determination of East Europe to orient itself to the West, particularly the European communities, these developing countries may well fail to exploit these evaporating comparative advantages. This is regrettable, as there should certainly be room for combining the market orientation of Vietnam, for example, with the determination of Central Europe to become "normal" market economies, as intimated in Section VI but obviously in the context of the much more constraining CPE format. Some more imaginative policies (see Brabant 1990b, 1991) will be required to transform these potential opportunities into mutual benefits, not only in the short- but also in the longer-term perspective.

REFERENCES

Brabant, Jozef M. van. 1978. "Le Rouble Transférable et son Rôle dans le Commerce Est-Ouest." In *Unités et Monaies de Compte.* Eds. J. L. Guglielmi and Marie Lavigne. Paris: Economica.

———. 1985a. *Exchange Rates in Eastern Europe—Types, Derivation, Application.* Washington, D.C.: World Bank Staff Working Paper No. 778.

———. 1985b. "Eastern European Exchange Rates and Exchange Policies." *Jahrbuch der Wirtschaft Osteuropas—Yearbook of East-European Economics* 11, no. 1, 123-72.

———. 1987a. *Adjustment, Structural Change, and Economic Efficiency—Aspects of Monetary Cooperation in Eastern Europe.* New York and Cambridge: Cambridge University Press.

——. 1987b. *Regional Price Formation in Eastern Europe—On the Theory and Practice of Trade Pricing.* Dordrecht, Boston, and Lancaster: Kluwer Academic Publishers.

——. 1987c. "Economic Reforms and Convertibility in Eastern Europe." Paper presented at the Fourth Congress of the Italian Association for Comparative Economic Studies, Sorrento, October 19-20.

——. 1988. "Economic Reforms, Monetary Cooperation, and Convertibility in Eastern Europe." New York, manuscript.

——. 1989. "Regional Integration, Economic Reform, and Convertibility in Eastern Europe." *Jahrbuch der Wirtschaft Osteuropas—Yearbook of East-European Economics* 13, no. 1.

——. 1990a. *The Planned Economies and International Economic Organizations.* New York and Cambridge: Cambridge University Press.

——. 1990b. *Remaking Eastern Europe—On the Political Economy of Transition.* Dordrecht, Lancaster, and Boston: Kluwer Academic Publishers.

——. 1991. *Integrating Eastern Europe in the Global Economy— Convertibility through a Payments Union.* Hemel Hempstead: Harvester Wheatsheaf. Forthcoming.

Dobozi, Istvan. 1988. "Patterns, Factors and Prospects of East-South Economic Relations." In *Global Challenges and East European Responses.* Ed. Pawel Bozyk. Warsaw: PWN.

Faddeev, Nikolay V. 1974. *Sovet ekonomicheskoy vzaimopomoshchi— XXV let,* 3rd Edition. Moscow: Ekonomika.

Kachanov, Aleksandr. 1989. "Sovety ekonomicheskoy vzaimopomoshchi—40 let." *Vneshnyaya torgovlya* 1, 2-6.

OECD. 1983. *Development Co-operation—Efforts and Policies of the Members of the Development Assistance Committee: 1983 Review.* Paris: OECD.

——. 1984. *Development Co-operation—Efforts and Policies of the Members of the Development Assistance Committee: 1984 Review.* Paris: OECD.

——. 1985. *Twenty-Five Years of Development Co-operation—A Review; Efforts and Policies of the Members of the Development Assistance Committee: 1985 Report.* Paris: OECD.

——. 1988. *Development Co-operation—Efforts and Policies of the Members of the Development Assistance Committee: 1988 Report.* Paris: OECD.

——. 1989. *Development Co-operation in the 1990s—Efforts and Policies of the Members of the Development Assistance Committee.* Paris: OECD.

Perczynski, Maciej. 1988. "Global Determinants of East-South Relations." In *Global Challenges and East European Responses.* Ed. Pawel Bozyk. Warsaw: PWN.

UNCTAD. 1976. *Proceedings of the United Nations Conference on Trade and Development, Fourth Session, Vol. I—Reports and Annexes.* United Nations Publication, Sales No. E.76.II.D.10. New York: United Nations.

Zevin, Lev. Z. 1988. "East-South Institutional Relations—Forms and Results." In *Global Challenges and East European Responses.* Ed. Pawel Bozyk. Warsaw: PWN.

Index

About the Contributors

V. B. BENEVOLENSKY is Senior Research Fellow, Institute for the Study of the USA and Canada, Moscow.

JOZEF M. VAN BRABANT is Chief, Centrally Planned Economies, United Nations.

SHARAM CHUBIN is Professor, Graduate Institute of International Studies, Geneva.

EDME DOMINGUEZ REYES is Professor, University of Barcelona.

TOM J. FARER is Professor, Washington School of Law, The American University; and Former Head of the Human Rights Commission, Organization of American States.

FREDERICK HELDRING is Chairman, Global Interdependence Center, Philadelphia.

OSVALDO HURTADO is President, Corporacion de Estudios para el Desarrollo; and Former President of Ecuador.

VICTOR A. KREMENYUK is Deputy Director, Institute for the Study of the USA and Canada, Moscow.

COLIN LEGUM is Professor, School of Oriental and African Studies, University of London.

GENERAL EDGARDO MERCADO JARRIN is Director, Instituto Peruano de Estudios Geopoliticas y Estratégicos, Lima; and Former Prime Minister of Peru.

GEORGE MIRSKY is Senior Research Fellow, Institute for the Study of the USA and Canada, Moscow.

CARLOS M. VILAS is High Commissioner for Refugees, Chargé de Mission–Nicaragua, United Nations; he is also affiliated with the Instituto de Ciencia y Cultura, Buenos Aires, and the Asociacion Nicaraguense de Cientificos Sociales, Managua.

FRANCISCO VILLAGRAN KRAMER is Member of the International Directory of IRELA; Researcher at the Universidad de San Carlos, Guatemala; and Former Vice President of Guatemala.

VIKTOR VOLSKY is Director, Institute of Latin American, Soviet Academy of Sciences, Moscow.

BORIS Y. YOPO is with Programa de Sequimiento de las Politicas Exteriores (PROSPEL), Santiago.

About the Editors

EDITOR JOHN F. WEEKS is Senior Research Fellow at the Geonomics Institute and Professor of International Politics and Economics at Middlebury College. He is editor of a previous book in the Geonomics Series, *Debt Disaster* (New York University Press, 1989), and author of several books on Latin America and economic theory, including *The Economies of Central America* (Holmes & Meier, 1985) and *A Critique of Neoclassical Macroeconomics* (Macmillan and St. Martins, 1990). In addition to his academic work, he is a frequent consultant to U.N. organizations. He received his Ph.D. from the University of Michigan, Ann Arbor, and has taught at universities on four continents, including the University of London, Universite Catholique de Louvain, and universities in Peru and Nigeria.

SERIES EDITOR MICHAEL P. CLAUDON is President and Managing Director of the Geonomics Institute and Professor of Economics at Middlebury College. He is the author of numerous articles and books on economics, and he serves as series editor for the Geonomics Institute for International Economic Advancement monograph series. He received his B.A. from the University of California, Berkeley, and his Ph.D. from The Johns Hopkins University.